D1187771

Reading and Responsibility

The Frontiers of Theory

Series Editor: Martin McQuillan

The Poetics of Singularity: The Counter-Culturalist Turn in Heidegger, Derrida, Blanchot and the later Gadamer
Timothy Clark

Dream I Tell You
Hélène Cixous

Scandalous Knowledge: Science, Truth, and the Human
Barbara Herrnstein Smith

Geneses, Genealogies, Genres and Genius
Jacques Derrida

Insister of Jacques Derrida
Hélène Cixous

Not Half No End: Militantly Melancholic Essays in Memory of Jacques Derrida
Geoffrey Bennington

Death-Drive: Freudian Hauntings in Literature and Art
Robert Rowland Smith

Of Jews and Animals
Andrew Benjamin

Reading and Responsibility: Deconstruction's Traces
Derek Attridge

The Romantic Predicament
Paul de Man

The Book I Do Not Write
Hélène Cixous

The Paul de Man Notebooks
Paul de Man

Veering: A Theory of Literature
Nicholas Royle

Reading and Responsibility

Deconstruction's Traces

Derek Attridge

Edinburgh University Press

In Memoriam
JD

© Derek Attridge, 2010

Transferred to digital print 2012

Edinburgh University Press Ltd
22 George Square, Edinburgh

www.euppublishing.com

Typeset in Adobe Sabon
by Servis Filmsetting Ltd, Stockport, Cheshire
Printed and bound by CPI Group (UK) Ltd, Croydon, CR0 4YY

A CIP record for this book is available from the British Library

ISBN 978 0 7486 4008 9 (hardback)

Contents

Acknowledgements   vii
Series Editor's Preface   ix

Introduction   1

1. Derrida, Deconstruction and Literary Criticism   15

2. Deconstruction Today: Literature, Postcolonialism and the Secret   34

3. Following Derrida   51

4. The Impossibility of Ethics: On Mount Moriah   56

5. Arche-jargon   78

6. Deconstruction and Fiction   89

7. Posthumous Infidelity: Derrida, Levinas and the Third   97

8. Roland Barthes's Obtuse, Sharp Meaning and the Responsibilities of Commentary   117

9. Nothing to Declare: J. Hillis Miller and Zero's Paradox   131

10. Radical Atheism and Unconditional Responsibility   138

11. The Place of Deconstruction: A Conversation with Jean-Michel Rabaté   149

Bibliography   163
Index   175

Acknowledgements

I am grateful to the many colleagues and friends whose invitations to speak or to contribute to journals and collections prompted the explorations of Jacques Derrida's work and legacy that underlie these chapters, and to Martin McQuillan and Jackie Jones for their enthusiasm and efficiency in taking this book on board.

I acknowledge the previous publication of parts of the book as follows:

An earlier version of Chapter 1 was published in *Critical Encounters: Reference and Responsibility in Deconstructive Writing*, eds Cathy Caruth and Deborah Esch, Rutgers University Press, 1995.

Part of Chapter 2 was published in *Etudes Anglaises*, Special issue on 'Littérature et theories critiques', ed. Catherine Bernard, 58.1 (2005): 42–52.

Chapter 3 was published in French translation in *L'Herne: Jacques Derrida*, eds Marie-Louise Mallet and Ginette Michaud (2004), and in English in *Khoraographies for Jacques Derrida* (*Tympanum* 4), ed. Dragan Kujundzic (2000).

Parts of Chapter 4 were published in *The Politics of Deconstruction: Jacques Derrida and the Other of Philosophy*, ed. Martin McQuillan (Pluto Press, 2007) and *Derrida's Legacies: Literature and Philosophy*, eds Simon Glendinning and Robert Eaglestone (Routledge, 2008); part of the Introduction also appeared in the latter publication.

Chapter 5, 'Arche-Jargon', appeared in *Qui Parle: Critical Humanities and Social Sciences*, 5.1 (1991), and is reprinted with permission from the University of Nebraska Press. Copyright 1991.

Chapter 6 originally formed part of a chapter in *Deconstructions: A User's Guide*, ed. Nicholas Royle, published by Palgrave and reproduced with permission of Palgrave Macmillan.

An earlier version of chapter 8 appeared in *Writing the Image after Roland Barthes*, ed. Jean-Michel Rabaté (University of Pennsylvania Press, 1997).

Chapter 9 was first published in *Journal for Cultural Research* (Routledge), Special Issue on 'Zero and Literature', ed. Rolland Munro, vol. 8 (2004), reprinted with permission, http://www.informaworld.com.

A version of Chapter 10 appeared in *Derrida Today* (Edinburgh University Press), 2.2 (2009).

A French translation of Chapter 11 appeared in *Derrida d'ici, Derrida de là*, eds Thomas Dutoit and Philippe Romanski (Galilée, 2009).

Series Editor's Preface

Since its inception Theory has been concerned with its own limits, ends and after-life. It would be an illusion to imagine that the academy is no longer resistant to Theory but a significant consensus has been established and it can be said that Theory has now entered the mainstream of the humanities. Reaction against Theory is now a minority view and new generations of scholars have grown up with Theory. This leaves so-called Theory in an interesting position which its own procedures of auto-critique need to consider: what is the nature of this mainstream Theory and what is the relation of Theory to philosophy and the other disciplines which inform it? What is the history of its construction and what processes of amnesia and the repression of difference have taken place to establish this thing called Theory? Is Theory still the site of a more-than-critical affirmation of a negotiation with thought, which thinks thought's own limits?

'Theory' is a name that traps by an aberrant nomial effect the transformative critique which seeks to reinscribe the conditions of thought in an inaugural founding gesture that is without ground or precedent: as a 'name', a word and a concept, Theory arrests or misprisons such thinking. To imagine the frontiers of Theory is not to dismiss or to abandon Theory (on the contrary one must always insist on the it-is-necessary of Theory even if one has given up belief in theories of all kinds). Rather, this series is concerned with the presentation of work which challenges complacency and continues the transformative work of critical thinking. It seeks to offer the very best of contemporary theoretical practice in the humanities, work which continues to push ever further the frontiers of what is accepted, including the name of Theory. In particular, it is interested in that work which involves the necessary endeavour of crossing disciplinary frontiers without dissolving the specificity of disciplines. Published by Edinburgh University Press, in the city of Enlightenment, this series promotes a certain closeness to that spirit: the continued exercise of critical thought as an attitude of inquiry which counters modes of closed or conservative opinion. In this respect the series aims to make thinking think at the frontiers of theory.

Martin McQuillan

Introduction

I

At the outset, it seems appropriate to ask why I wrote this book and why anyone should want to read it.

There are two answers (at least) to the first question. The chapters that make up the volume were all initially responses to invitations – to give a talk, contribute to a collection, participate in a dialogue. I hope they retain the sense of direct address and of focus on a specific issue that marked their original production, even though they have been revised and in some cases considerably expanded. The other answer is that they trace a constant engagement with the work of Jacques Derrida over nearly two decades and reflect an interest in that work going back a further two decades. They thus exemplify a set of responses to or elaborations of Derrida's writing, registering a few of the many ways in which it remains productive for our thinking about literary questions today and about culture more generally. To use Derrida's own metaphor, they are my counter-signatures to his signature: attempts to affirm what is singular about his writings in a manner that does not simply repeat them but brings to bear on them my own peculiar situation, individual history and distinctive knowledge and interests.

To attempt to answer the second question is perhaps presumptuous, but let me say that – leaving aside the obvious readership of those who already have an interest in Derrida and deconstruction – I would like to think that anyone who is curious about the monster called 'French theory' (or worse, 'Parisian theory') will find here some indications of why it has proved to be such a fascinating and rewarding resource for so many and for such a long time, and that those who come to the book with questions about some of the topics it treats – topics such as the nature of ethical obligation, the language of literary theory and the distinctiveness of fiction – will find that it provides a stimulus for fresh thought. Running through the entire book is a concern with reading: readings of Derrida, of course, but also Derrida's reading of others and the question of reading itself. A central question is: what does it mean to do justice of a work of literature or philosophy or photography? I've argued elsewhere that reading is not just an act, nor just an event, but a combination of the two, and that to read a text as *literature* (which is not limited to works classified as 'literary') is to read inventively, in a manner parallel to the inventiveness that characterised the author's act-event of creation.[1] This book continues the argument, taking deconstruction to be a name for that inventive mode of reading.

Since this book is the record of a long period of involvement with Derrida's thought, it will perhaps help to contextualise the chapters that follow if I sketch the beginnings and course of that involvement. I first encountered Derrida's writing, as did many of my generation, in the proceedings of a 1966 Johns Hopkins conference entitled *The Languages of Criticism and the Sciences of Man* (edited by Richard Macksey and Eugenio Donato).[2] Derrida's lecture, 'Structure, Sign and Play in the Discourse of the Human Sciences', became one of the most anthologised (which is not to say the best understood) of his short texts. My interests at the time when I first read the essay as a graduate student at Cambridge in the early 1970s were primarily in Renaissance poetry and the possibilities for poetic analysis offered by new developments in linguistics; in theoretical matters, Derrida was of less importance to me than Roman Jakobson, Noam Chomsky or Thomas A. Sebeok. However, French literary theory was in the air, and I was fortunate in those years in getting to know a young Fellow of Selwyn College who was completing an Oxford DPhil thesis on French literary theory and who lent me a copy to read when it was done. His name was Jonathan Culler, and the thesis, 'Structuralism: A Study in the Development of Linguistic Models and their Application to Literary Studies', was later published as *Structuralist Poetics*, one of the most influential works of literary theory of its decade. (I remember reading not long after its publication in 1975 that it was the most-stolen book from American bookstores.) Derrida does not feature greatly in Culler's book – nowhere near as extensively as Roland Barthes, for instance – but I was intrigued by the way in which Derrida's arguments, summarised by Culler in the final section of the thesis, seemed to undermine most of the positions taken by the theorists who had featured up to that point. I also made what I could of *Signs of the Times*, a special issue of the Cambridge magazine *Granta* produced in 1971 by Stephen Heath, Colin MacCabe, and Christopher Prendergast which introduced to a largely bemused readership the stringencies of French semiotics.

It wasn't until around ten years later that I started reading Derrida systematically, encouraged by my new colleagues at Southampton University, Isobel Armstrong, Maud Ellmann and Robert Young. Strong links were established with literary theorists in Paris, Frankfurt, Toronto and various centres in the United States, and we ran a series of conferences that proved to be important proving-grounds for the burgeoning interest in the UK in 'poststructuralist' theory. My particular concern was with the question of the distinctiveness of literature as a discursive and linguistic practice (in the work of James Joyce in particular), and I found the theoretical work I was reading, and the discussions I was having in connection with it, highly stimulating and productive. The first opportunity I had to hear Derrida speak was in 1982 at the Royal Philosophical Society in London; the lecture was entitled 'Devant la loi' – on Kafka's fable of the same name – and it has remained, only partly because of its personal associations, one of the texts I admire most.[3] My first meeting with him wasn't until two years later, first at the New York launch of Richard Rand's translation of *Signéponge* (Derrida's book on the poetry of Francis Ponge), then at the James Joyce Symposium in Frankfurt, where I proposed to him a project I had been considering for some time, a collection of his writings on literary texts – oddly neglected by his readers in Britain and North America in favour of his work on philosophers (see Chapter 2 below) – and received his warm approval. His only cautionary comment was that Peggy Kamuf was engaged on a collection of his writings as well, and I would need to take care not to come into conflict with what she was doing. (In fact, she and I were able to discuss our projects, which were significantly different, to make sure this didn't happen.)[4]

Derrida also suggested that we might conduct an interview, a suggestion I was able to follow up on in 1989 when, having moved to the United States, I visited him in Laguna Beach (his home while he spent a short period at the University of California, Irvine every year). We met for two mornings, and he spoke at considerable length about his longstanding interest in literature, advancing arguments about the role of the literary in philosophical, political and cultural contexts whose importance and implications I believe have still not been fully registered.[5] From the early 1980s, then, my work – whether on aesthetic theory, stylistics, Joyce or South African literature – has been undertaken in a constant, and constantly fruitful, interaction with Derrida's writing, and, indeed, with Derrida himself, as I was lucky enough to know him through these twenty years as a friend.

But why Derrida? Why not Barthes, Blanchot, Adorno, Kristeva, Habermas, Deleuze, Foucault, Jameson, Williams? A number of other philosophers and literary theorists have had a significant influence on my thinking, but as this volume suggests, none has played so central a role as Derrida. No doubt there are purely fortuitous reasons – happening to be in a particular place at a particular time, to read this and not that, to get to know this individual and not that individual. I can't discount my admiration for Derrida as a person, for his generosity, his openness, his energy, his sense of humour, his loyalty: it's hard to imagine devoting a great deal of one's time to the work of an individual one dislikes. But I wouldn't use these reasons in a defence of my commitment to Derrida's philosophical arguments, except to the extent that his personal qualities are reflected in his work – which they certainly are. Above all, I think, what keeps drawing me back to Derrida's work is his combination of extraordinary sharpness in reading, exacting rigour in argument and exceptional flair in writing. The common ground of Derrida's effectiveness in these three areas – reading, argument and writing – is responsibility: responsibility to the text being read, responsibility to the protocols of rigorous argument and responsibility to the reader.

As Derrida himself insisted, responsibility is not a simple ethical concept; it makes impossible demands, and is nevertheless – or consequently, rather – urgent and exigent (see Chapter 4 below). Responsibility in *reading* (which includes responsibility to its author, whether known or not) involves a fidelity to the singularity of a work, that which marks it as distinctive and of importance; yet in order to register that singularity one has to respond with an answering singularity, not with a mere extension or copy of what one has before one, and so with a degree of infidelity.[6] As I noted above, one of Derrida's favourite metaphors for this process and this demand was the signature and counter-signature; and a counter-signature, in order to do its job of validating a prior signature, has to be the unique imprint of someone who signs quite differently from the original signatory. Responsibility in *argument* means following the logic of a concept even to the point where it subverts logic, resulting in a position which is both based on rational thought and a challenge to rational thought. (One example discussed below, in Chapter 10, is hospitality; others Derrida has explored include the gift, forgiveness, justice and responsibility itself.) Responsibility to *the reader* is the least discussed of these three: it requires an awareness that one's words are not produced for one's own benefit but in order to be read by another, not always in ideal circumstances, and that one creates pleasure for the reader in language that is inventive without being inscrutable, lively without being ludicrous.

Other philosophers I admire have one or two of these qualities, but not many exhibit all three to the extent that Derrida does. Some are not particularly good readers, and use the texts they read as springboards for their own thinking. Some produce a series of propositions and neologisms that spill out one after the other rather than offering the reader a deductive sequence; ideas generated in this way may be stimulating and productive, but lacking any necessary argumentative base, they remain mere pronouncements. And many have no sense of responsibility to the reader, writing in clogged hermetic prose, dry-as-dust analytical formulae or dispiritingly 'playful' flamboyance. True, Derrida's flair as a writer sometimes resulted in excess, or so it seems to me; especially in his later work, I sometimes have the feeling that the argument presented in ten pages could have been as effectively – if not more effectively – presented in one. Some part of me enjoys the pared-down, painstaking logical deductions of the analytic tradition, and that part can get impatient with Derrida's wordiness. However, in the field of aesthetics, the analytic tradition, whatever its strengths, suffers from the huge disadvantage of not being able to tolerate the possibility that art may be an institution and a practice in which the norms of rational accounting to which it is wedded are tested and challenged – and that this capacity to put the norms of logical argument on trial is precisely what is valuable about the arts.[7]

Literature was immensely important to Derrida. Not that he consumed large quantities of it – he wasn't particularly interested in novels, for instance. But in his experience of a number of works, he found his understanding of central philosophical issues such as representation, identity, truth, law and belonging put to the test. Shakespeare, Joyce, Mallarmé, Celan, Artaud, Blanchot, Baudelaire and many others had this effect on him. His writings on literary works don't, however, offer themselves as models to literary critics (see Chapters 1 and 3 below); they are singular responses to the singularity of the works on which he is commenting. In my own literary criticism, while I have been constantly aware of Derrida's example, I have resisted any temptation to write like Derrida. My responsibility to his legacy, I take it, is not to imitate but to look for a singular response, arising from my own past history, my present situation and my hopes for the future of reading that will do justice to his inventive achievements.

II

Faced with what seemed like the impossible task of preparing a short talk for the Tate Modern series 'Derrida's Legacy' in February 2005, a few months after his untimely death, I found myself indulging in the kind of delaying tactic everyone is familiar with: it suddenly seemed extremely important that I should count the books by Derrida on my shelves, both French originals and the English translations which, in many cases, stand next to them. There turned out to be 122. A few of the books are made up of interviews, two or three are co-authored, and some are very short, but it remains a staggering number for one man to have written – all the more staggering when one considers the range of topics and authors treated. A look at the 'By the same author' pages in one of his last Paris-published books tells the same story – around seventy books in French, as well as numerous other contributions to other people's volumes. I can't think of any philosopher or literary critic writing in English today whose life's work is likely to come anywhere near this total.

The sheer quantity of Derrida's work, though it conveys something important about his intellectual energy and range, doesn't, of course, say anything about its significance or its uniqueness. But my diversionary exercise led to something else: I found myself scrutinising the first page of many of the French books, re-reading the words inscribed there in barely decipherable handwriting, running sometimes to several lines. For once we became acquainted, through our work together on *Acts of Literature*, he sent me, as he did a number of his friends, a copy of every book when it appeared, and usually added a short note on the half-title – always addressed not just to me but to my wife and to my two young daughters, for whom he played the role of surrogate grandfather. This happened frequently enough for his inscriptions to be a means of conveying recent news or responding to something I had sent him.

Through the painful sense of loss that the re-reading produced, I was struck by the thought that this combination of public utterance – on a vast scale – and private communication, of the general and the singular, is indicative of an important aspect of Derrida's work, one that is particularly relevant to the field of literature and literary criticism. Although he always thought of himself first of all as a philosopher, and although that's how he will no doubt always be primarily remembered, his legacy in the field of literary studies is, and will continue to be, substantial. And one rather crude way of summing up the importance of literature to him is to say that while philosophy has its eye always on the general, the literary work is inescapably singular.

So while Derrida examined the tradition of Western philosophy for the traces of the various singularities it has never been able to overcome in its reaching for universality, he approached literary works as singular stagings of many of the issues that philosophy has perennially grappled with. And not only philosophy: for these issues are of immediate concern to any thought about how we live our lives – issues of language

and signification, translation, hospitality, friendship, ethics and responsibility, lying and telling the truth, giving and forgiving, faith, sacrifice,
death and putting to death, and many more. At a time when literary
study in some parts of the academy seems be dissolving in a tepid bath
of cultural commentary, and when our paymasters are more and more
wedded to the enumerable and the assessable, Derrida reminds us of
the challenge of the inventive literary work: the pleasurable demands
it makes on us to see things differently and to think along new paths.
This is not a call to return to an old valuation of the literary masterpiece
– though there remains much of interest in those old valuations – but
an argument about singularity itself, which, for Derrida, is inseparable
from what he called 'iterability'. Whatever has meaning – from the simplest sign to the most complex literary text – has to be repeatable, but,
Derrida showed us, has also to be open to change in new contexts. This
implies infinite change, since the possibility of new contexts is an infinite
one. A word, a poem, a novel, if it were not open in this way, would
simply die, permanently closed in upon itself. His readings – themselves
open to ever new contexts, of course – often move in unexpected direc-
tions, but always strive to register and respect the singular inventiveness
of the work.

The lecture that I heard Derrida deliver in 1982 will serve as an
example – although 'example' is the wrong word, for Derrida's engagements with literary works are so varied that one cannot stand for all
the others. (This, as it happens, is one of the issues addressed in the
piece I've chosen to comment on here.) Kafka's fable 'Vor dem Gesetz'
('Before the Law'), which is not much more than a page long, tells of a
'man from the country' who comes to a doorkeeper standing 'before the
Law'. The man stays there for many years, all the while trying to gain
admittance through the open gate. Just before he dies, still outside the
gate, he asks the doorkeeper why, in all this time, no one else has begged
for access to the Law, and is told, 'No one else could ever be admitted
here, since this gate was made only for you'. On this, he shuts the gate
and the story ends.

Derrida's discussion of this story, in an essay which takes its name
from the story itself, is a richly detailed exploration both of textual
minutiae – down to the pointed nose of the doorkeeper – and of the
large questions that are posed within it. One of these questions is that of
the relation of literature to the law: both the determination of literature
by the law (the legal status of the title, the institution of copyright and
so on) and the not-so-obvious dependence of the law on literature (the
narratives that underlie the law's apparent autonomy and timelessness).
Kafka gives us a literary work that is recognised as such because of the

laws that govern literature, but which challenges, both in its singularity and in its narrative staging of singularity, those very laws. The law is open to all and yet at the same time inaccessible (what would it mean to be in the presence of the law itself, as distinct from its various doorkeepers?); the law is both wholly general – or it would not be law – and yet meaningful only in so far as it applies to (or refuses access to) singular individuals.

Derrida's essay explores these and other related issues, always returning to Kafka's words to puzzle out what they might mean. Like any good literary critic, his aim is constantly to do justice to what is unique and surprising in the work. And like any good literary critic, the writing he produces is itself unique and surprising: a singular response to a singular text. He has not told us the truth about Kafka's story, since truth is always dependent on the context in which it is framed, but he has conveyed its meaningfulness for him in a particular time and place. The readers of Derrida's essay are implicitly invited in their turn to do justice to the singularity of this extraordinary piece of literary and philosophical commentary. We can never articulate its laws, or the laws of literature, in wholly general terms, but each of us can, like the man from the country, find ways of creatively inhabiting the space outside the particular gate that it presents.

Derrida's legacy in the literary field does not, therefore, take the form of the model or paradigm. His essays on literary works cannot be imitated for the reasons just given: they are unique responses that call not for replication but for an answering inventiveness. An imitation would therefore not really be an imitation at all, as it would lack the inventiveness of the original it was claiming to imitate. He has left us, as I have stressed, a huge amount of writing to explore and respond to; and the work published during his lifetime is only part of his legacy, as will become evident as the massive project of the publication of his seminars unrolls.[8] But perhaps even more important is the spirit in which he engaged with texts and ideas, in the face of widespread misunderstanding and repeated denigration. (Did any major philosopher of the twentieth century suffer from such a vast quantity of ill-informed, mean-spirited abuse?) The generosity which he showed in inscribing his books to my family and me is not separable, I believe, from the generosity of his thought (a quality which is entirely compatible with scrupulousness and rigour) when he read Plato, or Shakespeare, or Joyce. It's this generosity – an aspect of the responsibility to the other I have already mentioned – that I would like to emulate in responding to Derrida and some of those who have worked with him, or on his writing, in this book.

III

But isn't the heyday of deconstruction long past? Don't we have a new canon of impressively foreign-sounding names (still mostly male) to conjure with today – Žižek, Agamben, Badiou, Negri, Rancière, Esposito, Meillassoux . . .? It is certainly true that deconstruction is no longer fashionable, but it is also true that this is a very easy thing to say, implying as it does that deconstruction was nothing *more* than a fashion, thankfully, like all fashions, of limited duration. The further implication in such a remark is that the speaker is superior to the intellectual marketplace, favouring a currently fashionable school of thought not because of its fashionableness but because of its inherent rightness and his or her own astuteness in appreciating this. We need to be a little more subtle in thinking about academic fashion, which, after all, operates as a powerful motor driving original thinking as well as spawning a great number of derivative productions. When I was excited by the new modes of reading I was being exposed to in the early 1980s this was no doubt largely because they showed me the limitations of those I had absorbed up to then and opened up new territory for intellectual exploration, but it was no doubt also partly due to an awareness that I was participating in a movement inspiring anger and dread in an older generation and fascination in the brightest of my students. (Little did we know then, of course, fighting our institutional battles as a beleaguered minority, that our cause would in due course become an orthodoxy against which younger forces would be mounted. These younger forces are a response, once more, to what the current orthodoxy has excluded but also to the excitement of the new; and once more, the result is a quantity of recycling and name-dropping but also some path-breaking innovations in thought.) If deconstruction in its heyday was *more* than a fashion, however, its value will have outlasted its glory days of trendsetting glamour. One of the aims of this book is to demonstrate that this is the case.

Derrida is, however, a problem for those who follow him, a problem some of whose lineaments I sketch in Chapter 3. His work is so wide-ranging and so forcefully argued that to engage fully with it is to leave little time to strike out on one's own path. This may be one reason why many of the philosophers most frequently quoted in current literary and cultural theory, although their work is unthinkable without Derrida's, devote little attention to it, or, worse, refer to it in garbled forms. One of the most forceful of current voices is that of Quentin Meillassoux who, in *After Finitude*, mounts an attack on the argument, inherited from Kant, that the absolute is unknowable and therefore a matter of faith.

Although one of his main targets is clearly Derrida, and in particular the notion of an 'other' that is, in principle, unknowable, the name Derrida doesn't appear anywhere in his book.

Meillassoux's argument – briefly, that scientific statements about entities existing prior to the emergence of life on earth undermine the fundamental Kantian proposition that the world can be described only as it appears to a living being – seems designed to clear a space for thinking in a mode very distinct from Derrida's, but its failure to engage with the latter's work is a signal weakness.[9] Another important work that appears to connect at many points with Derrida's writing is Roberto Esposito's *Bíos*: both philosophers discuss community – and especially the community of the present – in terms of immune systems, but Esposito makes only one brief reference to Derrida. Esposito's translator, Ray Brassier, however, devotes six pages of his introduction to a comparison of Esposito's and Derrida's arguments. (Meillassoux's book, incidentally, has a preface by Badiou and a puff by Žižek, while Esposito's is endorsed by Negri and Hardt. Žižek offers fulsome praise on the jacket of many of Badiou's books. Occasionally one feels – unjustly, no doubt – that all this mutual public admiration is designed to reassure both readers and the writers themselves that Derrida can be safely disregarded . . .)

Let us spend a moment with the example of Giorgio Agamben. (I should note that the tendency to think of a group of philosophers who 'come after' Derrida, as if they belonged to the following generation, is not chronologically sound: Agamben was born only twelve years after Derrida, Rancière ten years, Badiou seven years and Negri three. This tendency arises from the eagerness with which these thinkers have been seized on as alternatives to what is seen as the now superseded phase of Derrida, Blanchot, Nancy, Foucault, Barthes et al. Agamben ends *Stanzas*, first published in Italian in 1977, with a brief summary of Derrida's arguments in *Of Grammatology*. The critique that follows is to the effect that Derrida has failed to transcend metaphysics, a somewhat odd objection since the impossibility of transcending metaphysics is a key point in Derrida's readings of the tradition. We have here an example of what Derrida, in 'Limited Inc', calls the *reapplication* of an argument taken from the work being (supposedly) critiqued. Agamben writes 'Even if it were possible to reveal the metaphysical inheritance of modern semiology, it would still be impossible for us to conceive of a presence that, finally freed from difference, was only a pure and undivided station in the open' (156). Derrida has shown, in many different readings, just this: attempts from Plato to Husserl to conceive of such a form of presence always break down, always reveal that presence is divided from the start.[10]

In another piece, entitled 'Friendship', Agamben relates a conversation with Derrida while the latter was giving the series of seminars on which his book *Politics of Friendship* was based. The topic of their exchange was a statement, central to Derrida's discussion, attributed to Aristotle by Diogenes Laertius and translated variously as 'O my friends, there is no friend' or 'He who has friends has no friend', depending on whether the omega at the start of the sentence has an iota subscript and a rough breathing or no subscript and a smooth breathing. Agamben tells us that he had later resolved the problem to his satisfaction – he found that Isaac Casaubon's seventeenth-century edition introduced an emendation giving the latter meaning to the sentence, thus making it 'perfectly intelligible' – and informed Derrida of what he had discovered (3). He continues: 'I was astonished, when his book was published under the title *Politiques de l'amitié*, not to find there any trace of the problem' (3). Perhaps Agamben stopped reading halfway through Derrida's (admittedly rather long-winded) book, for on page 189 Derrida raises just this problem, citing (in the original) the two versions of the Greek. (Unfortunately, the translator or copyeditor has misunderstood Derrida's discussion – 'esprit', for instance, is translated as 'spirit' and not 'breathing', and the Greek characters are mangled – and the result is meaningless for the reader of English. Agamben, reading the French original, had no such excuse.) Derrida could hardly have laid more stress on the question of the two versions; he writes, 'We shall have to approach prudently . . . the difference created by this trembling of an accent, this inversion of a breathing, the memory or the omission of an iota' (190, translation modified). And he takes an entire chapter, 'Recoils', to do this. Here he points out that the version he has found more troubling and more suggestive – the earlier, unemended version – was the version relied on by Montaigne, Florian, Kant, Nietzsche, Blanchot and Deguy in their discussions of friendship. His research also turned up translations into French, German and Spanish that appeared to assume this version, while many others, in English, Italian, German and Latin, preferred the emended version. It is precisely the absence of 'perfect intelligibility' in the unemended version that interests Derrida, and Agamben's rebuke – which is presumably meant to say something about the quality of the friendship, or of the lack of friendship, between the two men – misses its mark.

IV

As I've said, the chapters of this volume are revised versions of talks or essays written in response to specific invitations; they reflect Derrida's evolving interests as well as my own repeated engagements with his thinking. (Although I have worked with both French originals and English translations, I refer throughout to the translations only, as this book is addressed to Anglophone readers; the only exceptions are when I am making a specific point about the French text.) The first three chapters are concerned with the general question of the importance of Derrida's work for literary criticism and other humanistic fields. The earliest to be written (in the late 1980s) was Chapter 1, 'Derrida, Deconstruction, and Literary Criticism'; it belongs to the period in which I was working on *Acts of Literature*, a period at which Derrida's 'deconstructions' of texts by Saussure, Lévi-Strauss, Rousseau, Plato, Hegel, Austin and other philosophers or linguists were having a profound influence on literary studies while his many readings of literary works were being regularly passed over. Although there is now a much wider awareness of the distinctiveness and suggestiveness of his literary readings, the question of their methods and claims remains an important one. Chapter 2, 'Deconstruction Today', and Chapter 3, 'Following Derrida', were both written for French publications; the first was commissioned for a special issue of a French journal on 'Littérature et theories critiques', and appears here in an expanded form, and the second was a contribution to an issue of *Cahiers de l'Herne* dedicated to Derrida. The next three chapters take up a series of specific topics in relation to Derrida's work: ethical obligation, theoretical jargon and fiction. Chapter 4, 'The Impossibility of Ethics', reflects Derrida's growing attention to ethical questions in the 1990s, at a time when I was beginning to study the work of Emmanuel Levinas, and Chapter 5, 'Arche-jargon', was written for an MLA panel on 'Critical Jargon' and takes up the question of the responsibility of the writer to his or her readers. Chapter 6, 'Deconstruction and Fiction', which arose from my reading of J. M. Coetzee's memoir *Boyhood* and a fascination with its problematic relation to fiction, was a contribution to a collection edited by Nicholas Royle entitled *Deconstructions: A User's Guide*. (The reader will note that Coetzee's name crops up from time to time in this book; my long engagement with his work has been another important element in my thinking about literature and responsibility.)

Chapters 7 to 11 engage, in one way or other, with literary theorists who have been strongly influenced by Derrida. I had followed with interest the sequence of Derrida's commentaries on Levinas, starting with his early essay 'Violence and Metaphysics'[11] – like many others, it was through this extended discussion that I was alerted to the importance of Levinas's ethical philosophy – and continuing until Levinas's death in 1995, and I was deeply moved by his tribute in *Adieu*, which appeared in French in 1997 and in English in 1999. I was also fascinated by Derrida's rewriting of some of Levinas's principal arguments – a perfect example of a reading responsible in its very lack of fidelity, which at the same time included an argument for understanding such perversion as necessary rather than contingent. In considering this complex response by Derrida to another thinker, Chapter 7, 'Posthumous Infidelity', originally written for a conference in Brisbane entitled '*After*: Mourning and Its Hospitalities', effects a transition between the two groups of chapters.

Roland Barthes was a Parisian colleague of Derrida's, and his work bears the marked imprint of the latter's thinking in its shift from a structuralist ambition to produce a science of the literary to a questioning of the premises of structuralism. Barthes's last work, *Camera Lucida*, is one of his most powerful and haunting, and Chapter 8 offers what might be called a Derridean reading of its most significant concept, the *punctum*. Chapter 9 turns to one of Derrida's most faithful American followers, J. Hillis Miller; in writing admiringly about Miller's constant pursuit of clarity in his readings of Derrida, and the necessary failure of this pursuit, I am no doubt projecting some of my own concerns and goals. Chapter 10, 'Radical Atheism and Unconditional Hospitality', addresses one of the most important of recent re-readings of Derrida, that of Martin Hägglund, who goes to the heart of Derrida's far-reaching argument concerning space and time – or, more precisely, the becoming-time of space and becoming-space of time – to indict those who would enlist Derrida as a negative theologian, a promoter of Levinasian ethics or a Schmittian political theorist. This is a discussion which will no doubt continue for some time: further evidence that there is a great deal in Derrida's work that we have not yet mined.

The book ends with a conversation that took place by e-mail with Jean-Michel Rabaté on the question of deconstruction and place, initially written to be performed by the two of us at a conference in Paris in 2003 – the last time, incidentally, that I saw Jacques Derrida, participating in a long and energetic public discussion with Hélène Cixous, in spite of the debilitating effects of the pancreatic cancer that was to kill him a year later.[12] (I last heard his voice on the telephone some weeks before his death, when he informed me that he wouldn't, after all, be able to join me in a question-and-answer session at the opening of the 2004 conference of the European Society for the Study of English in Zaragoza – characteristically, he had refused to back out until there was absolutely no possibility of participating.) Rabaté is both one of the most eminent and energetic commentators on Derrida's work, as well as someone who knew him well over a much longer period than I did; he was also among those whose friendship when I began to read Derrida in earnest was most valuable to me. This exchange seems, therefore, an appropriate way to end the book, though it by no means closes the conversation.

Notes

1. See *The Singularity of Literature*, and, for an exemplification of these arguments in an engagement with a single author, *J. M. Coetzee and the Ethics of Reading*.
2. It was later reprinted with a new title, *The Structuralist Controversy*, reflecting a growing awareness that humanistic study in the Anglophone world was irrevocably changing under the impact of recent French thought.
3. See Derrida, 'Before the Law'.
4. Kamuf's collection, *A Derrida Reader: Between the Blinds*, was published by Columbia University Press in 1991, a year before mine, which I called *Acts of Literature*.
5. See '"This Strange Institution Called Literature"'.
6. This question is further discussed in Chapters 1 and 7.
7. For an attempt to address this issue in a publication addressed to analytic philosophers, see Attridge, 'Singular Events'.
8. The first volume in English, *The Beast and the Sovereign*, was published by Chicago University Press in 2009. (The French originals are being published by Galilée ahead of the English translations.)
9. Martin Hägglund provides a cogent critique of Meillassoux's implicit disagreement with Derrida in 'The Arche-Materiality of Time', while resisting any assimilation of Derrida's thinking to the kind of fideism Meillassoux rightly rejects.
10. In his response to John Searle's bad-tempered attack on him, Derrida identifies a recurrent procedure in the former's argumentation: '*Sec* [Derrida's abbreviation of his essay title, 'Signature Event Context'] furnishes Sarl [Derrida's abbreviation of Searle's name] with an argument that the latter attempts to oppose to it' ('Limited Inc', 51). For a fuller discussion of Agamben's responses to Derrida, see Wortham, 'Law of Friendship', and Johnson, '*As If* the Time Were Now'.
11. 'Violence et métaphysique: Essai sur le pensée d'Emmanuel Levinas' was one of Derrida's first publications, appearing in *Revue de métaphysique et de morale* in 1964; it was reprinted in *L'écriture et la différence* in 1967 but did not appear in English until the publication of *Writing and Difference* in 1978.
12. The discussion has been published as Cixous and Derrida, 'Bâtons rompus'.

Chapter 1

Derrida, Deconstruction and Literary Criticism

I

We literary critics are doubtless always a little intimidated by philosophy: it refuses us the pleasures by which we set most store – the sensuous movements of language, the hilarious accidents of comedy, the surge and release of narrative, the intimacies of shared emotions, the particularities of concrete observation – and demands instead, with joyless exigency, the abstractions of pure thought, the progressions of cold logic. True, we read many philosophers with pleasure, but we do so with an edge of guilt, as we relish the modulations of their phrasing, trace their metaphorical patterns, respond to their intimations of feeling and take delight in the minute precision of their representations. At the backs of our minds is the discomfiting thought – implanted by three millennia of cultural history – that in the largest scale of things, the practice of literature can provide only an attractive garnish for the strong meat of philosophical enquiry.[1]

When a philosopher speaks up for literature, therefore, we are quick to take notice. The literary critic who defends the status of literature is inevitably suspected of special pleading, even if the defence is couched in impeccably philosophical terms; but when we find an accredited member of the institution of philosophy – someone who in his work traverses the entire tract of Western philosophical writing – arguing that literature might hold a key to the problems with which philosophy has never ceased to grapple, our reaction is understandably different. Perhaps we're not as peripheral as we feared; perhaps we weren't wrong to believe that Dante probes as deeply as Descartes, that Aristophanes' insights are as profound as Aristotle's. This, at least, is one possible reason why, in the late 1970s and throughout the 1980s, Jacques Derrida's words found within the literary academy such fertile ground.[2]

In accordance with the same logic, of course, Derrida's words found among philosophers, at least in the dominant schools of the English-speaking world, only the stoniest of ground. I can't say if philosophers suffer from a mirroring sense of inadequacy to that of critics, a sense that their own poker-faced efforts are always vulnerable to the sprightly corrosions of the literary, but it's clear that appeals for philosophy to open itself to an other called 'literature' fall mostly on deaf ears, as if what was endangered in the contemplation of such a prospect was not only the *traditions* of philosophy (philosophy is hardly loath to challenge its own traditions) but the very possibility of philosophical activity.[3] Even philosophers in the analytic tradition who make literature their special focus find it difficult to grasp the significant role played by literature in Derrida's thinking; thus Peter Lamarque, in *The Philosophy of Literature*, can claim that 'Literary Theory' (an apparently homogeneous body of philosophical work by Derrida and nine or ten others) 'rejected the notion of literature as art' and 'became increasingly remote from literature as such' (9) – and can in any case be dismissed as 'either anti-philosophical or at times philosophically suspect' (11).[4] This general picture is not significantly altered by the fact that philosophers who choose to regard philosophy as a kind of ongoing conversation rather than a quest for truth have found Derrida's literary bias appealing – a somewhat surprising fact, given Derrida's relentless engagement with traditional philosophical questions in what one must assume is the belief that they matter to the human community in fairly traditional ways.

Turning back to the early reception of Derrida's work by literary critics, which is the main concern of this essay, we find some rather surprising configurations.[5] Let us recall that by the early 1990s Derrida had written widely on literary as well as philosophical texts (using these categories for the moment in an entirely conventional sense): not only on Plato, Aristotle, Leibniz, Kant, Hegel, Husserl, Heidegger, Austin and many others who unquestionably nail their colours to the philosophical mast, but also on Shakespeare, Baudelaire, Mallarmé, Valéry, Joyce, Kafka, Artaud, Celan and many others whose work clearly answers to some notion of the literary.[6] Let us recall, too, that Derrida had on several occasions stressed the importance of literature to his work. For instance, in one of the interviews in *Positions* (an interview which first appeared in 1967), it is to certain literary works that he gives the leading role in the contemporary activity of deconstruction: 'If we had the time, we could . . . ask ourselves too, why the irreducibility of writing and, let us say, the subversion of logocentrism are announced better than elsewhere, today, in a certain sector and certain determined form of "literary" practice' (11). In his thesis defence of 1980 he commented:

'My most constant interest, coming even before my philosophical interest I should say, if this is possible, has been directed towards literature, towards that writing which is called literary' ('The Time of a Thesis', 37). And in the 1989 interview I included in *Acts of Literature* ('"This Strange Institution"') he elaborated at length on the centrality of literature to his intellectual development and philosophical concerns. 'It's the most interesting thing in the world', he said of literature, adding only half-jokingly, 'maybe more interesting than the world' (47).

In the light of Derrida's constant emphasis on literary writing, the first surprise we encounter when we consider his initial influence on literary studies in the English-speaking academy is the place of his own work on literature. Jonathan Culler provided an economical formulation of the situation in 1982: 'Derrida's own discussions of literary works draw attention to important problems, but they are not *deconstructions* as we have been using the term, and a deconstructive literary criticism will be primarily influenced by his readings of philosophical works' (*On Deconstruction*, 213). This is not, of course, a simple objective statement: not only was it uttered in defence of the selectivity of Culler's own representation of Derrida, but given Culler's influence *as* a representative of Derrida in the Anglophone world, it helped to fulfil the very prediction it claimed to make. Nevertheless, it does serve to mark a peculiar feature of the reception of Derrida's work: Derrida the reader of *philosophical* texts was much more important for literary critics than Derrida the reader of *literary* texts.[7]

Another conventional subdivision of Derrida's writing – equally problematic, and problematised by Derrida, but widely assumed nevertheless – is into a more 'philosophical' portion and a more 'literary' portion, the criterion this time being not the text under consideration but the mode of Derrida's own writing. One's first expectation might be that the influence upon literary criticism would be exercised largely by the 'literary' works – those that exploit language in a way traditionally regarded as the preserve of literature, and as inimical to philosophy's task of passing through the veil of language to truth itself. We must remember, however, that literary criticism is not itself traditionally 'literary'. Indeed, it relies for its identity on a clear separation between its mode and that of the works it comments on; in our schools, student criticism which doesn't achieve this distance from literature, which isn't properly analytical and objective, is criticised as being merely an extension or repetition of the literary work. In other words, literary criticism, even of the most bread-and-butter variety, operates as a kind of philosophy, though its procedures usually lack the peculiar rigour to which philosophy aspires. So perhaps we need not be too surprised that it was Derrida's 'philosophical' writing that was most important for literary criticism. A few critics claim to have been encouraged by Derrida's 'literary' example – in *Glas*, for instance – to write texts that play ingenious games with the signifier,[8] but they appear to have had relatively little interest in one of Derrida's major concerns, which is also one of my concerns here: the place of philosophy in relation to literature, and of literature in relation to philosophy. Such critics were influential in one respect, however: the view of 'deconstructive criticism' from the outside, from those who haven't read much Derrida or his more philosophically inclined mediators, is heavily coloured by a notion of something called 'freeplay', as if this meant some kind of escape from all the demands of careful thought that Derrida in fact continually exemplified and insisted upon.

This double discomfort with the more 'literary' Derrida led to another surprising phenomenon: we find literary critics (or at least academics speaking from the institutional site of the literature department) not only encouraging us to concentrate on the 'philosophical' Derrida, in both senses, but stressing the importance of Derrida *for philosophy* rather than for literary criticism. Thus in 1986 Rodolphe Gasché informed readers of *The Tain of the Mirror*, having admitted at the outset that he had 'given greater prominence to the more philosophically discursive texts' (4), that 'Derrida's marked interest in literature . . . has in his thinking never led to anything remotely resembling literary criticism or to a valorization of what literary critics agree to call literature' (255). And in 1987 Christopher Norris, in one of his introductory books read widely in literature departments (though probably less widely in departments of philosophy) focused his attention on what he called the 'more substantial and significant portion of [Derrida's] work' (*Derrida*, 20) – that is, the texts which do not employ a 'literary' style (which he believed, rather quaintly, was adopted to gratify the peculiar taste of American readers) – and went on to assert that he was 'more interested in the philosophical consequences of deconstruction than in its current high prestige among literary critics' (22).[9] Both writers were reacting against much of what had been done in the name of deconstruction: Gasché accuses so-called 'deconstructive literary critics' of having 'chosen simply to ignore the profoundly philosophical thrust of Derrida's thought' (3), while Norris assails 'those zealots of a limitless textual "freeplay" who reject the very notions of rigorous thinking or conceptual critique' (27). While I'm not sure that it's appropriate to describe the non-philosophical cast of much of what passes for deconstructive criticism as the result of a simple choice as Gasché does, and while I find Norris's phrase 'conceptual critique' doubly unapt for Derrida's engagements with texts, this reaction is understandable and largely justified. But it doesn't seem to follow with any philosophical rigour that Derrida's *own* use of a more literary style, and his writing on literary works, needs to be set aside, nor that Derrida's work is of only limited interest to literary criticism.[10]

II

Now that a good thirty years have passed since the impact of Derrida's work was first strongly registered in the literature departments of the English-speaking world, we know – or have no excuse for not knowing – that deconstruction is not a technique or a method, and hence that there is no question of 'applying' it. We know that it is not a moment of carnival or liberation, but a moment of the deepest concern with limits. We know that it is not a hymn to indeterminacy,[11] or a life-imprisonment within language, or a denial of history: reference, mimesis, context, historicity are among the most repeatedly emphasised and carefully scrutinised topics in Derrida's writing. And we know – though this myth perhaps dies hardest of all – that the ethical and the political are not avoided by deconstruction, but implicated at every step. None of what we have learned has been easy, and this above all has conditioned the reception of Derrida's work within the domain of literary criticism; the temptation to substitute a simple formula for laborious intellectual activity is understandably powerful and ever-present.

Derrida isn't, it turns out, saying that we literary critics are doing better than the philosophers; on the contrary, we are probably more damagingly caught up in the centuries-old philosophical presuppositions and practices he has questioned than are most philosophers. Our literary pleasures don't hold any simple lesson for philosophy, and what we like to term 'reading philosophy as literature' doesn't begin to engage with the issues that deconstruction – like the philosophical tradition it participates in while contesting – repeatedly broaches. How, then, do Derrida's dealings with works of literature differ from those we might consider characteristic of literary criticism?

We can start with some comments in one of the *Positions* interviews, where Derrida claims that criticism is dominated by such typically philosophical categories as 'the values of meaning or of content, of form or signifier, of metaphor/metonymy, of truth, of representation' (69), and some of its 'reductions and misconstruings' of literature are listed as 'thematism, sociologism, historicism, psychologism', as well as a 'symmetrical reaction' to this closure on the signified, an isolation of the literary in formal terms (70). (It is no doubt this allegiance of literary criticism to philosophy which explains the relative weakness of the impact of Derrida's 'literary' essays upon it.) One prevalent reductive approach to literature, which Derrida terms 'mimetologism' and links to the tradition of philosophical discourse on truth, he discusses and exemplifies at length in 'The Double Session'. In other words, we spend a great deal of our energy as critics (professional or casual) responding to literature as something else: as social history, as personal confession, as formal object, as ideological weapon, as moral lesson, as cultural instruction, as linguistic exercise, and so on. The texts of literary criticism down the ages would no doubt offer the same opportunities for deconstruction as philosophy: one could demonstrate their reliance on logocentric, phonocentric, phallocentric assumptions – their domination by the signified as meaning or by the signifier as form, or some organic or dialectical relation between them, for instance – and at the same time the exclusions on which those assumptions depend, as well as the structural necessity for that exclusion.

Deconstructive criticism, by contrast, would be an attempt to do justice to what is 'literary' about a literary work (though not just as a formal category), and in so doing to put into play, and reinforce, its potential for unsettling philosophical categories – and with them, of course, a whole series of political and ethical positions. Much that has passed for deconstructive criticism in the past thirty years operates just as much on the basis of philosophical assumptions as the more traditional modes it attempts to displace, whether it evinces its deconstructive allegiance by verbal frolics and open-ended interpretations or by the strenuous teasing-out of metaphysical oppositions. To treat the literary work as an indeterminate self-referential game is to reinforce the philosophy/literature, or serious/non-serious, opposition by which philosophy constitutes itself (the notion of literature as ungoverned rhetoricity being a philosophical notion par excellence), and to treat the literary work as a structure of thematic oppositions is to turn it into a philosophical argument. But what sense can we give to the apparently tautological notion of doing justice to literature 'as literature' in the light of Derrida's own readings of literary works? And what has literary criticism to gain from the difficult task of familiarising itself with Derrida's dealings with literature – if those strange texts could ever be said to become familiar? All I can do in this limited space is offer a few preliminary pointers to a future practice.[12]

First, a caution about the term 'literature'. Derrida uses the word in three distinct but related ways: sometimes to refer to a specific Western historical institution whose beginnings lie in the eighteenth century, in which case he contrasts it with 'poetry' (as an earlier term for a different institution); sometimes it means the body of texts from Homer to the present that have come to be called 'literature', or the concept that governs this textual classification; and sometimes the term is reappropriated (like the terms 'writing' or 'trace') to signal a movement or a moment that exceeds (while at the same time it makes possible) what we call 'philosophy', which Derrida identifies with 'logocentrism' and the 'metaphysics of presence'.[13] The shiftiness of the term 'literature' is frequently evident in Derrida's writing; thus in the statement to his thesis jury quoted earlier one should note the cautious qualification of the word: '. . . towards literature, towards that writing which is called literary'. And in *Positions*, having referred to a recent '"literary" practice', he adds:

> But you can very well understand why I would write this word ['literary'] between quotation marks, and what equivocality must be brought into play. This new practice supposes a break with what has tied the history of the literary arts to the history of metaphysics. (11)

This linking of the history of literature – in the first two senses – with the history of metaphysics is a constant and crucial emphasis in all Derrida's dealings with the question of the literary work. Here is an early statement, from *Of Grammatology*:

> With the exception of a point of advance or a point of resistance which has only been very lately recognized as such, literary writing has, almost always and almost everywhere, in accordance with diverse fashions and across diverse ages, lent itself to that *transcendent* reading, that search for the signified which we here put in question. (160, translation modified)

'Literature' does not, therefore, name a privileged body of texts in which the hold of metaphysics on Western thought is loosened; on the contrary, literature has generally been read (and not *mis*read) in terms of the presuppositions of logocentrism, phallocentrism, presence and transcendence that Derrida has traced as a ubiquitous impulse in the philosophical tradition. (Bad news for those critics who thought that deconstruction spelled the revenge of literature on philosophy.)

Derrida insists that there is no 'essence' of literature, however, nothing that could protect a privileged corpus from the inroads of its changing discursive contexts. Here is a relevant passage from 'The Double Session':

> This text [Mallarmé's 'Mimique'] could be read as a sort of handbook of literature . . . If this handbook of literature meant to *say* [*voulait-dire*] something, which we now have some reason to doubt, it would proclaim first of all that there is no – or hardly any, ever so little – literature; that in any event there is no essence of literature, no truth of literature, no literary-being or being-literary of literature. (223)

Depicted in this way, literature doesn't appear a very potent ally for the practice of deconstruction, and the emphasis placed by Culler, Gasché and Norris on Derrida's work on, and within, the *philosophical* tradition might seem to be vindicated. Yet we need to place against this apparent disqualification Derrida's repeated insistence on the importance of literature, especially of the 'point of advance or point of resistance' mentioned in passing in the passage from *Grammatology*. In *Positions* he comments more fully on this claim:

> It is incontestable that certain texts classed as 'literary' [again in quotation marks] have seemed to me to operate breaches or infractions at the most advanced points. Artaud, Bataille, Mallarmé, Sollers. Why? At least for the reason that induces us to suspect the denomination 'literature', and that which subjects the concept to belles-lettres, to the arts, to poetry, to rhetoric, and to philosophy. These texts implement, in their very movement, the demonstration and practical deconstruction of the *representation* that was made of literature. (69, translation modified)

And the passage from 'The Double Session' that I quoted earlier, although it asserts that there is hardly any literature, ever so little literature, asserts that it is a *literary* text – Mallarmé's 'Mimique' – that would tell us this, if texts could tell us things.

Some works, then, largely works of modernity, do *not* lend themselves to the transcendent reading that has dominated the history of literature, thwarting the urge to move through the writing to a self-sufficient, pre-existing theme, intention, historical or psychological cause, referent, model or moral, and thwarting too the formalising drive that would divorce the text from questions of reference, ethics and history. (Of course, they *are* subjected to transcendent readings, often applied with impressive skill and conspicuous success – one only has to glance at the critical corpus on writers like Joyce, Stein, Woolf or Beckett. If these works of literature performed the task of deconstruction on their own, Derrida's strenuous texts would be unnecessary.) Instead these texts pose these very questions, and in a way that does not permit of philosophical answers, because they shake the ground upon which philosophical thought rests: they question the very question, 'What is?' In doing so, Derrida argues, they expose the inescapable 'ground' of philosophy – which is not a ground at all, but a primordial movement or structure of differing/differentiating/deferring/being-deferred (all these, together with a challenge to phonocentrism, are implied in Derrida's invented word *différance*) that both makes philosophy possible and renders its task of totalisation and mastery unachievable. This exposure does not present itself as a substantive feature of the literary work, however. It is not a particular *place* in the work, since there is no law that forces every text to show its literary hand at some specific point; dreams may have navels, if Freud is right on this point, but texts are not organic unities, and can be endlessly cut and regrafted without excising what I'm calling the literary moment – indeed, as Derrida has shown, the capacity to be so cut and regrafted is constitutive of all textuality. And its evanescent quality is suggested by the unstated statement of 'Mimique' ('there is no – or hardly any, ever so little – literature'): not that the quantity of literature among the texts of the Western library is small, but that the literary event, the one that shakes the 'is' before you are able to ask 'What is?', can hardly be said to 'take place' at all, is exiguous, minimal, gone before you know it is there.

Our term 'literature', in so far as it names not an institution, a body of writing, or a concept, but a structural logic that breaks through the limits of institutions and textual categories, remains appropriate, in the same way that Derrida is willing to retain a number of the terms of metaphysical discourse which mark moments of uncertainty or excess, however suppressed, within that discourse. It is not incorrect, therefore, to say that Derrida's readings of philosophical texts are particularly concerned with their 'literary' dimension; but only if we have understood that 'literature' here is not a matter of sensuous movements or narrative satisfactions, nor of the inevitable recourse to metaphor,[14] nor even of 'textuality' (in Barthes's sense) or the 'materiality of the signifier'. Questioned in a 1981 interview whether literary and poetic language can be the 'non-place which would be the "other" of philosophy' he is trying to discover, Derrida replied:

> I think so, but when I speak of literature it is not with a capital L; it is rather an allusion to certain movements which have worked around the limits of our logical concepts, certain texts which make the limits of our language tremble, exposing them as divisible and questionable. This is what the works of Blanchot, Bataille or Beckett are particularly sensitive to. ('Deconstruction and the Other', 162)

However, we should not think in terms of an *opposition* between literature and philosophy; this is already itself a philosophical structure needing to be undone. No text, for Derrida, is completely dominated by metaphysics, just as no text can completely escape metaphysics.[15] From this perspective, 'literature' is not confined to the institution or corpus of literature; it is a moment or a structural possibility in every text, whatever its public genre. Those texts which qualify neither as literature nor as philosophy – Derrida has written on letters, autobiographies, notebooks, dialogues and other uncertain or mixed modes – offer peculiar opportunities of their own to exploit the 'literary'. Of course many of Derrida's own texts are equally uncategorisable and take advantage of devices associated with literature without marking themselves as belonging to a recognisable genre. In 'Deconstruction and the Other' he says of *Glas*, 'I try to compose a *writing* which would traverse, as rigorously as possible, both the philosophical and literary elements without being definable as either' (122). And in '"This Strange Institution"' he states:

> Still now, and more desperately more than ever, I dream of a writing that would be neither philosophy nor literature, nor even contaminated by one or the other, while still keeping – I have no desire to abandon this – the memory of literature and philosophy. (73).

To the extent that his texts do avoid generic categorisation, they avoid reinstating the categories of metaphysics, but by the same token they call for a 'reading' which is not governed by those categories – the kind of reading of which Derrida's texts on literature offer a number of instances.

III

Does this leave us with, on the one hand, a mass of texts called 'literature' which merely reproduce logocentrism and thereby sustain the ethical and political structures which depend on and follow from logocentrism, and, on the other hand, as 'a point of resistance which has only very lately been recognized as such', a few 'radical' works, largely of the twentieth century, which subvert it and challenge its ethico-political corollaries? Since Derrida has used philosophical texts from all periods to demonstrate the unsettling of logocentrism at the very moment it is being reinforced, while devoting relatively little attention to literary works from earlier periods, are we to assume that literature has been, for most of its history, even more complicit with metaphysics than philosophy?[16]

In beginning to answer this question, we might pay particular attention to the careful phrase by means of which literature's solidarity with metaphysics is described in the passage I quoted earlier from *Of Grammatology*: 'Literary writing has . . . *lent itself* to this transcendent reading' (*s'est prêtée d'elle-même à* . . .). This phrase signals the *possibility* of other kinds of reading, or other ways of dealing with a text, which go against the metaphysical grain to find, or rather to produce in collaboration with one aspect of the writing, a movement that would unsettle philosophy's assumptions – and therefore those of the bulk of literature (and, of course, literary criticism) as well. In 'The Double

Session', in the course of a discussion of imitation, Derrida comments that it is 'the precedence of the imitated . . . that governs the philosophical or critical interpretation of 'literature' [yet again in quotation marks], if not the operation of literary writing' (192). In that 'if not' we have the same hesitation about the degree of literature's domination by philosophy and metaphysics, in contrast to the indubitably logocentric tradition of literary criticism. Let us note, too, the phrase in the passage from *Positions* already cited: 'These texts implement, in their very movement, the demonstration and practical deconstruction of the *representation* that was made of literature' ('la manifestation et la déconstruction pratique de la *représentation* qu'on se faisait de la littérature' – not very clearly translated in the published English version). What these modern texts deconstruct is not literature *as such* – there is no literary essence, no being-literary of literature, 'Mimique' has (almost) told us – but what has been made of literature: a 'representation' of literature (as a type of representation, among other things). The passage continues:

> it being well understood that long before these 'modern' texts a certain 'literary' practice was able to operate against this model, against this representation. But it is on the basis of these last texts, on the basis of the general configuration to be remarked in them, that one can best reread, without retrospective teleology, the law of the previous fissures. (69)

Derrida's interest in a particular set of modern texts springs, then, from his sense that here, more prominently than elsewhere in literature, is perceptible the rupturing of the classical scheme of presence and transcendence. However, they draw this quality not just from their modernity, but also from their being literary: no non-literary text, according to Derrida, stages this rupturing as forcibly. And he leaves open the possibility of examining that 'certain "literary" practice' of earlier periods, though warning us against the danger of 'retrospective teleology': we should not read earlier texts as if they were imperfect realisations of what has finally been achieved in modernity. Their specificity is to be respected, and the 'literariness' whereby logocentrism is put in question takes a unique form in each text. If we read a text along with a contemporary (or more recent) commentary that works in the reductive, 'philosophical' way typical of the tradition of literary criticism, we might find that the literary text being read has 'lent itself' to such a reading, but we might also be able to show that it exceeds or undermines such a reading by its own 'literariness', its own staging and unsettling of the issues of interpretation, form/content relations, etc. The objective in every case would be to examine how *this* reading of *this* text at *this* time engages with or evades these issues, and thence to understand more fully the differences between readings, styles of reading, historical periods, cultural sites, and so on.

When Derrida writes on *Romeo and Juliet* (in 'Aphorism Countertime'), for instance, he focuses on, and weaves together, two motifs: 'aphorism' and 'contretemps', by means of which he engages with some of the best-known features of the play: the plot of unlucky accidents, the absoluteness of the declarations of love, the question of the 'name' in the balcony scene, and so on. But what he writes is also a text of thirty-nine aphorisms, or aphoristic paragraphs, conveying in their own dissociated definitions the unmastering rhythm of the contre-temps, the truncating stroke of the aphorism. As in Derrida's treatments of modernist literature, there is an *alliance* here between his text and the text he writes on: an alliance which, like Romeo's and Juliet's, is subject to chance and contretemps, but which clearly involves an answering, a commitment, an acknowledgement of a certain responsibility. Most of Derrida's writing on philosophical texts is more guarded, less open to the chance of contretemps, and therefore more summarisable, more teach-able, more transferable. But what the writing on literary works offers the reader – in concert with the works themselves – is something like the *experience* of the testing of the limit, the shaking of the frame (though we have to divest the notion of 'experience' of any simple, originary, 'natural' force). It is not an experience that can be conveyed by descrip-tion or summary; there is no substitute for reading the text itself.

We can trace this double movement – all literature offering the pos-sibility of readings which shake the metaphysical grounds of philosophy and criticism, yet some works offering particular opportunities for such readings – in the 1981 interview from which I've already quoted. First, the more general statement:

> In literature, . . . philosophical language is still present in some sense; but it produces and presents itself as alienated from itself, at a remove, at a dis-tance. This distance provides the necessary free space from which to interro-gate philosophy anew; and it was my preoccupation with literary texts which enabled me to discern the problematic of *writing* as one of the key factors in the deconstruction of metaphysics. ('Deconstruction and the Other', 109)

Then, in the next reply, a narrowing of focus as Derrida explains his dif-ference from Heidegger partly in terms of the writers who interest him (he names Mallarmé and Blanchot) and those who interest Heidegger (Hölderlin and Rilke) – a distinction, in other words, between a lit-erature that foregrounds the relays and mediations of all knowing, all thought, and one that strives (or at least appears to strive) for some kind of unmediated access to Being.[17]

Thus the peculiar ontological status of literature – without essence, without boundaries – does not entail levelling and homogenisation: 'If one can re-read everything as literature, some textual events lend themselves [that phrase again] to this better than others, their potentialities are richer and denser' ('"This Strange Institution"', 46). But the word 'potentialities' signals that the process of *reading* is crucial, and Derrida emphasises that our readings, too, always take place in specific contexts:

> Even given that some texts appear to have a greater potential for formalization, . . . works whose performativity, in some sense, appears the greatest possible in the smallest possible space, this can give rise only to evaluations inscribed in a context, to positioned readings which are themselves formalizing and performative. Potentiality is not hidden in the text like an intrinsic property. (46–7)

Derrida's focus on modernist works does not constitute a claim for some absolute superiority, but a recognition that, as a particular reader in a particular time and place, he can most productively respond to literature as manifested in these works.

IV

The way remains open, then, for the reading of *any* literary work – just as of any philosophical or critical work – in an attempt to track down, or at least make evident the tracks of, the 'literary' moment or movement. These encounters with texts would not be 'readings' in any conventional sense of the term, of course; they would not attempt an interpretation, or an evaluation, or a cultural placing of the text, nor would they make any claim to dominate other, past or future, encounters with the text. We might get a better sense of the status of these encounters if we hold on to Derrida's word *events*, events of reading responding as responsibly as possible to the event of the text, answerable to the uniqueness of the text and thus producing their own uniqueness. (As I noted in the Introduction, Derrida uses the terms 'signature' and 'counter-signature' in '"This Strange Institution"' and elsewhere in relation to literary response: the text is that unique but iterable structure that requires an equally unique but iterable response to validate it, to allow it to speak its 'own' name.) The responsibility involved in such an event of response is a responsibility to the other, a notion which plays an important part in Derrida's thought (derived partly from Levinas's extended interrogation of the term), and at the same time a responsibility to the future, since it involves the struggle to create openings within which the other can appear beyond the scope of any of our programmes and predictions, can come to transform what we know or think we know.[18] But responsibility for Derrida is not something we simply take: we find ourselves summoned, confronted by an undecidability which is also always an opportunity and a demand, a chance and a risk.

It is important to stress this concern with the otherness and singularity of the work, its difference from all other works, its historical particularity and irreducibility, since this aspect of deconstruction is often overlooked; for Derrida, the question of the relation between the singular and the general, the unique and the universal, is one of the questions that literature persistently stages in its full undecidability.[19] But at the same time, such responses to literary works would be very different from the responses of the critical tradition to literary objects seen as unique forms: they would make evident the fact that, far from being punctual and self-enclosed, both events, the work and the reading, have a structure that renders them repeatable, readable, misreadable, divisible, graftable within an infinite variety of contexts, open to an unpredictable future. Their uniqueness is not opposed to their iterability and citability, it is constituted by it. The event of the 'primary' text is brought about by the event of the text that answers to and affirms it, thus complicating the opposition of a pure primariness and a pure secondariness on which traditional criticism depends. The encounters I am describing would not be attempts to 'prove' some general philosophical truth, or to illustrate some general movement of deconstruction; rather, they would be engagements with the specificities of texts in order to dramatise, to make happen, each in its own unique way, the staging, the self-dividing, of presence, of meaning, of reference. They would, of course, be themselves 'literary' texts.

This sense of what a deconstructive criticism might be has a clear ethico-political dimension. It's not a question of the moral power of great literature as traditionally taught in humanistic criticism, nor of the detection of morally and politically suspect ideological positions concealed in literary works that is typical of many more recent approaches, but of the supremely difficult ethical act of responding to the singularity and otherness of the unique instance – whether person, act or text – while bringing to bear on it, without merely *applying* them, all the general laws and norms which constitute both it and the judging discourse. Philosophy – and both literary criticism and ethics count here as domains of philosophy – can offer little help; its founding principles and its continuing institutions are undermined by any such act. This is not to decry critical analysis which operates by means of the application of rules under the aegis of philosophy; most of what we do as critics is just such an activity and the skills involved in this activity form the basis of all reading. But just as no *literary* work is ever entirely the programmable reaction to events or experiences but reinvents the very conditions which enable it to come into being, surpassing the logic of computers or psychological and sociological rules, so no *critical* work that does justice to what is literary in literature, and to the specific literary work it's answering to and affirming, can be solely a skilful application of existing rules. Its singularity affirms, countersigns, makes possible the singularity of the other, of the text, but also necessarily betrays it, does violence to it (otherwise it could not be a singular, but merely an algorithmic reaction); and we touch here on the difficult, and essential, question of the violence at the heart of any ethical relation.[20]

An obvious question is whether Derrida's published writings on literary works could provide a model for such an activity of literary response and responsibility. Since one of the metaphysical relations that they would work to undermine is that between a model and an imitation, it's hard to give a positive answer. To do so would be to imply that from Derrida's diverse texts some useful paradigm could be produced, and then reproduced, whereas any such paradigm would leave out precisely what constitutes the efficacy of Derrida's engagements: their unique responsiveness to the uniqueness of the text. One might just as well try to produce a paradigm of the literary work by abstracting from, say, Blanchot's *La folie du jour*, Mallarmé's 'Mimique' and Kafka's 'Vor dem Gesetz'. But Derrida's texts, too, call for a response, not only as one reads them, but in going on to read other texts as well; and this response may produce further texts that also possess a singular respect for singularity, an iterable recognition of iterability, and a deconstructive concern with deconstruction. No one is ever going to be able to say with finality: these critical texts are deconstructive and these are not, because there is no place outside the chain of signatures and countersignatures, responses and responses to responses, from which such a statement could be made. It's tempting to replace the word 'literature' in some of Derrida's formulations by the term 'deconstruction': there is no essence of deconstruction, no truth of deconstruction, no being-deconstructive of deconstruction, by which a deconstructive text could be infallibly recognised. All one can do is testify to the deconstructive effect, which is to say the 'literary' effect, of a certain text (literary or critical), in a certain reading, and to attempt to fulfil one's obligation, as a responsible reader who is also a writer, to do justice to that quality, trusting to future readers to confirm, and re-enact, one's testimony.

Let me return, then, to the question I posed earlier: what has literary criticism to gain from becoming more fully acquainted with Derrida's texts on literature? The existence of these texts, it should be clear, does not imply an injunction to put a halt to all the many things that make up the diverse activity of literary studies in order to do something else (though it's hard to imagine any intellectual activity that would not be touched in *some* way by as fundamental a rethinking of the grounds of thought – and action – as Derrida's). Even limiting the question to the tradition of critical interpretation and evaluation, it would hardly be responsible to ignore the importance of work that has been done, and will continue to be done, by way of literary commentary and explication, the kind of work that Derrida calls, in *Of Grammatology*, an 'indispensable guardrail' (158). (The last thing Derrida does with the philosophical tradition, after all, is to dismiss it.) But anyone who finds that Derrida's claims for the deconstructive potential of literature carry some weight (and this implies also some acceptance of his more general arguments concerning the role of metaphysical thinking in our history and contemporary culture), and who experiences in reading his texts on literary works a series of events which seem to manifest, however fleetingly, that potential, may feel impelled to work toward strategies of literary engagement which produce events of a similar sort (though always, of course, singular events – with a singularity that is crucial to their effect).[21] The result may be less recognisable as literary criticism than most of the 'deconstructive criticism' written in the wake of Derrida's texts on philosophy (and here we see the force of Gasché's insistence, cited earlier, that Derrida's writing on literature is far removed from literary criticism), but, in combining a concern for that which marks literature as a site of resistance to metaphysics and transcendence (an ethico-political as well as an intellectual resistance) with a response to the iterable singularity of the literary work, it would be a way of allowing the work to speak that does not immediately subject it to history, sociology, dogmatics, aesthetics or some other philosophically determined discipline.

It's not just philosophy which, since Plato, has marginalised literature; our political and social histories show that no matter how radical or progressive a literary work is in terms of *content*, its being placed in the category of 'literature' – as traditionally understood – functions to take away its potential force as praxis. Derrida refers in '"This Strange Institution"' to the space of literature in our culture as the space where, in principle, *anything and everything may be said*, the space of '*tout dire*' (36–9), a cultural positioning which gives literature enormous power by means of the same act which takes all power away. A deconstructive literary criticism will not be one that apes Derrida's writing on literature;

it will be, in fact, one that does *not* ape Derrida, or anyone else (and so I should talk of deconstructive literary criticism*s*, with of course both the words 'literary' and 'criticisms' doing duty for as yet unnamed activities). It will be a series of events allowing literature, that 'so little' literature, to be heard in a way that, for once, actually matters.

Notes

1. The fact that for many years philosophers have been increasingly marginal-ised in certain cultures is perhaps in part a delayed revenge for what Plato did to the poets. Not that anyone would suspect governments of acting in the name of literature as they shut down philosophy departments, but there is a certain degree of continuity between a political attitude which can claim 'There is no such thing as society' (one of Margaret Thatcher's more memorable utterances) and what have traditionally been thought of as the (un- or anti-philosophical) pleasures of literature. See Eagleton's discussion of the way in which in Britain 'the aesthetic becomes a weapon in the hands of political reaction' (*Ideology*, 60).
2. Even the texts of a number of quite unphilosophical literary critics have been invested with a philosophical aura by the invocation of Derrida's name. Perhaps all major critical movements during this century have claimed some authority from an allegiance that can be called, in the broad-est sense, philosophical, whether openly as in the scientific pretensions of I. A. Richards's 'practical criticism', the appeals to Marxism in leftist criticism and the use of linguistics in structuralism, semiotics and stylistics, or covertly, as in the Wittgensteinian cast of F. R. Leavis's criticism and the quasi-technical approach of New Criticism. More recently, physics, biology, evolutionary science and neuroscience and other 'hard' sciences have been employed to stiffen theoretical arguments about literature.
3. A notorious instance of the philosophical establishment's perception of Derrida as the most potent of all imaginable threats was the opposition by a number of senior philosophers at Cambridge University to the award of an honorary degree. Their names appeared below a statement which included such comments as 'By denying the distinctions between fact and fiction, observation and imagination, evidence and prejudice, [Derrida's 'doc-trines'] make complete nonsense of science, technology and medicine . . . These doctrines threaten the very basis of all subjects' (flysheet circulated by the Council of Cambridge University, 1992). Readers of such comments might well wonder whether the blatant failure to read the texts at issue does not constitute a somewhat graver threat to 'all subjects'.
4. I have engaged more fully with Lamarque's work in a special issue of the *British Journal of Aesthetics* devoted to his book; see 'The Singular Events'.
5. What follows is, inevitably, a highly simplified sketch of the impact of Derrida's work on North American literary studies in the 1980s; in particu-lar, it omits the crucial mediating role played by a number of critics based in the USA. It might be said that the shape taken by 'deconstructive literary criticism' in the United States was determined more by Paul de Man than

by Derrida – though Derrida was the seminal influence on the phase of de Man's work that had this effect. A more detailed sketch is offered by Leitch in *American Literary Criticism*, chapter 10; by his silence with regard to Derrida's writings on literature and the issues they raise, Leitch confirms my sense of the slightness of their impact in the USA in this period.

6. For a selection of Derrida's writings on literary texts and an annotated bibliography of works by Derrida of special relevance to literature up to 1992, see *Acts of Literature*.

7. In Culler's 1997 introductory book, *Literary Theory*, Derrida continues to feature as the author of essays on Rousseau's *Confessions*, J. L. Austin and metaphor in philosophy rather than as a reader of literary works. However, in 2005, in a short essay entitled 'Derrida and the Singularity of Literature', Culler foregrounds Derrida's engagements with literature.

8. The following comment points to the basic (and highly problematic) dichotomy assumed by any such approach, while establishing the link between two of its most important practitioners, Geoffrey Hartman and Gregory L. Ulmer: 'Like Hartman [in *Saving the Text*], I approach Derrida through his style rather than his philosophical arguments' (Ulmer, *Applied Grammatology*, 318).

9. Norris somewhat surprisingly claimed that Derrida's more overtly 'literary' kind of writing represented the dominant way in which his work had been used in literary criticism: 'Hence their [deconstructive critics'] strongly marked preference for those texts where the deconstructive groundwork (so to speak) is very largely taken as read, and where Derrida most thoroughly exploits the resultant opportunities for experiments in style' (*Derrida*, 21). Perhaps this was a necessary falsification in order for Norris to be able to dismiss the field of literary studies and concentrate on Derrida's importance for philosophy.

10. Since the completion of the first version of this essay in 1989, it is pleasing to report, a number of writers have responded fruitfully to Derrida's literary readings, including Nicholas Royle (*After Derrida*, *Jacques Derrida*, *In Memory of Jacques Derrida*), Rodolphe Gasché ('On Responding Responsibly', 'A Relation Called "Literary"'), J. Hillis Miller ('Deconstruction and a Poem', 'Derrida and Literature'), Claire Colebrook ('Literature'), Peggy Kamuf ('"Fiction" and the Experience of the Other'), Leslie Hill (*Radical Indecision*) and Timothy Clark (*The Poetics of Singularity*).

11. The sticking-power of the term 'indeterminacy' is visible in the republication in 1988 of Derrida's 'Signature Event Context' and 'Limited Inc a b c . . .' in *Limited Inc*, with an 'Afterword' in which he makes abundantly clear his distance from the word; all in vain, for the back-cover blurb exults in 'Derrida's most controversial idea, that linguistic meaning is fundamentally indeterminate . . .'

12. I consider these issues from a different perspective, and at somewhat greater length in 'Derrida and the Questioning of Literature', the introduction to *Acts of Literature*.

13. This is not the place to rehearse Derrida's arguments about the history of philosophy since Plato as a history of 'the metaphysics of presence', of 'logocentrism', of the privileging of the signified, of the reliance on origins,

teleology and transcendence, and so on; in using such terms, I'm obliged to take those extended and complex discussions as read.

14. The notion that deconstruction involves the demonstration that philosophical texts are, in spite of themselves, metaphorical or rhetorical, is a widespread one, but not one that could be derived from Derrida's writing; indeed, the essay most explicitly concerned with metaphor and philosophy, 'White Mythology', works hard to make such a simplification impossible. The idea persists in introductions to Derrida, however; thus Norris can represent Derrida as 'arguing that philosophy – like literature – is a product of *rhetorical* figures and devices' ('Deconstruction', 7).

15. Discussing 'transcendent' and 'non-transcendent' readings in '"This Strange Institution"' (that is, readings which do or do not close upon the meaning or referent), Derrida insists both that 'One can do a nontranscendent reading of any text whatever' (44) and 'A literature which forbade . . . transcendence would annul itself' (45).

16. The point about Derrida's focus on twentieth-century literature should not be exaggerated, however; the authors he has written on include Shakespeare (in 'Aphorism Countertime'), Marvell and Milton (in *Memoirs of the Blind*), Baudelaire (in *Given Time*), Flaubert (in 'An Idea of Flaubert') and Mallarmé (in 'The Double Session' and 'Mallarmé').

17. De Man, however, prefers to see Romantic literature as equally alert to the relays and mediations of thought and Heidegger's reading of Hölderlin as one example of a repeated misreading of Romanticism; see, especially, 'Heidegger's Exegeses of Hölderlin'.

18. I present a longer discussion of this set of issues, which I can only briefly allude to here, in 'Modernist Form'. For a brilliant account of the futurity implicit in reading literature in the wake of Derrida's thinking (and that of Barthes and Blanchot), see Hill, *Radical Indecision*.

19. See, in particular, 'Before the Law', *The Gift of Death* (especially 57–88), and the discussion of singularity in '"This Strange Institution"' (58–70).

20. The issues addressed in this paragraph are central to Derrida's 'Force of Law', though they are not discussed there with any reference to literature. Derrida's essay was published in a special issue of *The Cardozo Law Review* entitled *Deconstruction and the Possibility of Justice* with a gathering of accompanying essays, a number of which appear in the volume of the same name edited by Carlson, Cornell and Rosenfeld. See also the follow-up selection of essays entitled *On the Necessity of Violence for Any Possibility of Justice* in a later issue of the same journal. The question of violence at the heart of the ethical is also raised by Derrida in *Adieu* – see Chapter 7 below.

21. Or, indeed, to seek out texts of the past that function, or can be shown to function, in a similar way. 'Deconstructive' responses to literature, in the sense in which I am using the term, did not come into existence with Derrida's writings. A fruitful place to look would be literary works themselves.

Chapter 2

Deconstruction Today: Literature, Postcolonialism and the Secret

I

What would a map of deconstruction today look like? If deconstruction is, as both its enemies and its friends have claimed, a kind of virus and we were able to produce – on the model of the colourful mappings one might see in a treatise on global diseases – a large chart of the intellectual world with its presence marked in red, how would the result appear?

Before attempting to answer this question, we have to be sure we know what deconstruction is, or, if this is not possible (because deconstruction might be said to cause problems for the act of definition), at least in what sense the term is to be used in this book. It will help to begin by following Jacques Derrida, writing in 'Some Statements and Truisms', in distinguishing between *deconstruction* and *deconstructionism*. The latter is a word often used by opponents of Derrida's work, or by those who are ignorant of it; deconstructionism is practised, such people tell us, by deconstructionists, who believe that there is no such thing as meaning, or truth, or knowledge (and often, by implication, morality). (After his death, Derrida was called in some newspapers 'The father of deconstructionism'.) But it's also a useful word to apply, as Derrida himself does, to a certain critical methodology – usually addressed to literary texts – that was very popular in English-speaking cultures in the late 1970s and 1980s, notably the United States, where it functioned as a kind of Indian summer prolonging the reign of New Criticism. The very fact that it was a method of interpretation applied in this manner made it very different from deconstruction as it is to be found in Derrida's work, which has never offered a set of procedures or a toolbox for the analysis of literature. Although it survives in some guides to literary theory and first-year university classrooms, deconstructionism as a way of gaining academic credit is dead and little mourned.

Deconstruction without the -ism is something else – indeed, 'it' is not a 'thing'. Its widest interpretation is very wide indeed. In the course of his argument in 'Some Statements' Derrida offers, as an example of what one might say about it (and therefore as a less than wholly adequate way of representing the topic under discussion), the following assertions:

> Deconstruction is neither a theory nor a philosophy. It is neither a school nor a method. It is not even a discourse, nor an act, nor a practice. It is what happens, what is happening today in what they call society, politics, diplomacy, economics, historical reality, and so on and so forth. (85)

This understanding of what 'deconstruction' means would result in our map being coloured almost entirely red.

If, however, we wish to think of deconstruction in slightly less encompassing terms, we can legitimately limit it to the influence of Derrida's work on intellectual, cultural, social and political practices. It is true that a number of other thinkers have laid claim to the term, or without necessarily using the term itself have deployed and developed Derrida's arguments and examples in interesting and important ways. But the word 'deconstruction' is inseparably associated with Derrida: not only did he make it his own by reinventing an old French locution, but in spite of some hesitation at times ('It is a word I have never liked and whose fortune has disagreeably surprised me' ('The Time of a Thesis', 44)) he has continued to make use of it in a variety of intellectual enterprises. Nearly all serious work that calls itself, or is generally accepted to be, 'deconstructive' acknowledges Derrida. If there were to be a second name attached to the term, it would probably be – at least in the English-speaking world – that of Paul de Man, who developed his own unique mode of reading that has some similarities with Derrida's (though perhaps not as many as Derrida himself liked to claim), and who, after becoming acquainted with Derrida's work, started to associate his own reading procedures with Derridean deconstruction. However, the question of de Man's influence and importance is a very different one (a chart of the viral penetration of de Manian deconstruction would today indicate only sporadic infection), and it is not my concern in this chapter.

It is also important to register the fact that Derrida undertook a wide range of different projects, not all of which can be called 'deconstructive'. However, this need not inhibit an account of deconstruction today. Unlike 'deconstructionism', a term which could be applied only very occasionally to Derrida's *oeuvre* (and usually at moments where he undermines the very applicability he is making possible), 'deconstruction' is appropriate for a great deal of Derrida's output, and certainly that part of it that has been most important in other fields. In the literary field, our particular interest here, 'deconstruction' and 'Derrida's work' are near enough to being exchangeable for us to take them as one.

With this clarification of what we mean, let us turn to our task of mapping deconstruction today. Thirty years ago, the project would have been a much simpler one. An intense red dot in Paris would have signalled the home, and the institutional and intellectual base, of Jacques Derrida, a few other dots around the city and around France would have indicated the locations of his early collaborators and followers, and more red spots would have featured in the United States, Great Britain and a few other countries. The American spots would have been largest in Baltimore and New Haven – after early visits to Johns Hopkins, Derrida began a regular annual visit to Yale in 1975 – and the British ones more widely dispersed, though Southampton, Sussex, Warwick and Essex would have been among them. If our map could show the importance of deconstruction in different disciplines, the redness in France would be largely in philosophy; in the USA and Britain largely in literary studies. If we had another colour, say blue, to signal the presence of an antibody fiercely resisting the virus of deconstruction, it would be widespread through both philosophy and literature departments in all countries.

But today, the map would look very different. Rather than red dots we would have to paint large areas of many countries and many disciplines in varying shades of pink, to show how widely deconstruction has permeated intellectual and creative activity even when no direct acknowledgement is made. Superimposed on the pink would be the red dots indicating the large number of teachers and scholars around the globe whose work is influenced directly by deconstruction; these would be more numerous, if perhaps more scattered, than in 1975. There would be fewer blue areas, though they would still be as intense.

I use this rather contrived metaphor because it seems to me that the significance of deconstruction today is very different from what might have been predicted in the heady 1970s – heady, at least, for those, like me, whose sense of the discipline they were involved in was transformed by an encounter with the work of Derrida. (Other French thinkers were important at the time – for instance, Michel Foucault, Jacques Lacan, Roland Barthes and Julia Kristeva – but none had quite the effect that Derrida did.) Who could have foreseen that Derrida's highly demanding engagements with his philosophical forebears and contemporaries, and occasionally with literary figures, would lead to a situation where it is almost impossible to enumerate exhaustively the fields that his work has touched? Apart from philosophy and literary studies, one has to include theology, legal studies, architecture, musicology, cultural studies, postcolonial studies, ethical theory, political theory, theatre studies, film studies, media studies, geography, nursing, historiography and art history and criticism – and doubtless many more of which I am unaware. In creative fields, too, Derrida's influence is widely perceptible (and even where there is no real influence, his name is frequently invoked as a talisman or claim to intellectual depth): these include the visual arts, music, theatre, poetry and fiction, and new developments in electronic art forms. Linguistically, too, the spread of Derrida's work has been remarkable: I haven't found any figures about the number of languages into which it has been translated, but it is no doubt the equal of any twentieth-century philosopher or cultural critic.

Much of this influence is of the kind that would produce only a faint shade of pink on our map. The spectre of deconstruction is present – or perhaps somewhere between present and absent – whenever a wariness is expressed about too-simple appeals to categories such as truth, meaning and, indeed, presence, whenever there is a willingness to attend to that which has been marginalised in the constitution of a dominant entity or power, whenever there is a suspicion of neat binary oppositions. Of course, in such tendencies one can trace many other influences, both ancient and modern, but the fact that they are so widespread today has something at least to do with the effect the work of Derrida has had on our habits of thought.

More intense pinks and reds would indicate the work of those who have developed Derrida's insights, of whom there are a great many, for one of the remarkable features of deconstruction, and one of the signs of its genuine originality, has been its invigoration of other inventive thinkers. There are those who are more or less Derrida's contemporaries, and who continue to be productive and innovative, such figures as Jean-Luc Nancy, René Major, Hélène Cixous, J. Hillis Miller and Hayden White. There are those who have left an important legacy in which the significance of Derrida's work is evident (if not fully acknowledged in every case), such as Barthes, Foucault, Lacan, de Man, Jean-François Lyotard, Emmanuel Levinas and Gilles Deleuze. There are others who have taken their work in a different direction after an early impetus from Derrida, such as Kristeva and Tzvetan Todorov. There are those who have felt the need to define their work against Derrida's, such as Jürgen Habermas, Pierre Bourdieu and John Searle. There are three current academic superstars who owe more to Derrida than they are usually willing to admit, Alain Badiou, Slavoj Žižek and Giorgio Agamben.[1] And there is a large contingent of younger writers for whom Derrida has provided creative inspiration, including Geoffrey Bennington, Nicholas Royle, Jonathan Culler, Judith Butler, Maud Ellmann, Jean-Jacques Lecercle, Henry Louis Gates, Barbara Johnson, Thomas Keenan, Peggy Kamuf, Marian Hobson, Eve Kosofsky Sedgwick, Christopher Johnson, Diane Elam . . . the list could go on and on (and I haven't even begun to name those who write in languages other than English).

Then there is Derrida himself. Until very shortly before his death, he continued to teach and to write and to lecture with almost unbelievable energy; as I noted in the Introduction, the total number of his books is around seventy, and although nothing has had quite the effect of the works of his *annus mirabilis* of 1967 (*La voix et le phénomène*, translated in 1973 as *Speech and Phenomena*; *De la grammatologie*, translated in 1976 as *Of Grammatology*; *L'écriture et la différence*, translated in 1978 as *Writing and Difference*), some of his most influential work has been published in the last fifteen years. This recent work has had an impact in a variety of areas, including (to name just a few) political and social theory – *Spectres de Marx/Specters of Marx* (1993/1994) and *Politiques de l'amitié/Politics of Friendship* (1994/1997); ethics – *Adieu à Emmanuel Levinas/Adieu to Emmanuel Levinas* (1997/1999); theology – the collection which Derrida co-edited with Gianni Vattimo, *La Religion/Religion*, containing Derrida's essay 'Foi et savoir'/'Faith and Knowledge' (1996/1998); ethics *and* theology – 'Donner la mort'/ *The Gift of Death* (1992/1995 and 2008); and animal ethics – *L'animal que donc je suis/The Animal that Therefore I Am* (2006/2008).[2] We are a long way from deconstruction*ism* in this work, but the spirit of deconstruction is very much alive in it.

The topics that Derrida explored in his later work have no direct relation to literary studies in its more academic guises – but they bear an intimate relation to what we do when we read, write, teach, translate and make critical judgements. They all operate at the difficult juncture of the unconditional and the conditional; like the gift, treated in earlier works such as *Given Time*, they involve what Derrida calls 'an experience of the impossible'. Moreover, the very notion of the 'literary', which has fascinated Derrida from an early age,[3] shares many features with some of the topics Derrida examined late in his life, as I noted in Chapter 1: it too points to an activity or an event that, like welcoming or forgiving, goes beyond the norms of the rational accounting by which our lives are dominated, challenging the limited understanding of the possible that governs our calculations and programmes. If the writing and reading of literature are to be revalued in a world more and more driven by economic profit and objective assessment, deconstruction, in all its senses, will remain a crucial resource.

II

Out of this rich, not to say bewildering, array of influences and developments, let me single out one as illustrative of the way in which Derrida's work has invigorated intellectual enquiry (and often spurred practical action) well beyond the purview of the philosophical tradition that is his own disciplinary home. A striking development in literary and cultural studies in the English-speaking world over the past twenty-five years has been the growth of what is somewhat inadequately known as 'postcolonial studies'. An outsider to this field might speculate that its major philosophical influences would be from political theory, and in particular from Marxism and its descendants, in the theorising of colonial resistance and liberation. This assumption would not be wrong, in so far as the Marxist tradition was a powerful impetus to the analysis and theorisation of colonisation and the postcolonial condition. However, what spurred the new disciplinary field into existence was the impact of a number of interrelated theoretical discourses, deconstruction among them, in the 1970s and after.

The most cogent account of the growth of postcolonial studies out of what became known generically, and rather unsatisfactorily, as 'poststructuralism' is Robert Young's in *White Mythologies*. Young argues that 'deconstruction involves the decentralization and decolonization of European thought' (18), and sees Derrida's work as a profound challenge to the ethnocentrism of the West. (Young's title echoes an essay by Derrida on the question of metaphor.) Having begun his publishing career with a widely used poststructuralist anthology, *Untying the Text* (1981), and as co-editor of the journal largely responsible for introducing Derrida's work to Britain, the *Oxford Literary Review*, Young has gone on to become one of the leading scholars of postcolonialism: besides *White Mythologies* (1990), subtitled *Writing History and the West*, he has published *Colonial Desire: Hybridity in Theory, Culture and Race* (1995), *Postcolonialism: An Historical Introduction* (2001) and *Postcolonialism: A Very Short Introduction* (2003). He also helped to found and is serving as General Editor of one of the most important journals in the field: *Interventions: International Journal of Postcolonial Studies*, which began publication in 1999. Although Young's recent work has turned from the largely theoretical and textual to the political and empirical, often with a strong narrative impulse, deconstruction remains one of the major resources of his thought.[4]

A critic who was associated with the *Oxford Literary Review* as it set about establishing itself as a leading vehicle for French literary theory and philosophy was Homi Bhabha, then a lecturer at the University of

Sussex. In the last fifteen years, his has become one of the most promi-
nent voices in postcolonial studies, an obligatory reference for anyone
seeking to engage with the field. The importance to Bhabha of Derrida's
work was evident right from the start, and Derrida remains, with Lacan,
Foucault and Fanon, among the most fruitful reference points for his
writing. In his highly influential book *The Location of Culture* he argues
for a more subtle understanding of the relations between coloniser and
colonised than has traditionally been put forward (by both sides), and
in so doing he finds a number of Derrida's strategies helpful; among the
terms that contribute to his argument are 'supplement', '*différance*', the
'parergon' and '*sur-vivre*'.

The Derridean genealogy of another leading figure in the field of postcolonialism is even clearer. The publication that brought Derrida's challenge to prevailing modes of thought into the English-speaking world
more fully than any other – though it was not the first of Derrida's books
to appear in English – was Gayatri Chakravorty Spivak's translation of
Of Grammatology in 1976. The heroic effort of a young Indian academic
who had made a home for herself in the United States and undertaken
a PhD dissertation on W. B. Yeats, the translation was preceded by an
eighty-page introduction in which Spivak wrestled with the strangeness
and difficulty of Derrida's work. The book's impact was extraordinary,
even though its argument about speech and writing quickly became
oversimplified and travestied in its spread across the campuses of North
America. Spivak's subsequent career, like Young's and Bhabha's, shows
an increasing commitment to questions of coloniality and migration,
capitalist exploitation and popular resistance. In addition, she has
devoted much attention to questions of gender and pedagogy. All these
topics feature in her major books, including *In Other Worlds* (1987),
Outside in the Teaching Machine (1993), *A Critique of Postcolonial
Reason* (1999) and *Other Asias* (2008). Yet the connection with Derrida
and deconstruction remains unbroken: to take just one example, *A
Critique of Postcolonial Reason* has an Appendix entitled 'The Setting
to Work of Deconstruction' in which Spivak rather baldly summarises
Derrida's intellectual career, as if the arguments and positions she sets
out here are the necessary foundation for an understanding of the difficult, 400-page book that – the Derridean term is apt – they supplement.
In this Appendix, Spivak argues for the 'setting to work of deconstruction outside the formalizing calculus specific to the academic institution'
(431), and gives as examples the way it 'breaks hesitantly into an active
resistance to the inexorable calculus of globalization' and is 'engaged in
displacing the binary opposition between economic growth and well-
being by proposing alternatives to "development"' (430).

During the exponential growth of postcolonial studies in North America in the 1990s, there were many who spoke (with or without irony, and with or without the adjectives 'holy' or 'unholy') of a 'trinity' of theorists central to the field's success in the academic world. These were Bhabha, Spivak and Edward Said, whose book *Orientalism* (1978) is widely regarded as one of the founding texts of postcolonialism. To a large degree, Said represents a version of postcolonial studies that is less dependent on, and sometimes actively opposed to, the writings of Derrida; the metropolitan French theorist who is of most importance to this school of postcolonialism is Foucault. However, it is sometimes forgotten that the book with which Said made his name, *Beginnings: Intention and Method* (1975), is deeply indebted to French theoretical writing. Foucault is, as one might expect, the most obvious influence and Derrida gets somewhat short shrift, but Derrida is included in the roll-call of French writers who 'have sought to show that literature, psychology, philosophy, and language are too independent of direct and constant human intervention to be reduced to the traditional creeds of humanism for explanation or understanding' (374). One might hazard the thought that Said's account of the complexity of beginning would have benefited from a fuller engagement with Derrida's questioning of the notion of origin – a questioning that, as it happens, is very well encapsulated in Spivak's Appendix to her *Critique of Postcolonial Reason*.

Running counter to the Derridean influence on postcolonial studies is a strong current of resistance by those who feel that the pursuit of 'theory' has been to the detriment of material analysis and actual achievements on the ground. Benita Parry, for instance, has been a consistent critic of French theory, as may be seen in her collection of essays, *Postcolonial Studies: A Materialist Critique* (2004). (It is somewhat ironic that her most influential essay, the modestly titled 'Problems in Current Theories of Colonial Discourse', was originally published in the aforementioned *Oxford Literary Review*.) In her introduction, Parry takes Young to task for claiming a major role for poststructuralism in the coming into being of postcolonial studies. In *Postcolonialism: An Historical Introduction*, Young asserts of post-structuralism that 'its deconstruction of the idea of totality was born out of the experience of, and forms of resistance to, the totalizing regimes of the late colonial state, particularly French Algeria' (415), and he pays particular homage to Derrida, who, 'neither French nor Algerian, always anti-nationalist and cosmopolitan, critical of western ethnocentrism from *Of Grammatology*'s very first page, preoccupied with justice and injustice, developed deconstruction as a procedure for intellectual and cultural decolonization within the metropolis to which he had sailed on the *Ville d'Alger* in 1949' (416). Parry suggests that the rift between a deconstructive and a materialist approach to postcoloniality is less bridgeable than Young imagines. This is a debate that will undoubtedly continue.[5]

III

Postcolonial studies is just one area in which deconstruction in its earlier manifestation in Derrida's writing made a formative contribution, and in which it is still an active ingredient in creative debates. Derrida's engagements with questions of ethics, politics and religion – topics which always had a place in his writing but which became more central in his later work – have not yet had time to have their full impact. In particular, his thinking on a number of topics with wide relevance to several fields of intellectual enquiry – and, indeed, to our daily lives – deserves to have significant effects. Among these are his discussions of justice (for example, 'Force of Law'), faith (see the collection *Acts of Religion*), hospitality (see Derrida and Dufourmantelle, *Of Hospitality*; 'Hostipitality'; *Adieu*),[6] forgiveness (*On Cosmopolitanism and Forgiveness*) and animal existence (*The Animal That Therefore I Am*).

Some of these topics resonate in the work of another great writer of our time, the novelist J. M. Coetzee. It is perhaps no surprise that when several hundred people signed a letter to the *New York Times* to protest at its ignorant and narrow-minded obituary of Derrida, Coetzee was among the signatories. Coetzee's novels are by no means 'illustrations' or 'exemplifications' of Derrida's thinking; if they were, they would hardly be as profound and disturbing as they are. But Coetzee and Derrida are animated by some of the same concerns and haunted by some of the same fears. Derrida's continuing engagement with the question of responsibility to the other – perhaps most dramatically evident when, in *The Gift of Death*, he explores the consequences of the only apparently tautologous slogan *tout autre est tout autre*, which one might inadequately render as 'every other is wholly other'[7] – is also a thread that runs throughout Coetzee's work, from the American propagandist's relation to the Vietnamese enemy and the eighteenth-century hunter's treatment of South Africa's indigenous inhabitants in the two novellas of his first work of fiction, *Dusklands*, through the many master–servant relations and racial conflicts that occur throughout his writing and the irruption of unplaceable individuals like Friday in *Foe* and Vercueil in *Age of Iron*, to the devastating staging of one man's failure to acknowledge his responsibility to the other in *Disgrace*.[8] To turn to a Coetzee novel – *The Master of Petersburg*, say – after reading some of Derrida's discussions of ethics, hospitality and the future as *arrivant*, is to experience the fraught encounter with the other in a way that both confirms and tests the philosophical account one has been absorbing. When Dostoevsky, the central character of *The Master of Petersburg*, takes in a beggar for the night, aware that he is probably a spy in government employ, the question of one's responsibility to the other is posed in concrete terms that echo but also challenge Derrida's ethical stance. Readers who have no awareness of Derrida's work are still likely to find the novel powerful, of course, but there can be no doubt that one's experience of Coetzee's probing fiction is rendered richer by being juxtaposed with Derrida's explorations of related issues.

The same is true not just for all of Coetzee's fiction but for much other literary writing as well. Some of the earlier readings of literary texts influenced by Derrida's work – I think, for instance, of Barbara Johnson's brilliant reading of Melville's *Billy Budd* in 'Melville's Fist' – were concerned to tease out the contradictions that animate the narrative in a manner parallel to Derrida's deconstructive readings of Rousseau, Saussure or Plato. Derrida's own engagements with literature, however, tended to learn from the text, to treat literature not as an object for dissection but as a staging of some of the most significant and mysterious aspects of human (and sometimes non-human) experience.[9] This is an area in which we are still, I suspect, learning to be Derrida's contemporary, as Richard Ellmann famously said of Joyce. Take Derrida's repeated association of the literary with 'the secret'.[10] What does he mean by statements like the following?

> Here we touch on a structure of the secret about which literary fiction tells us the essential or which tells us, in return, the essential concerning the possibility of a literary fiction. (*Given Time*, 153)

> There is in literature, in the *exemplary* secret of literature, a chance of saying everything without touching upon the secret . . . Even if the secret is no secret, even if there has never been a secret, a single secret. Not one. ('Passions', 29–30)

> Literature is the place of all these secrets without secrecy, of all these crypts without depth, with no other basis than the abyss of the call or address, without any law other than the singularity of the event called *the work*. ('Literature in Secret', 157)

Although a number of theorists have commented on this aspect of Derrida's understanding of literature,[11] its implications still have to be followed through with any comprehensiveness. Derrida is clearly, as so often, taking a word with which we are extremely familiar and putting it to unfamiliar uses, so that the reader is obliged to puzzle out his meaning. This is not a gratuitous or wilful courting of difficulty, but a strategy to get recalcitrant language to deal with operations and relationships that do not conform to the norms of linguistic – or logical – construction. At times, Derrida distinguishes the secret of which he is speaking here from the common-or-garden secret by calling it the 'absolute' or 'unconditional' secret in contrast to the 'conditional' secret. The former is not a matter of concealing something that could be revealed or communicated, but of the apprehension of something that can never be known. Like the famous purloined letter in the Poe story of that name, it is in plain sight but invisible. It thus has a relation to the secret in the ordinary sense and yet it is clearly very different. The relation between the two uses of the term has a number of parallels in Derrida's work: words such as 'hospitality', 'forgiveness', the 'gift', 'democracy' and 'responsibility' can all be used of experiences or institutions that we encounter in our quotidian existence or they can be used of absolutes operating without conditions and not directly observable though essential to the operation of their mundane cousins. A similar relation – which is not simply a relation of intensity or quality or of the real to the ideal – exists between what Derrida calls 'justice' and what he calls 'law'.[12]

The two modalities of the secret emerge in an interview published in *Points*. Asked about a comment that he writes 'in the position of non-knowing rather than of the secret', he explains that this is

> a structural non-knowing, which is heterogeneous, foreign to knowledge. It's not just the unknown that could be known and that I give up trying to know . . . And when I specify that it is a non-knowing and not a secret, I mean that when a text appears to be crypted, it is not at all in order to calculate or to intrigue or to bar access to something that I know and that others must not know; it is a more ancient, more originary experience, if you will, of the secret. (201)

The first secret is that of hidden knowledge; the more 'ancient' experience of the secret, the secret of non-knowing, is the absolute secret.

Derrida provides a concrete example of the secrecy of literature in *Given Time*. Analysing 'Counterfeit Money', a story by Baudelaire, he speculates on the possibility that the narrator's friend, who has apparently given a counterfeit coin to a beggar, has in fact given him a genuine coin and lied to the narrator about it. Whether or not the coin was counterfeit remains a secret.

> If the secret remains undetectable, unbreakable, in this case, if we have no chance of ever knowing whether counterfeit money was actually given to the beggar, it is first of all because there is no sense in wondering what actually

happened, what was the true intention of the narrator's friend and the meaning hidden 'behind' his utterances. No more, incidentally, than behind the utterances of the narrator. (153)

The last sentence is important: it's not just a matter of a statement made within the fiction that might harbour a secret which we will never plumb; every statement made by the narrator is equally inscrutable, a quasi-statement that is both intelligible but unverifiable. The sentences in what Derrida calls 'literary fiction' have no depth, and can't be challenged by the reader who wants to know more. For the author, too, joins the narrator and the characters, in speaking a language which operates like a secret in open view: Derrida points out that 'Baudelaire does not know, cannot know, and does not have to know, any more than we do, what can be going "through the mind" of the friend' (153). Literature lives on secrets, through and through.

In 'Passions', Derrida approaches the question from a slightly different angle. In a remarkable footnote – some of his richest speculations occur in footnotes – he writes:

> Something of literature will have begun when it is not possible to decide whether, when I speak of something, I am indeed speaking of something (of the thing itself, this one, for itself) or if I am giving an example, an example of something or an example of the fact that I can speak of something, of my way of speaking of something, of the possibility of speaking in general of something in general, or again of writing these words, etc. (142–3)

It is this that makes the secret of literature exemplary, for it reveals a property of all utterances: the possibility that any one of them might be other than what it seems 'literally' to be. Any sentence can function as an example of a sentence, and it is a purely pragmatic decision to take it one way or other. Literature capitalises on and exploits to the full this undecidability:

> Literature can all the time play economically, elliptically, ironically, with these marks and non-marks, and thus with the exemplarity of everything that it says and does, because reading it is at the same time an endless interpretation, a pleasure [*jouissance*] and an immeasurable frustration: it can always mean, teach, convey, more than it does, or at any rate something else. (143)

Derrida also refers to this constitutive undecidability as the 'perhaps': 'Everything is given over to the future of a "perhaps". For this little phrase seems to become literature by keeping more than one secret, and a secret which might, *perhaps, perhaps, not be one*' ('Literature in Secret', 131).

Another closely related term pointing to the same quality – one I have used repeatedly – is *singularity*. The literary work harbours a secret because it is singular. And 'the secret is not the secret of representation that one keeps in one's head and which one chooses not to tell, it is rather a secret coextensive with the experience of singularity' ('Remarks', 80). Singularity is not simply a matter of difference or of uniqueness; it is not opposed to but participates in generality.[13] As Derrida puts it in 'I Have a Taste for the Secret':

> Somehow, this secret that we speak of but are unable to say is, paradoxically, like good sense in Descartes, the best-shared thing in the world; but it is the sharing of what is not shared: we know in common that we have nothing in common. (58)

The literary work is secret because it is singular: it cannot be exhaustively analysed in terms of general codes and conventions, no matter how relentless the analyser. (Here we have a clue to the limits upon the currently fashionable field of 'cognitive poetics'.) In 'Literature in Secret' Derrida further explores the Biblical account of Abraham and Isaac on Mount Moriah that he had discussed in *The Gift of Death*, again drawing on Kierkegaard's meditations and retellings in *Fear and Trembling*. He says of the secrecy which binds Abraham, 'For the secret of secrecy about which we shall speak does not consist in hiding *something*, in not revealing the truth, but in respecting the absolute singularity, the infinite separation of what binds me or exposes me to the unique' (122–3). It may seem a huge leap from here to the act of reading a literary work, but Derrida sees a parallel between Abraham's commitment to an absolutely singular other and the operation of the literary work in the experience of the reader.

The secret of literature is also closely connected, for Derrida, to his understanding of democracy. In 'Passions' he offers the maxim 'No democracy without literature; no literature without democracy' (28). In a democracy, literature is the space where anything and everything may be said, but at the same time the literary author is stripped of any responsibility, 'not even to himself, for whatever the persons or the characters of his works, thus of what he is supposed to have written himself, say and do'. The author, in a democracy, has a right to an absolute non-response when challenged on these matters – and this is where the secret arises: 'This non-response is more original and more secret than the modalities of power and duty because it is fundamentally heterogeneous to them' ('Passions', 29). It is not just that the literary author is allowed not to answer for his statements and his characters' statements; it is that he *cannot* answer for them. A writer who attempts to justify what he has said in the literary mode is treating his work as something other than literature.

Another way of approaching this knotty issue is to think of the singularity of the literary work not as an attribute but as an event.[14] Derrida implies this when he notes that he speaks of 'a secret without content, without content separable from its performative experience, from its performative tracing' ('Passions', 24), and he often uses the word 'experience' in talking about the secret – see, for example, the quotation from the *Points* interview above, which continues: 'It is not a thing, some information that I am hiding or that one has to hide or dissimulate; it is rather an experience that does not make itself available to information, that resists information or knowledge' (201). We misunderstand what is distinctive about reading literature if we think in terms of 'content' as such: the literary work happens, each time it is read or listened to, so it is not a matter of surface and depth but a movement of meaning and of feeling that has to be repeated to be apprehended again. But for Derrida an event worthy of the name – an unconditional or absolute event, we might say – is not simply a happening but a happening that could not have been foreseen, that is not part of a chain of cause and effect. The literary event, I would argue, is always an event of this kind.[15]

This linking of the secret, literature, singularity, democracy and the event is a rich resource for future thought, a process which has begun in a number of places. But there is one more element in Derrida's conception of literature which remains unassimilated within our theoretical and critical discourses and awaits future elucidation and development. I mentioned earlier that for Derrida, Abraham's silence with regard to God's instruction is an archetype of the secret at work, as an absolutely singular experience which cannot be reduced to the general terms of discourse. It is thus analogous to the experience of literary singularity: to the degree that I can convey in the language of rational accounting the event of a literary work as I experience it I fail to do justice to it as literature. But Derrida forges a more direct link than this. In 'Literature in Secret',[16] after a series of '*whereas*' clauses summarising the centrality of the secret to the operation of literature in the context of democracy (or what he calls 'democracy to come'), he enunciates the following conclusion, as in a legal affidavit:

> Be it understood that literature surely inherits from a holy history within which the Abrahamic moment remains the essential secret (and who would deny that literature remains a religious remainder, a link to and relay for what is sacrosanct in a society without God?), while at the same time denying that history, appurtenance, and heritage. It denies that filiation. It betrays it

in the double sense of the word: it is unfaithful to it, breaking with it at the very moment when it reveals its 'truth' and uncovers its secret. (157)

At this point, I have to confess, I find myself at a loss. Literature as a 'religious remainder' has, of course, been a well-aired hypothesis at least since Matthew Arnold; but literature as descended from the Abrahamic moment? And as being unfaithful to it while revealing it? (Here we have a secret that *can* be uncovered, apparently.) And there is more: 'Literature can but ask forgiveness for this double betrayal. There is no literature that does not, from its very first word, ask for forgiveness' (157). And here Derrida returns to the gnomic phrase with which he began the essay, 'Pardon de ne pas vouloir dire', an untranslatable utterance which David Wills renders 'Pardon for not meaning (to say)'. All literature begs to be pardoned for its betrayal of its Abrahamic origins.

How are we to understand this? I have not found any satisfactory explanation of what Derrida is up to here. Gil Anidjar cites this passage but does not elucidate it, nor does Miller on his first mention of it.[17] Gideon Ofrat does offer a paraphrase (*The Jewish Derrida*, 110–11): 'The reader', he says, 'makes a covenant with the vanished author, but simultaneously betrays him by interpreting the work and trying to reveal its utmost secret' (111). But Derrida speaks not of the reader's asking for forgiveness but of literature's doing so, and not for the reader's attempt to expose the work's secret but for literature's denial of its origins. Leslie Hill follows Derrida closely in his summary of this essay, listing the latter's six '*whereas*' (or '*given that*') clauses, and commenting:

> But given all this, given this giving, and given this gift of literature, both donation and poisoned chalice, what was it, then, that followed? What followed, writes Derrida, is that literature was inseparable from the double logic of betrayal: from betrayal as truth, and truth as betrayal, for which literature asks forgiveness. As it does so, however, it accentuates simultaneously, and without end, both its responsibility and its irresponsibility, its burden and its gaiety, its complicity and its innocence. (*Radical Indecision*, 324)

This is finely put, but it doesn't get us very far in understanding what Derrida means by literature's request for pardon. Like much commentary on Derrida's more difficult writing, it repeats, with great elegance, rather than analyses or explains.

Miller, one of Derrida's readers who always does his best to explain the complexities and obscurities of the original (see Chapter 9 below), returns to Derrida's claims in his essay 'Literature and Scripture', and has a shot at turning them into something more easily graspable, though it's noticeable that questions remain:

The word 'pardon' in the phrase suggests, according to Derrida, that literature, as the betrayal of Scripture, sacred texts, the Bible, must continually, in
one way or another, beg pardon (from whom? from God? from constituted
authorities? from the reader?) for falsely imitating Scripture, for pretending
to be what it is not. Or, on the contrary, literature must beg pardon just
because it does, blasphemously, succeed in being Scripture, in hiding secrets
just as Scripture does.

That literature has, as Derrida asserts, an 'Abrahamic' origin is a conceit
that can be accepted as a way of associating it with the tradition of
sacred writings and highlighting the operation of secrecy in it. One could
say that because Abraham is willing to sacrifice everything, nothing on
earth remains sacred for him – and this sacrifice is repeated in literature's
desacralisation or secularisation of Scripture. But how does literature,
from its first word, ask for forgiveness for this process? Here is one
place, among many, where deconstruction today has much work to do,
a spur for deconstruction to come.

Notes

1. In the aftermath of Derrida's death, however, both Badiou and Žižek
   published tributes; see Douzinas, (eds), *Adieu Derrida*. This is not to
   say that they modify their own positions in favour of those they disagree
   with in Derrida's work. I discuss Agamben's response to Derrida in the
   Introduction above.
2. I have listed only the English translations in the bibliography. *L'animal que
   donc je suis*/*The Animal That Therefore I Am* is a compilation of four texts
   of Derrida's on the question of the animal, brought together by Marie-
   Louise Mallet after this death and later translated by David Wills.
3. Derrida describes his early interest in literary writing in '"This Strange
   Institution"', 33–75. (The French original of this interview can be found in
   Dutoit and Romanski (eds), *Derrida d'ici, Derrida de là*, 253–92.)
4. See, for example, his essay 'Deconstruction and the Postcolonial', in Royle,
   Deconstructions, 187–210. This volume gives a good sense of the current
   range of areas in which deconstruction is important, as does *Jacques
   Derrida and the Humanities*, edited by Tom Cohen.
5. Derrida's own late work *Monolingualism of the Other* has played an important part in discussions of postcoloniality; see, for example, Syrotinski,
   Deconstruction and the Postcolonial, chapter 1. Syrotinski's book is a valuable contribution to the debate about the role of deconstruction in postcolonial studies; see also Harrison, *Postcolonial Criticism*, and, for a study
   which endorses Badiou rather than Derrida (and uses the term 'singular' in
   an unfortunately idiosyncratic way), Hallward, *Absolutely Postcolonial*.
6. See also Derrida's important distinction between hospitality and tolerance
   in the dialogue with Giovanna Borradori, 'Autoimmunity', 124–30.
7. See Chapter 4 below.

8. I have discussed some of these questions in *J. M. Coetzee and the Ethics of Reading*.
9. See the previous chapter for a discussion of Derrida's responses to literary as distinct from philosophical works.
10. See 'Passions', 20–5; *Given Time*, 151–72; *A Taste for the Secret*, 57–9, 75; 'Literature in Secret'.
11. See, for example, Royle, *Jacques Derrida*, 119–28; Caputo, *The Prayers and Tears*, 101–16; Michaud, 'Literature in Secret'; Miller, 'Derrida and Literature'; Culler, 'Derrida and the Singularity of Literature', 874–5; Kronick, *Derrida and the Future of Literature, passim*.
12. See Chapter 10 below for a discussion of some of these pairs.
13. For an extended and illuminating discussion of singularity, including its relation to the secret in Derrida, see Clark, *The Poetics of Singularity*.
14. Derrida, in his essay on Joyce's *Ulysses*, states that 'in order to ask oneself what happens with *Ulysses* . . . it is necessary to think the singularity of the event': 'Ulysses Gramophone', 295.
15. See Attridge, *Singularity, passim*.
16. The original French is 'La Littérature au secret', which means 'literature locked up, incommunicado', suggesting its inability to communicate. 'In secret' would be 'en secret'.
17. See Anidjar, 'Hosting', 63–5; Miller, 'Profession', 286–7.

Chapter 3

Following Derrida

Derrida is hard to follow.

To begin a text with a sentence like that is, of course, to follow Derrida: to follow in his footsteps by finding an *incipit* that, shorn of context, proffers an undecidable choice of meanings, and which, moreover, stages the very issue the text is to take up. Some examples: '*Oui, oui,* you are receiving me, these are French words'; 'Pardon for not meaning (to say)'; 'What am I going to be able to invent this time?'; 'Genres are not to be mixed'.[1]

To follow in this sense is to redeploy a machine that someone else has invented, as Derrida demonstrates in 'Psyche' by varying the opening line of Francis Ponge's little poem 'Fable', 'With the *word* with commences then this text', as 'At the word *at* commences then this text,' adding, 'There would be other regulated variants, at greater or lesser distances from the model, that I do not have the time to note here' (334). But this possibility of variation does not simply *follow* an invention (here Ponge's invention), it constitutes the invention *as* an invention, by means of an achronological logic that we see everywhere at work in Derrida, a logic which does not allow for a simple process of following. If you follow this logic as you read Derrida, it becomes hard *not* to follow him, hard not to repeat him in your own thinking and writing – testimony, if testimony were needed, to the inventiveness of his texts. Yet to follow Derrida by repeating, by following out the logic of his inventions, is not to follow Derrida in the sense of *writing as he writes*: for he does not merely repeat what he reads, but invents afresh. So to truly follow Derrida, you have to be inventive too, to provide a singular counter-signature to testify to his singular inventiveness. For an invention not only makes a formula available for variations, it makes further inventions possible – though never easy.

In this sense, Derrida is hard to follow. It is hard to follow Derrida – to come after him, to write in his wake – because it is hard to follow him – to think and write in a way that does justice to his thought and writing – because it is so easy to follow him – to repeat his inventions without inventiveness. If the text I am writing now simply follows out some variations on Derrida's inventions – such as his ambiguous and self-referring *incipits* – it is nothing but an effect of those inventions (albeit a constituting effect); if it achieves inventiveness itself, it does justice to the inventiveness of those inventions. Of course, which of these it does emerges not in itself, but in the responses of those who read it, who follow it in turn.

To follow Derrida might also mean to pursue him, to be 'after' him in the third of the three senses so brilliantly teased out by Nicholas Royle in *After Derrida* (2), to find him always further on when one reaches a place he has been. In this sense, too, it is hard to follow Derrida because it is easy to follow him: he lures you on, but just when you think you have caught up with him, you find him further on, still inviting, still promising, still challenging.

I follow Derrida in saying 'Derrida is hard to follow', then, though I fail to follow him too. I also frequently fail to follow him whenever I read him, read those texts, try to respond to those events. There must be very few readers of Derrida who have not said to themselves while engaged with a work of his: this is hard to follow.[2] Most of the time, no doubt, this is because they – we – are not reading carefully enough, or we are reading translations based on careless readings. (When I began on the work of editing *Acts of Literature*, I had no intention of revising existing translations, but I found many instances where, in reading through a translation and finding a sentence that was hard to follow, I was able to turn to the French text to find an immediate solution to the problem.) But there are moments when it is difficult not to feel that the way is deliberately blocked, that no amount of careful reading would enable us to follow. These can be very powerful moments. One of my favourites is the ending of 'Aphorism Countertime', Derrida's response to Shakespeare's *Romeo and Juliet* which is also an exploration of the operation of the aphorism:

> The absolute aphorism: a proper name. Without genealogy, without the least copula. End of drama. Curtain. Tableau (*The Two Lovers United in Death* by Angelo dall'Oca Bianca). Tourism, December sun in Verona ('Verona by that name is known'). A true sun, the other ('The sun for sorrow will not show his head'). (433)

Turning to the French will help a little here, but not much: *tableau* in French conveys a transition from the theatre to painting in way that 'tableau' in English doesn't, being much more rooted in the world of the stage. The end of *Romeo and Juliet* (quoted from twice in the paragraph) presents a tableau of dead lovers mirrored in a painting by dall'Oca Bianca (to be seen by visitors to Verona): but why 'December sun'? An irreducibly personal memory? One that functions like a proper name, like an aphorism, like death, like the other?

I've been trying to follow Derrida for nearly forty years. Every new work I read (and I haven't read them all, by any means) throws down its challenges: both textual moments of opacity and movements of thought into what I would have thought were no-go areas. To take one example: I remember well my first reading of 'L'animal que donc je suis' in *L'animal autobiographique*, the introduction to the lengthy lecture (nine hours!) that Derrida presented at the ten-day conference on his work at Cerisy-la-Salle in 1997.[3] Not only are there particular passages that baffle me, where I find it hard to follow the logic of the sentences, but I find myself balking at – hesitating to follow – the larger argument even when I have no trouble in following sentence by sentence.

I should have seen it coming, of course: one of the things Derrida does in this essay is to show how the question of the animal, or of animality, has been surfacing in his work for a very long time. I should have paid more attention to the readings of Heidegger on animals in *Of Spirit*, and the 1988 interview with Jean-Luc Nancy, '"Eating Well"', in *Who Comes after the Subject?* ('after' in which sense?, I now want to ask, after Royle) – where Levinas, too, is challenged on the subject of animality.[4] I should have remembered the startled expression on Derrida's face when, before his delivery of the lecture 'Force of Law' at the Cardozo Law School in 1989, a technician testing the microphone yelled to his mate: 'HEY, ANIMAL!' I should have taken more fully to heart his response to a talk I gave in Alabama in 1995, which circled around the starving cats in *The Gift of Death*, a response which included cogent criticism of the treatment of animals by large-scale agri-business. Indeed, I should have thought more about those cats as cats, and not just as a convenient example for Derrida' argument about infinite responsibility.[5]

Yet it was not Derrida who finally made me face up to the question of the animal, but another writer whom I have always found ahead of me as I try to follow him: the novelist and critic J. M. Coetzee, to whom I have already referred in the previous chapter. In his case, too, there were premonitions I should have registered, notably the question he asked after a seminar paper I presented on Levinas in Cape Town in 1994: 'Are you being addressed by the face of the other when the eyes that are looking at you are those of the slaughter-ox?' As was the case with my writing on Derrida, I had written an essay giving a central place to an animal in Coetzee's work: the chained dog which Dostoevsky releases in *The Master of Petersburg*. But I did not acknowledge the force of the challenge that this moment and others like it in his novels offered to my long-held preconceptions until I read the two works he published in 1999, *Lives of Animals* and *Disgrace*. I now know I shall have to respond to these works, and to Derrida's 'L'animal que donc je suis', with some kind of writing of my own (whether I publish it or not): an attempt to follow these writers that does not simply follow out the logic of what they say (which is not only a matter of logic, of course) but tries to follow them in being inventive, inventively exploring their differences from each other. (Two memories: a 1990 lunch with Jacques Derrida in rue Linné, Paris, near the Galilée office, listening to him talk animatedly about carnophallogocentrism while eating with gusto a plate of steak tartare; a 1997 lunch with John Coetzee in Princeton, watching him consume a vegetarian meal before giving his first lecture on 'The Lives of Animals', in which he presented a fiction that included a lecture condemning the slaughter of animals on an industrial scale for consumption by humans.) These challenges, Derrida's and Coetzee's, to the human-centred version of ethics I have long held (I recall an undergraduate essay for a philosophy class in which I expounded at length such an ethics) demand a response; my responsibility as a reader is to do justice to each one's singularity, to follow each one's inventiveness as faithfully as I can, which does not mean just faithfully following them.

Jacques Derrida had and has a huge following, which he entirely deserves. I write this short piece as one of his followers, in homage and in gratitude for what he gave me during the twenty years I knew him, and the longer period I have been reading him. I do not expect to catch up, and I am grateful for that too.

Notes

1. From the openings of, respectively, 'Ulysses Gramophone', 'Literature in Secret', 'Psyche' and 'The Law of Genre'.
2. See Chapter 2 above for an example of a passage in Derrida I find hard to follow. And chapter 7 below for a discussion of an example of Derrida following another philosopher.
3. The essay's title puns on *suis*, which can mean both 'am' and 'follow'; it was translated by David Wills as 'The Animal That Therefore I Am (More to Follow)' in the collection of writings on the animal by Derrida, *The Animal That Therefore I Am*.
4. Another section of the Cerisy Lecture, in which Derrida examined the status of the animal in a number of earlier philosophers, including Heidegger and Levinas, is collected in *The Animal That Therefore I Am*, under the title

'"But as for me, who am I (following)?"' (The original has no title, but begins with the phrase Wills has chosen for a title, 'Mais moi, qui suis-je?' – another characteristic Derridean *incipit*, another pun on 'follow' and 'am'.)

5. See the following chapter for the cats.

Chapter 4

The Impossibility of Ethics: On Mount Moriah

I

What really got me hooked were the cats. This is the sentence out of which they sprang at me:

> How would you ever justify the fact that you sacrifice all the cats in the world to the cat that you feed at home every day for years, whereas other cats die of hunger at every instant?

Readers who have not been pounced on by these cats themselves will need to know that I am quoting from Jacques Derrida's *The Gift of Death*, and more specifically from the third chapter, 'Whom to Give to [Knowing Not to Know]'.[1] I recall vividly the first time the cats got their claws into me: it was in the attic lounge of the Normandy chateau of Cerisy-la-Salle in 1992, a day or two after Jean-Michel Rabaté had arrived with a trunkful of copies of *L'Éthique du don*, containing Derrida's work, hot from the Paris presses. I was playing truant from that morning's sessions of the Derrida *décade* in order to read 'Donner la mort', and I was most unjustly being rewarded for my lack of commitment by the gift of some of Derrida's most startling articulations.

Derrida introduces the cats as part of his radical quotidianisation, if I may call it that, of a short Biblical text, the *Akedah*, the story of the Binding of Isaac. This short narrative – nineteen verses of Genesis chapter 22 – has, of course, been subject to numerous and varied commentaries and retellings. For the faithful, it often exemplifies the virtue of human submission to the will of the deity, no matter how absurd or monstrous the form in which the latter appears;[2] for the sceptical, it may signify instead the unpalatable authoritarianism of the major monotheisms. Emily Dickinson speaks for the latter category, striking a sardonic note in her version of the story:

Abraham to kill him
Was distinctly told –
Isaac was an Urchin –
Abraham was old –

Not a hesitation –
Abraham complied –
Flattered by Obeisance
Tyranny demurred –

Isaac – to his Children
Lived to tell the tale –
Moral – with a Mastiff
Manners may prevail.

(*Poems*, 514)

For Kierkegaard and Derrida, however, the story of Abraham's willing-ness to kill his son in response to a divine command cannot be reduced to either of these postures; for them it exemplifies a terrifying paradox, the paradox entailed in *responsibility to the other*. Derrida follows, with great fidelity, Kierkegaard's rendition of the story in *Fear and Trembling* (which Kierkegaard presents as Johannes de Silentio's rendi-tion), drawing out clearly the proto-deconstructive force of Kierkegaard/Silentio's analysis. The other is absolute (its name in the story is God), and one's responsibility to the other is absolute. The realm of ethics, however, which is the realm of general laws of conduct and relation-ship, such as the law which forbids murder and which enjoins on the father the protection of his children, is, it seems, only relative and can be overridden by the obligation to the other, an obligation which always takes the form of the singular – here the singular command of Jehovah, 'Take now thy son, thine only son Isaac, whom thou lovest, and get thee into the land of Moriah; and offer him there for a burnt offering upon one of the mountains which I will tell thee of' (Genesis 22:2, Authorised Version). A command addressed to a single individual, enjoining a single act upon another single individual at a single time and place.

For Kierkegaard, Abraham is the prime exemplar of the knight of faith, who, having achieved 'infinite resignation', does not rest there, who takes the extraordinary step of believing in what Kierkegaard calls 'the absurd'; believing, that is, that in spite of all appearances, in spite of all rational calculations, performing the terrible deed will be for the good, because 'for God all things are possible' (46). And of course Abraham turns out to be right. 'And the angel of the Lord called unto him out of heaven, and said, Abraham, Abraham: and he said, Here am I. And he said, Lay not thine hand upon the lad, neither do thou anything unto him' (Genesis 22: 11–12). Abraham's faith is proved, God's blessing is ensured and the future – for this is, of course, a story about the future – is saved.

Kierkegaard's didactic use of the story to clarify his distinction between the knight of resignation and the knight of faith does not prevent him from retelling the story several times to heighten its drama and its horror, nor from asserting, in the voice of Johannes de Silentio, the continuing difficulty of coming to terms with it:

> Thinking about Abraham . . . I am shattered. I am constantly aware of the prodigious paradox that is the content of Abraham's life, I am constantly repelled, and, despite all its passion, my thought cannot penetrate it, cannot get ahead by a hairsbreadth. I stretch every muscle to get a perspective, and at the very same instant I become paralyzed. (33)

And later: 'Abraham I cannot understand; in a certain sense I can learn nothing from him except to be amazed' (48).

II

Like Kierkegaard, Derrida is horrified by the story of Abraham and Isaac.

> The story is no doubt monstrous, outrageous, barely conceivable: a father is ready to put to death his beloved son, his irreplaceable loved one, and that because the Other, the great Other, asks him or orders him without giving the slightest explanation. An infanticide father who hides what he is going to do, without knowing why, from his son and from his family, what could be more abominable, what mystery could be more frightful (*tremendum*) vis-à-vis love, humanity, the family, or morality? (68)

But it is at this point that Derrida makes his swerve from Kierkegaard, and the cats start their stealthy advance. Having emphasised how monstrous is the demand made on Abraham, how his responsibility to the absolute Other requires that, by sacrificing his son, he sacrifice the ethical obligations he is under as father, husband, patriarch, social being, Derrida comments:

> But isn't this also the most common thing? what the most cursory examination of the concept of responsibility cannot fail to affirm? . . . As soon as I enter into a relation with the other, with the gaze, look, request, love, command, or call of the other, I know that I can respond only by sacrificing ethics, that is to say by sacrificing whatever obliges me to also respond, in the same way, in the same instant, to all the others. . . . Day and night, at every

instant, on all the Mount Moriahs of this world, I am doing that, raising my knife over what I love and must love, over the other, this or that other to whom I owe absolute fidelity, incommensurably. (68–9)

The difference between Kierkegaard and Derrida here is crucial. For both, Abraham's intended action involves renouncing ethics – Kierkegaard calls it a 'teleological suspension of the ethical' – in the name of absolute responsibility to the absolute and singular other. (An extremely un-Kantian and at the same time un-Hegelian position, of course.) But whereas for Kierkegaard the absolute other speaks only in God's voice, for Derrida it speaks also, although differently, in Isaac's voice. (Here we become aware that Derrida's is to some extent a Levinasian reading of Genesis and of Kierkegaard: it is precisely in encountering the face of the other that I encounter God.[3]) The paradox is thus much tauter than it is for Kierkegaard: Abraham, *whether or not he obeys God's command*, will fail in his binding responsibility to the other. To spare Isaac is to defy God; to kill him is to murder the other, the other other, who is no less divine. It is no longer just a question of overriding the ethical, as some bloodless general code, in the name of singularity and alterity, for Derrida has complicated the distinction between those two orders. Ethics, Derrida states in the paragraph I have just quoted, is 'that which obliges me to also respond, in the same way, in the same instant, to all the others', and earlier in the same paragraph he had talked of the 'infinite number' of these others, constituting a 'general and universal responsibility (what Kierkegaard calls the ethical order)' (69). But if ethics is the simultaneous responsibility toward every other, *as singular other*, and if, as Derrida insists, *tout autre est tout autre*, 'every other is wholly other', ethical behaviour is, from the very first moment, from before the very first moment, utterly impossible – it is easier to do the bidding of a singular divinity, however outrageous, than attempt to live by the general norms of ethics.

Now we know well enough that to term a certain practice 'impossible' is not, for Derrida, the same as saying that it can never happen or is nugatory. Bismarck famously observed that politics is the art of the possible, and it's not difficult to agree. Determinate and achievable goals, practical and practicable policies, staged and cumulative programmes, these are the watchwords of a successful political platform. Politics happens squarely, it would seem, in the realm of the possible, the feasible, the achievable.

Deconstruction, on the other hand, involves a constant engagement with the impossible.[4] Here are a few statements by Derrida, out of many more I could have chosen:

From 'Psyche: Invention of the Other':

'Deconstruction loses nothing from admitting that it is impossible.' (328)

From 'Force of Law':

'Deconstruction is the experience of the impossible.' (15)

From 'Violence and Metaphysics':

'The impossible has *already* occurred.' (18)

The impossible is also a constitutive feature of many of the concepts or experiences on which Derrida dwelt in his later work. Another small selection (the use of bold is mine):

From *Given Time*:

'The **gift** is the impossible.' (7)

From *The Other Heading*:

'The condition of possibility of this thing called **responsibility** is a certain *experience and experiment of the possibility of the impossible*.' (41)

From 'Sauf le nom (Post-Scriptum)':

'The sole **decision** possible passes through the madness of the undecidable and the impossible' (59); '. . . **love** itself, that is, this infinite renunciation which somehow *surrenders to the impossible*.' (74)

From *Politics of Friendship*:

'This love that would take place only once would be the only possible **event**: as impossible.' (66, translation modified)

From *Of Hospitality*:

'It is as though **hospitality** were the impossible.' (Derrida and Dufourmantelle, *Of Hospitality*, 75)

And finally there is the subtitle of Derrida's second essay on Abraham and Isaac, included in the expanded *Gift of Death* and discussed above in Chapter 2: 'Literature in Secret: An Impossible Filiation'.

Some of the most valuable practices we engage in, then, are impossible, such as giving, judging, witnessing, inventing, loving, forgiving or deconstructing. These things happen all the time, in spite of, or rather because of, the fact that they are impossible. They happen, that is to say, not because someone knows in advance how to truly give, or finally judge, or fully witness, or completely deconstruct – to possess in advance a formula for any of these things is precisely to *prevent* it from happening – but because the realm of possibility (the realm, let us say, of thought, of knowledge, of philosophy, of cause-and-effect, of presence, of chronology, of calculation) depends on that which it excludes, the impossible. It is because possibility doesn't totally govern the scene that giving, judging, witnessing, deconstructing happen (however fleetingly, precariously and imperceptibly).[5]

But the question that has to be asked is whether the impossibility of ethical behaviour, as I have just represented it, is of the same order as these other impossibilities. If ethics enjoins on me equal responsibility to and for every person in the world, living, dead and unborn, and does this at every instant, it is hard to see how *any* act could be called, even fleetingly or imperceptibly, 'ethical'.[6] And Derrida gives some examples which make it very clear that he really *does* mean that my responsibilities are infinite and fulfilling them an impossible task:

> By preferring what I am doing here and now, simply by giving it my time and attention, by giving priority to my work or my activity as a citizen or professorial and professional philosopher, writing and speaking here in a public language, French in my case, I am perhaps fulfilling my duty. But I am sacrificing and betraying at every moment all my other obligations: my obligations to the other others whom I know or don't know, the billions of my fellows (*semblables*) (without mentioning the animals that are even more other than my fellows) who are dying of starvation or sickness . . . every one being sacrificed to every one else in this land of Moriah that is our habitat every second of every day. (69–70)

Derrida doesn't leave it there, however. To make it harder still, he brings in the cats. Here again is the sentence in which they make their appearance: 'How would you ever justify the fact that you sacrifice all the cats in the world to the cat that you feed at home every day for years, whereas other cats die of hunger at every instant?' (71). I don't even have a cat, but every time I read this sentence I feel momentarily appalled by the pitiful meowing of all those cats out there that, every instant of every day, *I am not feeding.* We are a long way from the terrible encounter with the almighty on Mount Moriah, and Derrida might seem to risk accusations of trivialising the Biblical narrative in translating it into this common domestic scene. But there is no escape from the implacable logic of his analysis. If there is a general law of ethics, how can its generality suffer limitation through a *more* general ethical law that allows it to apply only to humans? By what pre-emptive and violent stroke can the animal world be excluded? Or the plant world? Or the possible inhabitants of other planets? 'An *infinite* number', says Derrida, 'the *innumerable* generality', and he clearly means it. He even mentions places and languages; in being here, I am not in all the other places I might be in; in favouring English, I am discriminating against all the other languages I might use. Nor are the non-human others less important to the argument than the humans. If anything, they are *more* important; they are, as Derrida says, 'even more other than my fellows' (69).

The impossibility of the ethical act appears to offer, then, not the tiniest toehold for possibility to get a grip. The most universally benevolent deed I could ever perform would still be as nothing compared with the goal of complete ethical generality. As if this were not enough, Derrida tightens the noose even further. Although I can never begin to satisfy the demands of ethics, although my every action, indeed my very existence, breathing the air I breathe and occupying the space I occupy, is a falling short of the ethical, *there is no way I can justify my failure*. Here again, the cats enforce the point. My preference for the cat I call my 'own' over all the other cats in the universe is as inaccessible to the language of explanation and justification as Abraham's preference for God over Isaac (and over his own ethical obligations and paternal feelings). Once I begin to speak, I enter the discursive realm in which only the ethical as systematic code can be articulated and heard – the realm of law, of calculation, of generality. To comment on the story of Abraham and Isaac at all is to find Abraham guilty of a terrible crime. Only in silence, in secrecy, can one understand – no, that's not the right word, as Kierkegaard knew – take account of, countersign, affirm Abraham's appalling decision.[7] We cannot learn from it, says Johannes whose last name is Silentio.

My responsibility to the singular other, then, the centrepiece of the Levinasian thought that Derrida has absorbed and refashioned in many works, runs counter to ethics as a general system and cannot be justified. Moreover, it runs counter to my responsibility to other singular others. 'I can respond to the one (or to the One), that is to say to the other, only by sacrificing to that one the other', writes Derrida. This is a much more hard-nosed approach to the problem of multiple others than Levinas's invocation of 'le tiers', made so much of by Simon Critchley in his book on Levinas and Derrida.[8] It brings us back to the question of the impossibility of ethical behaviour. I asked earlier if this was the same order of impossibility as that which we associate, in Derrida's work, with the gift, justice, witnessing, deconstruction – and literature. We know that justice – justice to the absolute singularity of the other, the person, the case, the text – is impossible and that it happens.[9] Abraham does justice to the absolute singularity of Jehovah, of the command, the call. We can't say how he does it, he can't say how he does it, but he does it, and without hesitation. But he also decides, and it is the same decision, to do the worst possible *injustice* to his son. And if the act of doing justice is always also the act of doing an injustice, ethical acts – acts which involve no injustice – cannot happen. It might seem then, that the impossibility of being ethical belongs to a different order of impossibility from that of doing justice, giving, forgiving, deconstructing, writing or reading the literary, which do, after all, happen.

III

Derrida has spoken of the 'quasi-fictional' quality of this text, distancing himself to a degree from the philosopher or ethico-political commentator whose voice we hear – a stratagem which of course echoes Kierkegaard's own text, published under a pseudonym and composed in a style that is as literary as it is philosophical. Whether or not Derrida might, if pressed, say this about *every* text he has published, it is true that there is a certain extravagance, occasionally bordering on comedy, in some parts of this work. No matter how familiar one is with Derrida's writing, it's easy to find oneself asking at these moments, 'Is he being serious?', and thus to put oneself in the position of those many readers – including those looking for concrete political recommendations – who resist Derrida's thought because it pushes them beyond the point where they feel comfortable.

Someone whom one would certainly not think to include among such readers is David Wood, a respected philosopher in the continental tradition who has written with acuity and sympathy on Derrida's work and edited a number of collections devoted to Derrida. Yet Wood is among those who can't stomach the move I've just summarised. The following is an excerpt from his essay, 'Much Obliged':

> First problem: 'I can never justify the fact that I prefer or sacrifice any one (any other) to the other.' Can this be true? Suppose I have promised something to one person and not to another, in such a way that they rely on my support in ways that others do not. Does that not give me special obligations? Or, suppose one person (or animal) in need is in front of me, and the other is not? . . . The thought that there are no fixed boundaries here does not mean that there are none. Hospitality would self-destruct if it were 'infinite'. (136–7)

And again:

> Unless we are holding on to some source of absolute justification, which I thought had long since been abandoned, it is just not true that 'I can never justify this sacrifice', that 'I will always be secretive'. My justification for teaching my children about poison ivy is that they are my children and I care especially for them. (137)

In this response Wood is not far from the attitude of the impatient political activist who finds in Derrida's writing no guide to practical life, and who asks, 'How can an assertion of the impossibility of acting responsibly, and of justifying what one does, contribute to the needs of the here and now?' Wood, quite reasonably (at least quite reasonably as a practical man if not as a philosopher of deconstruction) believes that he is perfectly able to rank his responsibilities and, if need be, justify this ranking. And the implication is that, having got his responsibilities in order, he can act upon them without too much difficulty – irrespective of all this rigmarole about starving cats.

The worrying thing about Wood's essay is not just that it has difficulties with this text of Derrida's, but, as I've suggested, that its misreadings of the text imply an inability to grasp what is centrally radical about deconstructive thinking. One way of putting this would be that it does not acknowledge the consequences of the 'impossibility' of deconstruction and the associated impossibilities we have already noted. (I make no comment on the *ad hominem* aspects of his essay, the accusation that Derrida suffered from 'what one could almost call . . . hubris' and the peculiar suggestion that the argument of *The Gift of Death* sprang from a sense of guilt on Derrida's part (136, 137).)

There are two elements in Derrida's argument that Wood, and no doubt many other readers, find troublesome. The first is the claim that every choice I make in favour of a person, an animal, a culture, a language, a place, necessarily involves the sacrifice of every other person, animal, culture, language or place I might have chosen; the second is that I am unable to justify any such choice and sacrifice. The first claim follows ineluctably from Derrida's understanding of responsibility as unconditional and singular, a unique response to a unique other, manifested in an extreme form in Abraham's response to God but applicable to all instances of responsibility. (Wood appears to share this understanding: he says, 'I must acknowledge that at one level Derrida is right about responsibility – right, that is, to insist that it must exceed any prescribable algorithm' (138).) But if responsibility is unconditional, outside the operation of norms, conventions, discourse, rationality, there can be no fully reliable means whereby my responsibility to x can be calculated as greater or lesser than my responsibility to *y*. Responsibility, if it is not mere calculation, can never be anything other than absolute, whether it is responsibility to God, to humans, to cats or to languages. Derrida's apparently absurd examples are no more than the result of following through the consequences of this position.

The second stage of Derrida's argument, that I can never *justify* any of the choices and attendant sacrifices that I make, follows directly on from the first. It links the concept of responsibility to the singular other and the concept of the decision. Abraham's decision to obey the command of God is made as a singular response to a singular set of circumstances, absolutely heterogeneous to all laws and generalities. We cannot say whether it is more an act or an event, whether it is something Abraham does or something that happens to him. 'The instant of decision', Derrida quotes Kierkegaard as saying in a strikingly proto-Derridean moment, 'is madness' (*The Gift of Death*, 66). The decision here consists in placing one responsibility – to God, to the singularity of the absolute other – above another, or rather many others – to Isaac, to the family, to the state, to the human community, to the covenanted future (of which Isaac is the embodiment), to ethics as a general system.

Once we describe Abraham's decision in these terms, the impossibility of justification, the inevitability of silence, is obvious. To account for his decision in language, in the public discourse of what counts as justification, would be to cross from the unconditional to the conditional, from the incalculable to the calculable, from the impossible to the possible. But to assert that Abraham is, and cannot avoid being, 'silent' about his decision is not to assert that he does not, and cannot, speak. (Derrida notes that 'speaking in order not to say anything is always the best technique for keeping a secret' (*The Gift of Death*, 60).) What is more, Abraham is under an *obligation* to speak, to justify his action; once he descends from the lonely heights of Mount Moriah to the public spaces he has to pick up once more his familial and social existence, to move from the realm of the impossible to the possible, from, if you like, deconstruction to politics. He has to negotiate the unnegotiable.[10] Another impossible demand, in other words. Which does not mean it cannot be done – one must never forget that, for Derrida, the impossible (which of course has nothing to do with the very difficult) is what opens the possible. Were it straightforwardly *possible* for Abraham to justify his decision, if he could speak with no reserve, no secret, no silence inhabiting his words, we would know that he had not made a decision, in the strict sense, that it must have been a calculation, with no ethical force, no enactment of responsibility. His attempted justification will succeed only if it fails, if his account of what he has done bears a silence at its heart – one might even say *produces*, without producing, a silence at its heart. This is what Kierkegaard's account attempts to do, to testify to and thus produce without producing Abraham's secret, to bear witness to the enormity and importance of that secret. This is what Derrida's account attempts to do. This is what deconstructive writing does, testify to secrets.[11]

This is all very well, our political pragmatist may say, but Derrida carries the argument well beyond matters of life-and-death decisions, and that's when it becomes troubling. It may be correct to say that there is a structural aporia at the heart of every genuinely ethical decision, that the ethical act, as an absolutely singular event, as the Saying which exceeds the Said, cannot, by its very nature, be justified. But when Derrida applies his arguments to the most banal of daily actions, actions which one would not normally characterise as 'ethical', an understandable resistance ensues. I did not choose to speak the language I speak and so can hardly be accused of sacrificing all other languages to it; I have no option but to occupy the place I stand in, and so no sacrificial act in relation to other places is involved; I feed my cat out of sheer habit and have to take no decision to do so.

Thus David Wood tells us that us that he teaches his children about poison ivy and has a straightforward justification for doing so and for not making the hopeless attempt to ensure that all the children in the world know about poison ivy: 'They are my children and I care especially for them' (137). It's clearly not something he has to *decide* to do. No doubt he would have similarly down-to-earth justifications for virtually all his other actions that bear upon his responsibility to others. No impossibilities, no silences, no secrets. But Wood's insertion of a proviso just before this assertion suggests that matters are not quite so simple: 'Unless we are holding on to some source of absolute justification, which I thought had long since been abandoned'. His justifications are, it would seem, partial, or tentative, or provisional; at any rate, they make no claim to be 'absolute'.

This rather changes the picture. Partial, tentative, provisional justification can have no purchase on the ethical act; such justification is not particularly difficult and it happens everywhere all the time. It is the bottomless resource of the 'good conscience' that Derrida excoriates. It is the speech which simply covers over the secret. It's not to be dismissed – it's part of rational, practical discourse, and it can be legitimate or illegitimate, convincing or unconvincing. But its ever-present possibility depends on the *impossibility* of justification in the purity of its concept, which one can call 'absolute' if one wishes: the justification – and one has to add, if there is such a thing – that justifies, that makes immediately apparent, without shadow, the justness of the act in question. The same structure, as Derrida has shown, operates in the case of the gift, testimony, hospitality, justice itself, deconstruction. (I quoted earlier Wood's comment: 'The thought that there are no fixed boundaries here does not mean that there are none. Hospitality would self-destruct if it were "infinite"'. He doesn't seem to appreciate how right he is: hospitality, Derrida has argued, is both infinite and impossible.[12])

Wood's detour from Derrida becomes even clearer as the paragraph continues. He reasserts that there can be no such thing as absolute justification (in other words, absolute justification is impossible – something with which Derrida would clearly not disagree), and adds: 'To describe me as sacrificing all other cats when I feed my own is to mistakenly read my inability to justify this activity as some sort of deficiency' (137). One begins to sense what is making Wood bridle here: he believes that Derrida is accusing him of some ethical or intellectual weakness in his unjustifiably selective treatment of the potential objects of his responsibility. If this were the case, it would be a universally shared weakness, and so hardly something to get individually worked up about; but in any case there is no suggestion in Derrida's discussion that the impossibility of meeting all one's responsibilities as an ethical subject is a mark of 'deficiency'. There *is* animus in some places in his discussion, but there's no obvious reason why David Wood should think it's directed against him; Derrida inveighs, for example, against 'the structure of the laws of the market' and 'the mechanisms of external debt and other similar inequities' whereby so-called 'civilized society' sacrifices 'tens of millions of children' who die of hunger and disease (86), but there's no reason to think he wouldn't have been anything other than very pleased to know that the Wood children have been warned about poison ivy.

Nevertheless, Wood's response does point to the extravagance of Derrida's depiction of responsible choice and resultant sacrifice as everyday, in fact second-by-second, occurrences. If *The Gift of Death* has a fictional narrator prone to exaggeration, this is undoubtedly a place where we hear his voice, signalled, perhaps, by the throwaway irony of that 'what the most cursory examination . . . cannot fail to affirm'. But what is the point of this taking-to-extremes, in so far as it can be wrested into the domain of the thetic? It may help if we linger over the word 'ethics' for a moment. For Kierkegaard, ethics names the generality of laws which the knight of faith must succeed in transcending in the wholly ungrounded act that reaches from the finite into the infinite. (Abraham is the prime exemplar, but Kierkegaard himself in his love for Regine Olsen is a further, subtextual, instance.) Levinas proposes a very similar structure, but for him ethics names not the generality of laws but the act of transcendence towards the infinite, in response to the demand of the absolute other. Derrida always had a Kierkegaardian suspicion of the term as too compromised by systematic philosophy (voiced in the discussion in *Alterités*, for example) while remaining highly sympathetic to Levinas's project, and here he brings to a point of crisis the tension between the two uses of the term. He proposes an ethical system of the most generalising kind, one that demands absolute responsibility to every other, and that makes no distinction between my children and my neighbour's (or those of another country); and although this demand is given a Levinasian twist (a twist of the knife, to be sure) in Derrida's catchphrase *tout autre est tout autre*, the logic remains implacably general and systematic. Against this backdrop stand out the very specific obligations which Wood worries about – to my family, my cats, those whom I have promised to help, and so on. Now Derrida's point is hardly that these specific obligations should receive no privilege; on the contrary, his argument rests on the assumption that they will, just as the specific responsibility to God overrides every ethical norm that Abraham holds dear. What he is alerting us to is the fact that these obligations make themselves felt and have to be dealt with *in strict opposition to the ethical system, to the systematicity of ethics*. Furthermore, any attempt to justify these singular obligations must fail, for justification can be given only in discursive, public, rational, terms – that is to say, the systematic terms which the act in question has challenged.

Of course, most attempts to construct a practical ethics try to find a way to rank responsibilities; Derrida's point is that such systems are necessarily incoherent, for they use a systematic philosophical language in an attempt to capture and legislate for what is constitutively resistant to such language. But incoherence is not a reason for abandoning ethical systems; it may in fact be a reason for preserving and constantly refining them. Derrida has consistently devoted his energies to an exploration of the structural incoherence – an incoherence which is far from arbitrary or innocent – of central concepts in Western discourse, concepts which he thinks of as *legacies* that we have, whether we like it or not, inherited. These concepts have often been used to promote or disguise inequality and oppression – in *The Gift of Death* Derrida is scathing about 'the monotonous complacency of [civilized society's] discourses on morality, politics, and the law' (85–6) – but they also hold out the promise of a better future.

As Wood's response, and that of many other commentators, suggests, this is an aspect of Derrida's thought that is easily misunderstood. He is not trying to *describe* the psychological process of deciding (or giving, or promising, or forgiving, or acting responsibly). He is offering a *structural analysis* of these concepts, as they exist in Western discourse, as they have been passed down to us. Whether they name something that 'happens' is impossible to say – impossible not because we can't peer into our minds but for wholly structural reasons. But what is certain is that they are enormously productive concepts, precisely because of their impossibility.

IV

What, then, are we left with? Some kind of impulsive subjectivism or decisionism? Pick your favourite other, act responsibly to him, her or it, and let the rest go hang? Feed your own cat, *cultiver votre jardin* and forget about the state of the world? And don't even bother to justify or even discuss your choice? This would be a terrible misreading of the story of Abraham and Isaac, of Kierkegaard, of Derrida. The ethical, the responsibility toward the generality and therefore the political (as the construction and implementation of programmes to further the common welfare) remains an absolute and unavoidable demand. We need look no further than the word 'sacrifice'. You can sacrifice only what you value. Abraham's decision is an act of responsibility toward God *only because Isaac is his beloved son*, born miraculously to him in his old age, the promised beginning of the chosen generations, the embodiment of the future.[13] There is a fierce logic to God's command: of all the things Abraham could be asked to do, sacrificing Isaac, sacrificing ethics, sacrificing the future, is the most difficult; and of all the people who might have been asked to do it, Abraham is the person for whom it is most difficult. In that difficulty, in the horror that Kierkegaard depicts so powerfully, is the acknowledgement that ethics, as responsibility to the multiplicity of others, matters. Without the strongest possible commitment to ethical and political norms, acts of singular justice, of incommunicable responsibility to this or that unique other, cannot happen; there is nothing to sacrifice, no decision beyond the calculable to be made. The slightly ludic, or even ludicrous, nature of Derrida's image of a world teeming with famished cats should not mislead us; it is by no means a *reductio ad absurdum*. I believe that Derrida wants us to confront the situation in all seriousness. Starving cats are not a joke.

Taking the full measure of Derrida's sentence means acknowledging that there is no comfortable position vis-à-vis ethics, politics, responsibility, justice, no avoiding of the issue, no waiting till the storm blows over. It is not a question of weighing one duty against another, which would be to remain within the realm of calculable ethics, but of acting in the knowledge of the aporia implicit in every deed, 'the sacrifice of the most imperative duty (that which binds me to the other as a singularity in general) in favor of another absolutely imperative duty binding me to the wholly other' (71–2). Both duties are binding, and they cannot be judged against one another. And the cats are there to impress upon us that this aporetic space is not some rare and distant realm but right here where we live our daily lives.

To those who would resist this account, who would insist that there is no need for any sacrifice of individuals or of ethics in general, that the observance of moral norms is all that is necessary for responsible behaviour, Derrida has another answer, which he sketches in the following chapter of *The Gift of Death*, 'Tout autre est tout autre'. 'Civilized society', which would condemn any man who behaved as Abraham did on Mount Moriah (Derrida imagines a father taking his son up to the heights of Montmartre to kill him), and whose claim to civilisation rests on those moral norms, functions smoothly *only because* it sacrifices tens of millions of children (not to mention adults, animals and others) (85). This sacrifice is not performed out of responsibility, nor is it carried out in agony. (So it is not, properly speaking, if we can speak properly of these things, a sacrifice.) And, on TV screens, in newspapers, in public appearances, it receives endless justification.

V

So far, we have considered the situation of Abraham as he stretches out his arm. In deciding to kill Isaac, he has answered the call of the absolute other and betrayed every human obligation, including his obligation to the future. Now observe: in the feline version of the story, not only do I *decide* to feed my cat, but I *do* feed it, and the other cats starve. This is what happens in the world, where no angelic voice stays my feeding hand and offers me an alternative which will save both my cat and all the others. The Bible story, designed to reassure us of the goodness and wisdom of the divine plan, gives us a happy ending, but it is false to everyday experience, an 'ideological' resolution, perhaps, of a real and inescapable contradiction. On our daily Mount Moriahs, God is silent.

This would seem to be the logic of Derrida's position, departing from Kierkegaard's argument that faith in the absurd, in God's capacity to achieve the impossible, is what resolves everything – though in doing so he cleaves all the more strongly to the real force of Kierkegaard's text, which lies in its depiction of the inassimilable horror of the story. Actually, in this text, Derrida doesn't overtly draw this conclusion; his major interest in the chapter, following on from his discussion of Jan Patočka's linking of the secret and responsibility in the earlier part of the book, is in Abraham's necessary secrecy. But it is implicit in everything he says: we carry out our daily, unjustifiable sacrifices without any hope that the victims will be spared. Not *altogether* without hope, though, since acting out of responsibility to and in affirmation of the other is always acting out of responsibility toward and in affirmation of the future. It is acting in the spirit of what Derrida elsewhere calls a certain 'desert-like messianism (without content and without identifiable messiah)' (*Specters of Marx*, 28). Abraham's decision to kill Isaac evinces immense trust in the future, a trust which goes contrary to all predictability – for what is predictable is the instantaneous cancellation of the promised future of blessed generations.

We are not yet at the end of the difficulties that beset any attempt at responsible action, however. Answering the call of the singular other in such a way that other others are necessarily sacrificed is not justifiable, not ethically acceptable, not even comprehensible; it can be admired, however, it does bear witness to human worth, it does affirm the future. But what if the call is false or misheard? What if I am hearing a reflection of my own voice? (There is a midrash on Genesis 22 which suggests that this is actually what happened.) Or the voice of a death-dealing machine? What if Abraham is deluded? This is how Kant reads the story, and the point is made again by Lyotard in *The Differend*:

> Abraham hears: *That Isaac die, that is my law*, and he obeys. The Lord speaks at this moment only to Abraham, and Abraham is answerable only to the Lord. Since the reality, if not of the Lord, then at least of the phrase imputed to Him, cannot be established, how can it be known that Abraham isn't a paranoiac subject to homicidal (infanticidal) urges? (107)[14]

How can God's command to Abraham be distinguished from Nazi commands to kill Jews? A sceptic might say that Abraham's duty was to attend to the demand of a mysterious voice from the sky *last and least of all*. Perhaps the only way to read the story as a sceptic is to treat it as a fantasy: let us imagine that there was such a thing as an all-powerful God and that he ordered a man to kill his son – in this case, the genuineness of the call would simply be a given of the story. But we cannot escape in this way when we translate the problem to our daily wrestle with responsibility. Given that we cannot make ourselves answerable to every other in the world, how do we choose? Of all the demands made on us by others, which are genuine and which are spurious? (Remember Hamlet's agonising uncertainty about the ghost who summons him to kill a relative.) Clearly there is no answer to that question in the form of rules or calculus; the aporia we face is precisely the absence of rules. As Lyotard argues, obligation is necessarily and structurally incomprehensible.

John D. Caputo reflects on this dilemma in *Against Ethics*, taking his cue from Levinas, Blanchot and Lyotard as well as from Derrida. Reduced to two words, his response to the problem is 'obligation happens'. It cannot, finally, be explained, grounded, justified; but it happens all the time. And it is always singular: this person, this case, this demand obliges me, here and now. My cat, and not the millions of other cats in the world. To observe only this, however, is to risk leaving obligation in the realm of the capricious or the arbitrary, and Caputo has much more to say about it, none of which I shall attempt to summarise. (It is not primarily a book of arguments.) What is worth stressing, however, is what he draws from Levinas's emphasis on the other as *destitute* – 'the widow, the stranger, the orphan' – and from Lyotard's discussion of *les juifs*, with a small 'j', all the non-peoples rendered other by Western thought and Western history.[15] Obligation happens to me most authentically when I am confronted not by the all-powerful, as Abraham was, but by the powerless.

I find myself obliged, for instance, to reflect on the place of women in the story of Abraham and Isaac. In doing so I am helped by both Derrida and Caputo, who have also felt this obligation. (Kierkegaard too seems to have felt it, for the four rewritings of the Abraham and Isaac story which Johannes de Silentio gives in his Prelude all end with the figure of a woman and her breast-fed child – but his emphasis is not on feminine nurturing but on the necessary violence of the act of weaning, as an allegory of God's treatment of Abraham.) Derrida devotes a paragraph of *The Gift of Death* to the absence of women in the biblical story and in Melville's *Bartleby*, between which he is drawing some parallels. The speculative possibilities that this absence raises threaten to ruin the entire argument, but they remain as suspended questions:

> Would the logic of sacrificial responsibility within the implacable universality of the law, of its law, be altered, inflected, attenuated, or displaced, if a woman were to intervene in some consequential manner? Does the system of this sacrificial responsibility and of the double 'gift of death' imply at its very basis an exclusion or sacrifice of woman? A woman's sacrifice or a sacrifice of woman, according to one sense of the genitive or the other? (76)

Caputo has an answer, even though his reply – like many good replies – predates the question, *Against Ethics* having been completed just too early to take account of 'Donner la mort'.[16] His answer is yes, the introduction of a woman does alter the sacrificial system, and very significantly. Under the Kierkegaardian name of Johanna de Silentio he too rewrites the story of Abraham and Isaac, calling it 'The Story of Sarah' (*Against Ethics*, 139–46). In this version, the voice that stays Abraham's hand comes not from the same God who had ordered the sacrifice but from an alternative site of obligation, a site identified with Abraham's wife Sarah. The obligation in question – felt more strongly by women than men in the society which Genesis depicts – is the obligation toward the weak, the helpless, the victim, the child. Abraham's God is answered by Sarah's God, the violence of one against the gentleness of the other. In this way, 'the logic of sacrificial responsibility' is indeed troubled, as Derrida suggests it might be.

Responsibility to the other is not just a question of the obligation or demand that I feel most intensely because it addresses me with the greatest imperiousness. If this were the case, the existing system of power relations would determine the exercise of responsibility and would thereby reproduce itself endlessly. The subordination of female to male, of black to white, of poor to rich would continue unabated. The future would come not as the other, but as the same. Responsibility has an *active* dimension; it is not merely a passive response. I am obligated to *seek out* the other, to *learn* to hear its voice and see its face. Derrida has always stressed that, while one cannot make the other come, one can prepare for its coming. (One name for this activity of preparation is 'deconstruction'.[17]) When my cat comes meowing to me in the morning, there is nothing automatic about my responsibility to feed it; perhaps I have found out that the cat next door is hungry and sick, obliging me to sacrifice my own cat. That is to say, the generalised responsibility of ethics that Derrida talks of can become, at any moment, particularised and imperative – and to act responsibly (though this is now not clearly distinguishable from acting ethically) is to do the *work* necessary to produce such particularisations. The last thing the biblical story and its various readings do is to applaud spontaneity: Abraham has pondered for three days on the deed and has behind him a long lifetime of thought and labour. It requires work to acquire knowledge of the needs that surround one and of ways in which one might address them effectively. In a patriarchal society, such as Abraham's or ours, there is an obligation to labour to hear the voices of women, to attend to Sarah, who has been excluded, who will be sacrificed on the same altar as Isaac without achieving any of the glory of her husband. Every other systematic exclusion and oppression requires similar work. And so the impossibility of ethics does not, cannot, inhibit action: it is not different in kind from the impossibility of doing justice, giving, forgiving, deconstructing, writing or reading the literary. No justice, however, without the work of the law; no responsibility to the infinite other without the labour of ethics and politics. Even though law, ethics and politics go into the abyss with every act of justice and singular responsibility.

VI

Kierkegaard's writing in *Fear and Trembling* and Derrida's in *The Gift of Death*, like that of the biblical account they are responding to, is not, in any simple sense, philosophical. Both stress that the responsibility to the other which concerns them cannot be explained or conveyed in philosophical language. Kierkegaard even implies that it cannot be addressed in language *tout court* – 'As soon as I speak', he writes, 'I express the universal' (60) – but his text, performing rather than expounding, belies this. One word we might use to characterise the way these texts function is 'literature'. Let me simply end with another rewriting of the story of Abraham and Isaac, this time by a poet on active service during the First World War. What Wilfred Owen saw happening in that war was the generation of the old and powerful sacrificing the future by bringing about the deaths of so many of the younger generation, of all nationalities. Like Dickinson, Owen sees the story of Abraham and Isaac as a story about the failure of the old in their responsibility to the young. Like Caputo's Johanna de Silentio, he understands the command to sacrifice Isaac as a manifestation of the violent ideology of masculine force and pride. His version, however, offers no hope that an alternative voice will be heard. The poem, 'The Parable of the Old Man and the Young' – it will be familiar to many from Benjamin Britten's *War Requiem* – is, like much of Owen's poetry, itself an instance of responsibility to the other, a labouring to attend to the suffering on all sides, a bearing witness for the sake of the ravaged future.

> So Abram rose, and clave the wood, and went,
> And took the fire with him, and a knife.
> And as they sojourned both of them together,
> Isaac the first-born spake and said, My Father,
> Behold the preparations, fire and iron,
> But where the lamb for this burnt-offering?
> Then Abram bound the youth with belts and straps,
> And builded parapets and trenches there,
> And stretchèd forth the knife to slay his son.
> When lo! an angel called him out of heaven,
> Saying, Lay not thy hand upon the lad,
> Neither do anything to him. Behold,
> A ram, caught in a thicket by its horns;

Offer the Ram of Pride instead of him.
But the old man would not so, but slew his son,
And half the seed of Europe, one by one.

(*Collected Poems*, 42)

Notes

1. 'Donner la mort' first appeared in 1992 as a long contribution to Rabaté and Wenzel (eds), *L'Éthique du don,* and subsequently as the larger part of a 1999 book by Derrida also entitled *Donner la mort.* In English the original essay was published as a book, *The Gift of Death,* in 1995, and then in 2008, in a revised translation, as part of *The Gift of Death,* 2nd edn, an English version of Derrida's 1999 book. I shall quote from the revised translation; this sentence occurs on p. 71.
2. In the Qur'an, the centrality of the idea of submission is such that Isaac is *told* what is about to happen and accepts it.
3. Derrida's reading is perhaps more Levinasian than Levinas's own. In *Proper Names,* Levinas proposes that the most telling moment in the drama is the *second* command, the order to spare Isaac; Abraham's ability to hear this command, which returns him to the ethical order vis-à-vis Isaac, is the essential ethical point (74, 77). See also Derrida's note 6 on p. 79, and his discussion of the problematic distinction between the ethical and the religious in Kierkegaard and Levinas (83–4). Of course, for Levinas the term 'ethics' generally has a rather different signification from what it has for Kierkegaard, Heidegger and Derrida (at least until his more recent writing on Levinas). Derrida's discomfort with the term and the systematic philosophy it evokes (a discomfort which partially echoes Heidegger's in the 'Letter on Humanism') is concisely stated in *Altérités* (70–2). In *Adieu,* however, Derrida endorses Levinas's understanding of ethics more fully, though not without a certain rewriting whereby thirdness, and thus the juridico-political, become an integral feature of the ethical response to the Other (see Chapter 7 below). If it were not for this mediation, argues Derrida, the ethics of the face-to-face would threaten violence – but at the same time, in an inescapable double-bind, the juridico-political itself violates the purity of the ethical relation. We are back with the cats.
4. The force of the notion of impossibility in Derrida is something that is well brought out by John D. Caputo; see *The Prayers and Tears* and *Deconstruction in a Nutshell.*
5. One characteristic formulation of Derrida's is the following from *The Other Heading*: 'The condition of possibility of this thing called responsibility is a certain *experience and experiment of the possibility of the impossible: the testing of the aporia* from which one may invent the only *possible invention, the impossible invention*' (41). It will be evident from the discussion in Chapter 1 that literature, too, is an engagement with the impossible.
6. There is an intriguing moment in an interview when Levinas appears to come close to Derrida's position: explaining that the sixth commandment

is not limited to literal acts of murder, he says, 'For example, when we sit down at the table in the morning and drink coffee, we kill an Ethiopian who doesn't have any coffee' ('The Paradox of Morality', 173). This idea is not, as far as I am aware, developed anywhere in his work.

7. Derrida further develops the implications of Abraham's secrecy, and relates it to the (non-)category of 'literature', in 'Literature in Secret'. See Chapter 2 above.

8. Simon Critchley, *The Ethics of Deconstruction*, 225–37. In more recent work, Critchley somewhat revises his view that Levinasian ethics provides a grounding for politics absent from Derrida's deconstruction; see *Ethics – Politics – Subjectivity*. Levinas does not extend the ethical beyond the dual relationship: 'Because there are more than two people in the world, we invariably pass from the ethical perspective of alterity to the ontological perspective of totality' ('Ethics of the Infinite', 187). Derrida's reworking of Levinas may be seen as an attempt to keep alive the thinking of alterity in the larger sphere. See Chapter 7 below.

9. One should add, perhaps, 'perhaps', for Derrida often qualifies statements about the occurrence of events such as the exercise of justice or hospitality, or the giving of a gift, with an 'if'. We cannot *know* that these things happen, but we can try to find ways of formulating how they happen if they do.

10. 'Responsibility . . . demands on the one hand an accounting, a general answering-for-oneself with respect to the general and before the generality, hence the idea of substitution; and, on the other hand, uniqueness, absolute singularity, hence nonsubstitution, nonrepetition, silence, and secrecy. What I am saying here about responsibility can also be said about decision' (*The Gift of Death*, 62). Derrida used the phrase 'negotiating the unnegotiable' in a seminar on *The Gift of Death* in Pietermaritzburg, South Africa, in 1998.

11. It may also be what literature does. See Chapter 2 above.

12. See, for instance, 'Of Hospitality'; and, for further discussion, Chapter 10 below.

13. Kierkegaard writes: 'Since God claims Isaac, he must, if possible, love him even more, and only then can he *sacrifice* him, for it is indeed this love for Isaac that makes his act a sacrifice by its paradoxical contrast to his love for God' (*Fear and Trembling*, 74). This passage is cited by Derrida, who also stresses that 'in order for there to be a sacrifice, the ethical must retain all its value' (67).

14. Kant poses a similar question in *The Conflict of the Faculties*, 115, and *Religion*, 175.

15. See Levinas, *Totality and Infinity*, and Lyotard, *Heidegger and 'the jews'*. As Jill Robbins points out, the destitution to which Levinas refers is primarily that of the face, irrespective of the condition of the human individual it belongs to: 'The face's destitution is an essential destitution' ('Visage, Figure', 283). To lay stress on literal destitution, therefore, is to move away from Levinas's more absolute formulations and to stress the contingencies of ethical life, which is what Caputo does.

16. After the publication of 'Donner la mort' Caputo published an essay, 'Instants, Secrets, and Singularities', which could be read as an extra

chapter of *Against Ethics*, focusing on the 'mad economics' of *Fear and Trembling* as read by Derrida. (A revised version appears in Caputo's *Prayers and Tears*, 188–222.)

17. See, for instance, 'Psyche', 340–3. Levinas also emphasises the unremitting exertion required by ethics: 'I have described ethical responsibility as *insomnia* or *wakefulness* precisely because it is a perpetual duty of vigilance and effort which can never slumber' ('Ethics of the Infinite', 195).

Chapter 5

Arche-jargon

I

I have a problem with jargon, or rather with its absence.[1] Like some stern deity, a comrade-in-arms of Duty and Conscience, the figure of Lucidity hovers threateningly above my computer screen, issuing imperatives, interfering with my progress, driving me back over my prose to revise and elucidate. 'Is it clear?' 'Will they see what you mean?' 'Do you *know* what you mean?' are questions that haunt my every keystroke. And perhaps it's out of envy that I'm drawn to writers who seem less bound to this tyrant's remorseless wheel – modernists in literature, Continentals in philosophy, deconstructors in criticism.[2]

As a slave, I inevitably harbour suspicions about my master and frequently murmur rebelliously as I rewrite a sentence for the tenth time. What's the source of this power, exercised over me as a force in need of no justification? Psychologically, in terms of my personal history, I can make some guesses; but the question is more interesting as a philosophico-politico-cultural one. This demand for clarity, perspicuity, accessibility, this attack on jargon, hermeticism, technical language: what's at stake here, for assailants and victims?

It goes without saying that shall try to deal with this question as lucidly as I can.

II

Most of those who use the word 'jargon' would probably acknowledge, at least after calm reflection, that it is not a neutral term, objectively naming a certain kind of discourse. No less than three times in its series of definitions, the *OED* invokes the distinctly non-objective attitude of 'contempt': 'Often a term of contempt for something the speaker does not understand'; 'Also applied contemptuously to a language by one who does not understand it'; and 'Applied contemptuously to any mode of speech abounding in unfamiliar terms, or peculiar to a particular set of persons'. A word that expresses an interest, then, a position, a *parti pris*; my writing is clear, yours is obscure, theirs is jargon-ridden. 'A mode of speech abounding in unfamiliar terms' is a definition that makes no sense outside a specific situation in which someone finds something unfamiliar, and 'terms peculiar to a particular set of a persons' are jargon only to some other set of persons. However, to agree on the relativity of the term 'jargon' is not to remove it from the realm of semantic enquiry. It is, after all, used of certain texts and not others; and we all know what kinds of text are most likely to attract this particular charge today. Most of us – and I certainly include myself – have been tempted to reach for the term in a moment of exasperation. And any invocation of 'jargon' – however easily it can be shown to be an ideological rather than an objective judgement – implies a philosophy of language and an ethics of reading.[3]

To complain about jargon in a text is to complain about the prominence of marks indicating a specific context – an institutional or political group, a closed discursive system, a current cultural trend. (It has even been associated with racism: writing about himself in *Roland Barthes*, Barthes states: 'He has often been dismissed by an accusation of intellectualist jargon. And hence he felt himself to be the object of a kind of racism: they excluded his language, i.e., his body' (103).) Those indicative marks will tend to be individual words and phrases rather than difficulties of syntax or argument (the implication, of course, is that larding one's discourse with obscure items of vocabulary is an easy task, a merely mechanical feat to be sharply distinguished from the torsion of language under the force of strenuous thought), and they will usually have a technical flavour – the discourse of a specific *techne*, an art or science, a kind of artificial or invented language, as opposed to the 'natural' language spoken by the community at large. The implication, again, is that a certain mechanical quality has been allowed into living speech: in a domain where sensitive human judgement is the appropriate mode, such as literary criticism, the terminology of the laboratory is making its angular, unlovely inroads.[4] (This interference is particularly marked when the offending terms come from a foreign language – as if our own wasn't good enough.) Also implicit here is an aesthetic charge; Fowler's *Modern English Usage* calls jargon 'talk that is considered both ugly-sounding and hard to understand' (315) – notice that Fowler too brings out the relativity of the term: 'talk that is considered . . .', not 'talk that is . . .' Not only do these obscure terms balk comprehension, they clot and clog the limpid flow of easy prose. Even if they're not foreign, they sound foreign. The use of jargon is thus a cardinal misuse of language: words are being selected – this is the implied accusation – not because of the appropriateness of their inner meanings, their relevance to an argument, but because of their external properties, sounds and shapes that signal exclusiveness, foreignness, technicality, artifice, but do no real intellectual work. Lazy immigrants in outlandish garb.

Or we might even say *Gastarbeiter*. The phenomenon of *Fremdwörter* in the German language offers close parallels to our topic: in German, words imported from other languages (especially Latinate words) remain more clearly marked than is usually the case in European languages, and provoke responses in many ways similar to those elicited by jargon. Adorno's 1959 radio talk 'Words from Abroad' is a particularly rich discussion of the phenomenon, presenting a judicious defence of the use of foreign words for specific, carefully judged purposes. Adorno himself makes the link between foreign words and jargon when he calls 'terminology' 'the quintessence of foreign words in the individual disciplines' (189). The term 'jargon' is, of course, inescapably linked with Adorno through *The Jargon of Authenticity*, his 1964 attack on the postwar German heritage of Kierkegaardian and Heideggerian existentialism that manifested itself in an ideal of *Eigentlichkeit*.[5] In this context, however, the word *Jargon* in German (another *Fremdwort*) indicates a use of language sharply distinct from jargon as we have been considering it, or from what Adorno, more neutrally, calls 'terminology': 'Nowhere do foreign words in German prove their worth more than in contrast to the jargon of authenticity, terms like *Auftrag*, *Begegnung*, *Aussage*, *Anliegen* [mission, encounter, message, concern] and the like. They all want to conceal the fact that they are terminology' ('Words from Abroad', 190). Jargon, in Adorno's sense, is terminology (jargon in *our* sense) masquerading as homely utterance.

A truly jargon-free text would therefore have to be a text that did not depend on a limited context for its intelligibility; it would be universally accessible, instantly and totally translatable into sense (the same sense that its author had in mind before putting it into language). Sounds and shapes would melt with perfect efficiency into their meanings, not drawing attention to themselves, not obstructing the natural process of understanding. It's not difficult to see what model of language is implied here: language as both natural and universal, without artifice or technique, immediately relating sound to meaning and vice versa. George Orwell, in what is probably the best-known attack on jargon and related style-crimes in English, offers the following recommendation to writers: 'What is above all needed is to let the meaning choose the word, and not the other way about . . . Probably it is better to put off using words as long as possible and get one's meaning as clear as one can through pictures and sensations' ('Politics and the English Language', 138–9).

What, then, if we were to acknowledge that even as an ideal – perhaps especially as an ideal – this model misrepresents the workings of language in the service of an essentially ideological suppression of difference and change? That it attempts to mask the heterogeneity of language, and of languages, universalising and essentialising what is mediated, contested, constructed? Then jargon would cease to be a sign of everything that can go wrong with language and become instead an index of how language actually works and should be seen to work. Adorno argues in a similar vein with regard to foreign words in German:

> By acknowledging itself as a token [*Spielmarke*], the foreign word reminds us bluntly that all real language has something of the token in it . . . Not the least of what we resist in the foreign word is that it illuminates something true of all words: that language imprisons those who speak it, that as a medium of their own it has essentially failed . . . Foreign words demonstrate the impossibility of an ontology of language: they confront even concepts that try to pass themselves off as origin itself with their mediatedness, their moment of being subjectively constructed, their arbitrariness. ('Words from Abroad', 189)

Hence the particular perniciousness of jargon in Adorno's sense: unlike self-acknowledged terminology, which entails a 'critique of concepts' claim to exist in themselves when in fact language has inscribed in them something posited' (189), jargon is terminology trying to pass itself off as language that is wholly unmediated.[6]

Every word in a text signals its dependence upon a circumscribed context, or rather a series of such contexts (including particular groups of language-users); if this weren't so it couldn't begin to function as an item of language, and would be dispersed meaninglessly across empty space. There's no clear division between 'native' and 'alien' terms; no word is purely natural, purely at home, purely given over to meaning. Language is *techne*, technique, artifice – except that these words have to be understood in a way that doesn't oppose them to a concept of self-sufficient and primary nature.[7] Let's take, for example, the word 'jargon'. Does it immediately yield itself to a meaning, independent of its user, its occasion, its history, its audience, its physical form? Certainly not: its effectiveness, we've already seen, lies partly in its invitation to the reader to take sides in a particular situation, to join a group pitted against another group. Moreover, it's not a word that melts easily into its environment, but one whose sounds have a force of their own – many would say it's an 'ugly' word, but that's probably an effect of the meaning upon our perception of the sounds rather than the other way round (we shouldn't forget the 'sweet jargoning' of birds in Chaucer and Coleridge). The *OED*, puzzled by the etymology of *jargon*, tentatively relates it to the word *jargle*, 'to utter a harsh or shrill sound; to chatter, jar', which in turn is speculatively related to the 'onomatopoeic base *jarg-*, *garg-*'. On that base are erected such words as *gargle*, *gargoyle*, *guggle*[8] and *gurgle*, with cognates in many languages. The onomatopoeic force is so great here that the etymologist's lines of descent in dealing with this cluster are more than usually hypothetical, allowing as they must for the possibility that at any given period the existence of the word in question represents a fresh imitative invention rather than a link in a historical chain. (Thus the extended etymological information given by the *OED* under *gurgle* is followed by the undermining comment: 'Whether the English word is a direct adaptation of any of those verbs or is a native echoic formation is not clear.')

Jargon is therefore an instance of jargon, or at least of the properties for which jargon is condemned. My coinage *arche-jargon*, besides being another instance of jargon, names the condition of the word *jargon* – as it names that of all words.

III

You will of course have predicted the shape of my argument as soon as you saw my title. Perhaps I should have added a subtitle, 'With apologies to Jacques Derrida'. 'Arche-writing' and 'arche-trace' are two terms in a Derridean series, naming – or I would prefer to say nicknaming – an originary condition or movement that doesn't function like an orthodox origin or *arche*, but like writing, like a trace. Or, I would add, like jargon.

For my comments to have been anything more than a parody, however, I would have had to examine in some detail instances of the word 'jargon' in critical discourse, showing how critics who use it to attack writing they dislike nevertheless rely on something very close to jargon – as I've described it – to pursue their critique.[9] This 'something' can't be spelled out with the jargon-free lucidity that those critics would demand, precisely because all notions of lucidity, and its opposite, depend on it. And hence the appropriateness of borrowing (or nicking, in English slang) the term 'jargon' itself from their pejorative vocabulary, and reapplying it at another level – turning 'jargon' into an indisputable instance of what they would call jargon by giving it a Greek prefix, and thus in addition alluding to the work of a notoriously jargon-ridden, non-native philosopher.

Derrida, as far as I'm aware, never advanced this view of jargon. But he did – not surprisingly, perhaps – show some interest in the term. (It is, of course, a French word too, as much, or as little, at home on either side of the English Channel – though more so on both sides than in Germany, where it signals its alienness by retaining something of its French pronunciation.) Here's part of one of the inserts in the right-hand column of *Glas*, the column which explores the works of Genet. (I cite the French first, for obvious reasons, then the brave English translation by John Leavy and Richard Rand, which necessarily loses some of the onomatopoeic force of the passage.)

J'argotise, je jargonne, j'ai l'air de produire des mots nouveaux, un nouveau lexique. Un argot seulement, un jargon. Ils sortent tous deux du fond de la gorge, ils séjournent, un certain temps, comme un gargarisme, au fond du gosier, on racle et on crache.

L'argot est un mot d'argot. Comme tous les mots d'argot, Littré ne le mentionne pas. Argotiser c'est travailler contre le lexique. Mais en argumentant, en élaborant, en alléguant, depuis le dedans de son corpus. Argot est un très vieux mot, enraciné dans la langue et dans la littérature. Comme jargon. Et pourtant, son usage est d'abord argotique, limité à une bande ou à une école. (246)

I argotize, I jargon, I seem to produce new words, a new lexicon. Merely an argot, a jargon. They both come from the bottom of the throat, they linger, for a certain time, like a gargling, at the bottom of the gullet, you rasp and you spit.

Argot is an argot word. As with all argot words, Littré does not mention it. To argotize is to work against the lexicon. But by arguing, by elaborating, by alleging, from within its own corpus. Argot is a very old word, rooted in language and literature. Like jargon. And yet its usage is argotic first of all, limited to a band or a school. (220)

One of the impulses of *Glas* is to challenge Saussure's relegation of onomatopoeia to the realm of linguistic irrelevance. Not that Derrida is defending the traditional poetic notion of onomatopoeia as the happy matching of sound and sense; rather, he's examining and exemplifying the disruptive operation of sound, its introduction of the physical body into that ideally harmonious, and harmoniously ideal, notion of language. He's interested, therefore, in the sounds of the word 'jargon', heightening our attention to them by means of the echoes in *gorge*, *séjournent*, *gosier*, *racle*, *crache* and *gargarisme*. (This last is yet another member of that cluster built on *jarg-* and *garg-*: *gargarise* and *gargarism* are good English words, inherited relatively unchanged from Latin and Greek, and eventually displaced by the verb/noun *gargle*.) He's also interested in the link between *jargon* and *argot*, a link not only of sound but also of function.[10]

The equivalent words in English seem inseparable, too – here's the *OED*'s brisk definition of *argot*: 'The jargon, slang, or peculiar phraseology of a class, originally that of thieves and rogues.' (The word is 'French. Of unknown origin.') And it places next to *argot* its symbol for words which are 'not naturalized' – that's its exact phrase – in English. That silent 't' also brands 'argot' as an unassimilated alien, a piece of jargon, an example of the argot of those who read too many French writers. Fowler, in his entry under *jargon*, has a discussion of *argot*, referring to the usual 'thieves and tramps in France', and continuing: '[It] is applied secondarily to the special vocabulary of any set of persons. There is in these senses no justification for its application to any English manner of speech instead of whichever English word may be most appropriate' (*Dictionary of Modern English Usage*, 315). Such as, presumably, that native – or at least long-settled – inhabitant, 'jargon', which Fowler thinks should be applied only to 'the sectional vocabulary of a science, art, class, sect, trade, or profession, full of technical terms,' adding: 'There is plenty of work for it there alone, so copiously does jargon of this sort breed nowadays' (315). The word 'jargon', it seems, is an industrious citizen, unlike those fornicating and proliferating immigrants which it names.[11]

Besides *argot*, Fowler discusses a number of other affiliated terms in his article under *jargon*, among them *cant* and *slang*, both of which exhibit a certain interchangeability with one another and with *jargon*. (For the *OED*, *cant* is, among other things, 'professional or technical jargon', while *slang* is 'the cant or jargon of a certain class or period' – and notice, incidentally, the recognition that time is one aspect of the contextual variation affecting the evaluation implied by and directed at these terms.) Here too, we find words that name a certain context-boundedness betraying the same context-boundedness – thus the *OED* gives six (widely disparate) senses for *slang*, telling us that all but the first occur 'only in slang or canting use'. *Slang* is, moreover, 'a word of cant origin, the ultimate source of which is not apparent'; the meaning of *cant* in this case being, presumably, 'The secret language or jargon used by gipsies, thieves, professional beggars, etc.' (The use of cant is presumably the badge of professionalism among beggars as jargon is among literary critics.) Faced with this hypersensitivity to context, etymology falters in its task of producing a coherent transhistorical narrative: *cant*, the OED informs us, 'presumably' represents Latin *cantus*, and derives from the contemptuous depiction of beggars' whining – 'or the word may have been actually made from Latin or Romanic in the rogues' jargon of the time'. As *slang* may be slang (and '*argot* is an argot word'), so *cant* may be cant. (For good measure, the *OED* adds further alternative sources in Irish and Gaelic *cainnt*, 'language', and two seventeenth-century Presbyterian Ministers, Andrew and Alexander

Cant. Perhaps even now, folk-etymology is busy adding Immanuel to this imaginary genealogy.) What these uncertain etymological labours show is that none of these words is stable across contexts and periods; they are words which demonstrate – while at the same time they name – the difference made to language by its changing situation.

If jargon highlights the issue of context and perspective, the question of audience is never far away. It is easy to say that jargon arises when the audience responding to a text is different from the one assumed by it, but harder to answer the question, 'In that case, what and to whom is the responsibility of the writer?' For Adorno, 'Only the word that takes pains to name its object precisely, without having an eye to its effect, has an opportunity to champion the cause of human beings by doing so' ('Words from Abroad', 191); and for Barthes, 'A writer has greater obligations towards a way of speaking which is the truth for him than towards the critic of the *Nation française* or *Le Monde*' (*Criticism and Truth*, 51–2). This precision, this truth, is unquestionably part of the responsibility of the writer; but don't Adorno and Barthes dismiss with suspicious ease all consideration of the effect of their writing on particular readers? Adorno writes with an understandable fear of the manipulative potential of language, but a myth of objectivity may end up being just as manipulative (and less consciously so) as a recognition of the other-directedness and – to put it in Bakhtinian terms – the other-inhabitedness of language. ('Words from Abroad' is, as one might expect of the brilliant writer Adorno, clearly directed towards its radio audience.) The responsible use of jargon, and language-as-jargon, far from refusing take into account effects on audiences, takes them into account in the fullest possible manner.

To argotise, to jargon is to work against the lexicon, says Derrida, to demonstrate the ideological character of those barriers between native and alien, natural and artificial, to bend thought into ways other than those sanctioned by a familiar and familiarising language. '"Jargon", says Barthes, 'is a way of imagining (and shocks as imagination does)' (*Criticism and Truth*, 52). It's a way of refocusing attention both on the medium of language, as technique, as artifice, as physical production, operating always in specific situations, and of reasserting the heterogeneity, the multiple specificities, of the human communities who use it.

IV

Having invented a jargon of 'arche-jargon', or 'arche-argot', to give it another nickname, or 'jargonicity', which would do equally well, am I in a better position to understand my own domination by the imperative of lucidity? Perhaps: for if jargonicity is the condition of all discourse, heterogeneity the condition of all communities, I can rely on no natural bond between my audience and me, the world and my language, to secure immediate communication. As I write I have to open myself to those who will be receiving these words, without homogenising or fixing them; and at the same time I have to open myself to the language I use, without transcendentalising or mystifying it. I've been arguing that to hurl the word 'jargon' at a text which uses terms unfamiliar to the reader represents a failure to acknowledge the properties of language and language-use; but I should add that when it can be demonstrated that those unfamiliar terms are being used vacuously or intimidatingly (and everything I've said should indicate the cautious and meticulous spirit in which such demonstrations need to be undertaken), jargon represents a similar failure, since it involves an inability or unwillingness to take into account the otherness of language and those who use it.

No doubt I shall continue to labour under the yoke of lucidity; but I shall try to hold myself subject only to a lucidity that acknowledges the jargonicity of all language. This is a lucidity that makes no implicit claim for universality or transparency; it accepts the operation of the random and contingent, it acknowledges the often unpredictable force of the physical, it is prepared, for specific purposes, to work against as well as with the lexicon. 'Clarity', writes Barthes in his defence of jargon, 'is not an attribute of writing, it is writing itself, from the very moment at which it becomes writing, it is the happiness of writing, it is all the desire which is in writing' (*Criticism and Truth*, 51, translation modified). Lucidity can never be lucidity for all and for ever, but can only be a sensitivity to context, a responsibility to the other, a recognition of difference, heterogeneity, mediation; something not very far removed from jargon, in other words.

Notes

1. This essay was written for an MLA session entitled 'Critical Jargon'; it has been only lightly modified for publication, and thus from the very start betrays the principles of sensitivity to context which it attempts to articulate – except to the extent that this note itself succeeds in transforming the context.
2. In Chapter 9 below, I address a similar drive for lucidity in a literary theorist I admire, J. Hillis Miller.
3. Roland Barthes makes some of the essential points in a vigorous counterattack on critics who had accused him of using jargon; see the section entitled 'Clarity' in *Criticism and Truth*, where he briefly delineates the 'myth'

of 'clarity': a particular class language promoted to the status of a 'natural' language, 'universality appropriated by the class of property owners' (49). In his discussion of the term, Raymond Williams, while acknowledging that 'specialized internal vocabularies' can be a problem, rightly insists that 'every known general position, in matters of art and belief, has its defining terms, and the difference between these and the terms identified as *jargon* is often no more than one of relative date and familiarity' (*Keywords*, 176). For a wide-ranging collection of essays on jargon, see the first issue of the online journal *World Picture*; and for a collection with a focus on academic writing, see Culler and Lamb (eds), *Just Being Difficult?*

4. Such attacks on jargon are related to the critique that finds an excess of technique over substance in a writer like Joyce – see chapter 13, 'Envoi: Judging Joyce', in Attridge, *Joyce Effects*.

5. The translation of *Eigentlichkeit* as 'authenticity' disguises the word's close relation to the basic terminology of *eigen*, 'own', and *eigentlich*, 'proper, real, actual, true'. *Authentizität* does in fact exist as a *Fremdwort* in German, and is cited by Adorno as one of the most striking and discomfiting examples of such words that he has used ('Words from Abroad', 197–9).

6. Adorno does not, however, attend as fully to the situatedness of language as he might, and when he turns to examples of his own employment of foreign words he seems in danger of falling back into a view of language as direct expression not very far removed from Orwell's. Thus he insists that 'only the foreign word that renders the meaning better, more faithfully, more uncompromisingly than the available German synonyms will allow a spark to flow in the constellation into which it is introduced' (192).

7. The apparent contrast between this position and that taken by Vološinov (Bakhtin?) in his discussion of the 'alien word' is largely a matter of emphasis. Vološinov finds the distinction between 'native' and 'foreign' languages useful when taking linguistics to task for modelling its analysis of living languages on that of dead languages – isolated, finished, monologic, written – and its analysis of native languages on that of foreign languages. While there is certainly a danger here of naturalising and privileging the (writer's) 'living' and 'native' language, Vološinov's aim is to assert the importance of contextual as against abstract meaning in linguistic study, and is hence consonant with the argument I'm putting forward here. See Vološinov, *Marxism and the Philosophy of Language*, 71–81.

8. 'Guggle: (verb) To make a sound like that made by liquid pouring from a small-necked bottle . . . To bring *up* or pour *forth* with a guggling sound; (noun) The windpipe . . . The epiglottis . . . A guggling sound ("The slow guggle of the natives' hubble-bubble . . . breaks the lazy repose", Russell, *Diary India* I. xiii. 211)' (*OED*).

9. Lee Edelman articulates an argument close to mine in the preface to his *Homographesis*:

> The demand, for instance, that critical writing be purged of 'jargon' and specialized language acquires its 'humanistic' or 'commonsensical' appeal only insofar as we are willing to ignore how the demonized term here, 'jargon', serves as the very thing it denounces: a jargonistic code, like

'family values' as used at the Republican National Convention in 1992, that assumes, disingenuously and with oppressive effects, the availability of a common ground of shared assumptions and understandings, of universally acknowledged truths and expressions, all of which are adequate to the expression of any concept worth our consideration . . . The fiction of a common language that can speak a universally available truth, or even a universally available logic, is the fantasy on which the structures of dominance anatomized throughout this volume rest. (xvii)

10. The same twinning is the basis of Pascal Singy's study, 'Le vocabulaire médical'. Singy defines *argot* in terms of a cryptic function, whereby the medical profession sustains its superiority over the lay world, *jargon* in terms of a communicational function, whereby technical accuracy is achieved. Not surprisingly, however, he discovers in medical discourse a 'rapport dynamique' between the two functions – one is always on the point of turning into the other.

11. One might assume that jargon would always be gendered male, given its proclivity towards the technical, but at least one of its opponents manages to imply that its unworthiness is in part due to its feminine qualities: 'The first virtue', writes Sir Arthur Quiller-Couch,

the touchstone of a masculine style, is its use of the active verb and the concrete noun. When you write in the active voice, 'They gave him a silver teapot', you write as a man. When you write 'He was made the recipient of a silver teapot', you write jargon. ('Interlude: On Jargon', 96–7)

Chapter 6

Deconstruction and Fiction

'Now, for the poet, he nothing affirms, and therefore never lieth' (123). This is how Sir Philip Sidney, writing an *Apology for Poetry* in the late sixteenth century, carves out a space for fiction, a space in which the accusation of telling lies (which Plato, for instance, had accused poets of doing) simply does not make any sense. This distinction between two primary modes of discourse, fictional and non-fictional, has often been made since Sidney's day, and it operates strongly in much thinking about language use in our own time.

The crucial difference that is articulated by means of this distinction is between two kinds of *claim*: some sentences claim to be telling the truth, making a statement about really occurring events or existing entities, and can therefore be judged in these terms; others make no such claim, and therefore escape any such judgement. Thus John Searle, in what has become a standard essay in analytic aesthetics, argues that the writer of fiction is 'pretending' to make assertions rather than actually making them, and in so doing is *not* committing himself or herself to the truth of the expressed propositions ('The Logical Status', 61–7). Sidney's sentence itself, for instance, carries with it the implication that an appeal to the criterion of truthfulness *would* be legitimate, and so does the sentence you are reading now. It is possible that these sentences are not true, that they are lies or errors; but no one would dispute that they operate within the arena of truth and its alternatives. However, the opening of James Joyce's *Ulysses* – 'Stately, plump Buck Mulligan came from the stairhead' – makes no such claim; anyone trying to assert that this sentence is untrue would be thought to be making a very odd statement indeed, perhaps one which itself was not meant to be judged true or false.

There have existed many names for discourse which makes no claim to the condition of truthfulness. Sidney calls it *poetry*, as did Chaucer (although the narrower meaning of 'composition in verse' was also common in medieval and Renaissance times); and as late as 1755 Samuel Johnson includes in the definition of *poet* in his *English Dictionary* 'an inventor, an author of fiction'. As this definition indicates, though, the term *fiction* was available by Johnson's time, providing a less slippery, less limitingly honorific name for writing that situates itself outside the true/false distinction. Originally a general term for inventing or feigning, *fiction* began to be applied to linguistic productions involving imaginary characters and events (whether in prose or verse) at the end of the six-teenth century.[1] (Neither term is coterminous with the even more prob-lematic term *literature*: at different periods in its history, this term could embrace a greater or lesser amount of non-fictional writing, and has always excluded some fictional writing, such as jokes and tall stories. We will not be concerned with literature in this chapter.)

Theoretically speaking, there seems no problem in distinguishing between the fictional and the non-fictional. The problems that arise with the distinction appear to stem largely from the pragmatic difficulties in given instances: how do we know whether a sentence or a longer text is or is not making a claim to be truthful (and hence whether or not it makes sense to judge it wrong or deceitful)? Languages, at least in their written form, don't usually include markers that indicate unambiguously the existence of such a claim; Joyce's sentence about Buck Mulligan could occur in exactly that form as a statement about a real individual. Although there are syntactic forms that are associated with narrative (such as the use of free indirect discourse – sentences like 'Tomorrow he would show them'), these may be used just as effectively in a historical narrative as in a fictional one.[2] Since sentences don't themselves advertise their status as fictional or non-fictional, the distinction depends entirely on the context in which they appear to the reader or listener, and the context may not furnish sufficient information. The same problem arises with *irony*, which is a use of language in which the literal assertion being made by the words is modified (or even contradicted) by some feature of the context – for example, circumstances which make it impossible for the statement to be literally true. Indeed, fiction could be considered a branch or type of irony, one in which the context informs the reader that the sentences are to be taken as referring to an imaginary reality.

What are the clues in the context, then, that lead us to the conclusion that a sentence or a text is fictional? The simplest answer would seem to be: features making it evident that the author of the sentence or text *meant them to be read* as fictional. (Thus John Searle asserts 'Whether or not a work is literature is for readers to decide, whether or not it is fiction is for the author to decide' ('The Logical Status', 59).) This would seem to be implied in the notion of a 'claim' being made by any sentence to be true or to be outside the realm of true and false: the claim is, presumably, made by the author of the sentence as he or she writes it. The context that tells us this could be in the form of other sentences or words, such as a title or a blurb, or the physical appearance of the publication, such as a scientific journal or a paperback novel, or it could be information gained from the circumstances under which we encounter the text, such as a recommendation by a friend or teacher. Of course, it is always possible to overlook or misread clues, and to reach the wrong conclusion about an author's intentions; but this would seem to be an inescapable problem about the pragmatics of reading, not a theoretical problem about the distinction being made. A writer does, or does not, expect any given sentence to be read as fictional or non-fictional, ironic or literal, and it is the job of the reader to find out, by whatever means possible, which of these it is.[3]

Alas, things are not so simple. A number of philosophical and critical traditions have shown that the writing process and the reading process are more complicated than this model suggests. One of the most powerful of these traditions is deconstruction. Jacques Derrida has examined a number of attempts to provide a philosophical grounding for the view of writing and reading I've just sketched, and found, again and again, highly instructive failures. Yet the word 'failure', like my 'Alas' at the start of this paragraph, conveys the wrong impression: deconstructive readings are not aimed at exposing inadequacies in arguments and intellectual limitations in their authors, and the fact that the simple model doesn't work is as much a cause for rejoicing as for regret. It is precisely in their forceful and meticulous engagement with these questions that a wide range of philosophers have demonstrated the complexity of such notions as 'meaning' and 'truth', and it is precisely on this complexity that we depend in all our cultural, political and economic practices.

One of the most effective ways in which Derrida has brought into focus the complicated operations of language as it is produced and received is by tracing in a number of philosophical works the role played by the notion of *writing* and its relation to notions such as *truth* and *presence*. The pure expression of truth, if there were such a thing, would be *immediate*: it would not rely on anything external to it, since the utilisation of some outside aid would always threaten to contaminate its purity. But the utterance of the truth – or of a statement making a truth-claim – is in fact always mediated by language, language which has its own sedimented history, structural properties and figurative potential. The truth in language is never simply present; it always has to pass through space and time, and this means that the context in which it is produced is always different from that in which it is received.

But why pick on writing? Historically, it has frequently been language in the form of writing that has been identified as the troublemaker, intervening between the author's attempt to enunciate the truth and the reception of this enunciation by readers distant in space and time and thereby subject to unpredictable vagaries of transmission. Speech, on the other hand, has seemed to philosophers at least since Plato (and to many an unphilosophical language-user) to be a guarantor of authenticity, of the here-and-nowness of one person's communication with another. Irony, for example, is often signalled by a particular way of speaking which is lost when the words are written down; and if the hearer is not certain, he or she can always ask, 'Are you being serious?'[4] There are also certain inflections of the voice associated with story-telling, so any difficulties we have in distinguishing between fiction and non-fiction could be said to be the fault of writing.

However, Derrida has shown in a number of works that philosophical arguments in support of this position always fall short of their goal: speech is revealed as subject to the same mediations as writing, in spite of the illusion of immediacy and presence. The signals whereby a speaker conveys the fictionality of an utterance, for instance, are as much part of the language system as the vowels and consonants, and are just as liable to reinterpretation in new contexts. The preferring of the spoken word as the locus of truth is, in fact, one aspect of a much wider tendency in Western thought that prefers presence to absence, the immediate to the mediated, originals to copies, and non-fiction to fiction – and in so doing creates simple oppositions where there is something more complicated, and more productive, at work.

Because of the mediated nature of all utterance, the difficulties besetting the distinction between fiction and non-fiction (or between the literal and the ironic) cannot, after all, be regarded as purely pragmatic. It is not just that sometimes it's hard to tell whether a sentence is meant to be taken as an assertion of the truth or not. Pushing the argument to the limit, it's more accurate to say that it's never possible to be sure, with absolute certainty, that it is (or is not) appropriate to regard a sentence as an assertion of a truth, for the type of context that would be necessary tell us this – a totally reliable and fully ascertainable context – does not exist.[5] Any context can always be further contextualised. Past contexts can never be wholly ascertained; future contexts cannot be wholly predicted. This condition even affects the act of writing: the writer does not have full access to the context which makes it possible – for instance, the unconscious motivations that underlie certain choices of words. Without realising it, writers who think of their work as entirely inside the non-fictional realm often write *as* this or that character, the hard-bitten journalist, the empathetic historian, the meticulous philosopher. Perhaps writing is only possible with at least this degree of the fictional – but then the same would be true of speaking. These conditions, which may seem a check on human ability, spring from the same structural properties that make the assertion of truth possible at all: if language were not a system of mediations, if utterances were not always open to new contexts, it could not begin to function. If a statement could not always be fiction, it could never make a claim to truth. In response to Searle's assertion that the relation between fiction and non-fiction is one of 'logical dependency', Derrida comments: 'The real question, or at any rate in my eyes the indispensable question, would then become: what is "nonfiction standard discourse", what must it be and what does this name evoke, once its fictionality or its fictionalization . . . is always possible (and moreover by virtue of the very same words, the same phrases, the same grammar, etc.)?' ('Limited Inc', 102, 133). He goes on to point out that the very rules or conventions governing the distinction between fiction and non-fiction partake of the fictional, as they are symbolic inventions, not 'things found in nature' (133–4).

The impossibility of keeping the fictional totally at bay in writing non-fiction has graver consequences for some genres than for others. If in reading a philosophical treatise or a scientific report, for instance, one finds one cannot be certain that there are no fictional statements among the non-fictional ones, the attainment of what is thought of as philosophical or scientific truth is imperilled. Another place where fiction is banned – but perhaps cannot be kept out – is the law. Derrida touches on all of these in his discussion of Kafka's brief story 'Before the Law', discussed above in the Introduction. He presents Kafka's text as a parable – a fiction – about the fictionality at the heart of the law, and shows that both Freud and Kant, scientist and philosopher, rely on something like fiction and cannot avoid doing so. Commenting on Kant's elaboration of a categorical imperative at the heart of moral law, he states: 'Though the authority of the law seems to exclude all historicity and empirical narrativity, and this at the moment when its rationality seems alien to all fiction and imagination . . . it still seems *a priori* to shelter these parasites' (190). As parasites, fiction and imagination are external to the law (and science and philosophy – all governed by rationality), but their hosts depend on them for their operation, even if that operation is not as smooth as, by their own lights, it should be.[6]

Another mode of writing where it would seem to be imperative that the reader be able to identify fictional moments is autobiography.[7] In autobiographical narrative, a narrator makes the claim: the events affirmed in these sentences happened to me. In a genuine autobiography it is possible to identify this narrator with the actual author of the sentences, and we are entitled, perhaps even encouraged, to judge each of the sentences as true or false. (In fictional autobiographies, of course, such as Defoe's *Moll Flanders* or Dickens's *Great Expectations*, we make a clear separation between the 'I' of the text and the author; the 'I' is capable of lying, but not the author.) Among autobiographies, those which stake most on this claim are those we call *confessions*: autobiographies where one is led to feel that the truth has been hidden – for good reason – until the moment of articulation in language.[8]

Here we would seem to be at the furthest remove possible from fiction. If we find in reading a confessional autobiography that we are uncertain whether we should be judging its statements on the basis of their truthfulness or enjoying it as fiction, we might as well give up all possibility of experiencing anything like confessional power. (The same is not true if we find ourselves *disbelieving* certain statements – to catch an autobiographer lying may be to register a moment of fierce internal struggle with memory and conscience, and to find the power of the confession enhanced.) Yet, as we have seen, what we think of as telling the truth is always mediated by linguistic and other systems – by the history of the genre of autobiography (including fictional autobiography), for instance – and we are likely to experience as truth only a work which successfully exploits those systems, and which is therefore to some degree a fiction, the elaboration of a believable character on existing models. For the writer, producing a convincing confession may mean the repudiation of conventional forms and fictional precedents, but this repudiation is itself thoroughly conventional. (The speaker in Sidney's sonnet sequence, *Astrophil and Stella*, who may or may not be identifiable with the author, repeatedly bases his claim to truthful utterance on his rejection of Petrarchan conventions.) Thus even the most powerful of confessional autobiographies cannot, and need not, escape fiction, and some of the most interesting confessions acknowledge this and yet manage to preserve the truth-telling power of the confession.[9]

Peggy Kamuf comments as follows on the problem of fiction:

> Fiction, the excessive mark of fiction, suspends the sign as sign of a referent, which otherwise, without the mark, would be presupposed. As such a mark, it has its 'being' only by virtue of an act of reading, whereby its mark gets remarked. It is thus less the name of an entity than the name of an *experience*. ('"Fiction"', 141)

But, following Derrida, she notes that this experience is equivocal, hanging 'between the suspension of the referent, as signaled by fiction's mark, and the persistence of the assumption of referential language' (143). Fictional language both *refers* and *deploys referentiality*; it may, for instance, demonstrate the immense power of the referential drive, or it may expose the frailty of our systems of referring. (We have, despite my earlier disclaimer, come round to talking about literature.) A sense of the writer's intention certainly enters the experience of fiction, and to this extent Searle and Lamarque are right, but it is an intention inferred, and never infallibly, by the reader from the markers in and around the text. The latter may include a statement by the author – 'I meant it as fiction' – but not only can this only ever be one among many clues, it raises the question of fictionality all over again. How do we know if this statement by the author about the fictionality of the text is or is not fiction?

Notes

1. There are other types of utterance besides fictional ones that do not make truth-claims; for instance, *performative* utterances make things happen (or attempt to do so). 'I name this child Catriona' does what it says (if the conditions are right); it doesn't assert a truth about something. However, performative utterances also occur in fiction, which can be troublesome for philosophical analysis – see Derrida's essay 'Signature Event Context'. For an extended discussion of speech acts – and in particular, performatives – in literature, see Miller, *Speech Acts*.
2. See Ann Banfield, *Unspeakable Sentences*, for a discussion of sentences of this type. It's sometimes claimed that only in fiction can the thoughts of person other than the narrator be related, but historians can legitimately use letters and journals to ascertain what a historical personage was thinking at a particular moment. Genette, in 'Fictional Narrative, Factual Narrative', considers a number of possible markers of fictional writing, but has to conclude that although such writing displays characteristic features, none can be taken as an infallible indicator of fiction.
3. Thus Lamarque concludes a discussion of various attempts within analytic aesthetics to distinguish between fiction and non-fiction with the somewhat lame conclusion, 'It seems implausible to remove intention altogether from an account of fiction' (186).
4. For a discussion of fiction that begins with the question 'How can we take fiction seriously?' see Kamuf, '"Fiction"'; this is an example of a question which, in writing, remains ambiguously poised between genuine enquiry and ironic dismissal.
5. Derrida adverts to one aspect of this undecidability of all utterances in the footnote from 'Passions' I quoted in Chapter 2: 'Something of literature will have begun when it is not possible to decide whether, when I speak of something, I am indeed speaking of something (of the thing itself, this one, for itself) or if I am giving an example' (142). The second option could be extended to the possibility that I am making a fictional statement.

6. Derrida notes that writing has always been treated as a 'parasite' by the philosophical tradition (Derrida, *Limited Inc*, 102). See also Miller, 'The Critic as Host'.

7. The necessarily fictional nature of autobiography has been the subject of a great deal of discussion. For a deconstructive treatment, see de Man, 'Autobiography as De-Facement'.

8. Interestingly, Derrida has associated both his own intellectual development and the institution of literature with the notion of confession. In an interview he talks of an adolescent desire to capture the memory of what happens – 'something like a lyrical movement toward confidences and confessions' ('"This Strange Institution"', 34) – and remarks that among the first texts he became interested in were confessions, notably the confessional writings of Rousseau and Gide. He then identifies literature as an institution (albeit a fictional institution) which in principle allows one to 'say everything' (*tout dire*), both in the sense of a total representation but also in the sense of speaking without constraints.

9. I have discussed Coetzee's memoirs *Boyhood* and *Youth* and his important essay 'Confession and Double Thoughts' in *J. M. Coetzee and the Ethics of Reading*, chapter 6, 'Confessing in the Third Person'. The third in Coetzee's trilogy, *Summertime*, is even less conventional as an autobiography, being a (fictional) record of a (fictional) biographer's attempt to ascertain the life-story of the (semi-fictional) John Coetzee in South Africa in the 1970s.

Chapter 7

Posthumous Infidelity: Derrida, Levinas and the Third

I

I begin with a quotation:

> All of Derrida's thought, from the beginning to the end, was a meditation on death, a meditation that diverted, disconcerted, and displaced everything in philosophy, from Plato to Hegel to Heidegger, that was also, and first of all, concerned with death.

A misquotation, in fact: this sentence was written not about Derrida but by Derrida about Emmanuel Levinas; however, it is perhaps even truer of the writer than of his subject. In a conversation with Gianni Vattimo in 1995, Derrida commented:

> I think about nothing but death, I think about it all the time, ten seconds don't go by without the imminence of the thing being there. I never stop analysing the phenomenon of 'survival' as the structure of surviving, it's really the only thing that interests me, but precisely insofar as I do not believe that one lives on post mortem. (Derrida and Ferraris, *A Taste for the Secret*, 88)

The sentence I quoted at the start comes near the close of Derrida's posthumous tribute to Levinas, 'Le mot d'acceuil' (120) – translated as 'A Word of Welcome' but also suggesting 'the word "welcome"' – which makes up the larger part of *Adieu*, the volume published in France two years after Levinas's death in 1995. As early as *La voix et le phénomène* (*Speech and Phenomena*) in 1967 Derrida was arguing that 'The possibility of the sign is this relationship with death' (54); and he continued in various ways to assert the structural implication of death in any textual entity whose operation depends on its inbuilt ability to survive beyond the mortal existence of its producer or addressee. In a related argument, his account of friendship puts at the centre of the relationship between friends the knowledge that one will die before the other. He can thus write of 'the mourning that follows death but also the mourning that is prepared and that we expect from the very beginning to follow upon the death of those we love' (*The Work of Mourning*, 147). This repeated invocation of death is only one example of Derrida's continuous project of demonstrating the constitutive function of that which is habitually excluded as the simple 'outside', but it represents one of the most original deployments of that argument.[1]

Death was not only a structural principle for Derrida, however: he was profoundly affected by the deaths of those close to him, and his writing bears many traces of both his grief and his attempts to conceptualise the experience of loss. While the fact that one friend must survive another is not, for most of us, a lived part of friendship, I suspect that for Derrida it was an actual, felt element of his relationships; parting was always coloured by the possibility of not meeting again. Some of Derrida's most telling works were written in response to the loss of friends, in a complex weave of tribute and meditation, eulogy and philosophy. The death of Paul de Man occasioned a substantial work, *Mémoires*; the imminent death of his mother was a major topic of 'Circumfession'; and several of his texts on the deaths of friends are collected in *The Work of Mourning*, published three years before his own death in 2004. The tribute to Levinas is another instance.

Time and again in writing after the loss of a friend, Derrida emphasises the impossibility of mourning, the necessary infidelity it entails.[2] In fact, he identifies *two* infidelities between which, impossibly, we have to choose. Thus in *Mémoires* he writes:

> Is the most distressing, or even the most deadly infidelity that of a *possible mourning* which would interiorize within us the image, idol, or ideal of the other who is dead and lives only in us? Or is it that of the impossible mourning, which, leaving the other in his alterity, respecting thus his infinite remove, either refuses to take or is incapable of taking the other within oneself, as in the tomb or the vault of some narcissism? (6)

Similarly, in 'The Deaths of Roland Barthes', he finds that in responding to the death of a friend one is faced with the impossible choice between doing nothing but quote the other or avoiding quotation altogether, betraying the dead one by offering nothing oneself or by making the dead one disappear again behind one's own words. 'We are left then with having to do and not do both at once, with having to correct one infidelity by the other' (275).

The challenge of writing a funeral oration or a tribute to a dead friend is only an extreme instance of the challenge of doing justice to the other, including the challenge of doing justice to the author, whether alive or dead, of a text one is reading. Derrida's strong emphasis on the notion of responsibility in his later work owes a great deal to Levinas, who understood ethics as a matter of absolute responsibility to a singular other – a responsibility whose impossibility does not diminish its exigency. There is therefore a double difficulty in attempting to do justice to Levinas's work on responsibility to the other – or, for that matter, in attempting to do justice to Derrida's writings on the same topic: one is subject to the very imperative that one is trying to give an account of.

II

The difficulty of doing justice to Levinas's thought was something Derrida had faced early in his career; his long essay on Levinas, 'Violence and Metaphysics', published when he was 34, was at once generous in drawing attention to the importance of Levinas's work and exacting in its critique of some of that work's central claims and methods. His later essay, 'At This Very Moment in This Work Here I Am', which first appeared in 1980, again demonstrated his fidelity to Levinas through infidelity, by means of a careful and respectful questioning of the older writer's mode of argumentation and his privileging of the masculine. In a transcribed discussion of 1986, Derrida explains that his hesitation about using the word 'ethics' arises from its genealogy, aligning himself with Heidegger's critique of ethics, and poses a question to Levinas: although you are clearly using the word in a different sense from that which it derives from its history, what is the legitimacy of using words extracted from their historical determinations? (*Altérités*, 70–1). (This is a replay of one of his major worries in 'Violence and Metaphysics': is it possible to write against the tradition of Western philosophy in the language of Western philosophy?) Yet in the same discussion he says, 'Before a thought like that of Levinas, I never have an objection. I am ready to subscribe to everything he says' (74).

As this last comment suggests, there is traceable a warming towards Levinas over the course of Derrida's career; in place of the uncompromisigly severe analysis of 'Violence and Metaphysics' one finds an increasing sense of indebtedness to the other man's work. The brilliant account of ethics in *The Gift of Death* (first published in 1992) owes a great deal to Levinas, even though Derrida is still using the term 'ethics' in a Kierkegaardian vein to refer to a universal category challenged by singular responsibilities. In 2000, five years after Levinas's death, he published *Le Toucher, Jean-Luc Nancy* (translated as *On Touching – Jean-Luc Nancy*) and devoted a long discussion to Levinas's passages on *eros* and the caress in which the tone is more accommodating, and Levinas's masculinism, although clearly still a problem for Derrida, is considered more sympathetically. And the year before his own death, Derrida gave an interview on Levinas to *Le Magazine Littéraire*, in which the cordial tone is very evident ('Derrida avec Levinas'). The interviewer, Alain David, who knew Levinas, begins by noting the closeness between the two philosophers; Levinas, apparently, was often heard to say, 'But what does Derrida think of it?' Although most of the interview is taken up with Derrida's account of the philosophical and cultural differences between himself and Levinas, there is an insistence throughout on the importance of the latter's work. Thus after summarising his objection to Levinas's use of a Graeco-Hegelian discourse at the very moment at which he is subjecting that discourse to a radical critique (the old worry), he adds that he has made this objection, 'without ever frontally opposing Levinas's "project", the necessity of which I have always believed in' (32). The other disagreements have to do, once more, with gender, with Levinas's treatment of animality, and with the question of politics. There is also a strong defence of the difficulty and riskiness of Levinas's endeavour, in contrast to what Derrida perceives as the merely fashionable employment of phrases like 'respect for the Other' or even the word 'ethics' itself – which he sees as too often providing an alibi allowing the speaker to neutralise questions of politics and justice.

One may surmise, then, that when Derrida was invited to give an oration at Levinas's funeral two days after his death, and a year later to contribute to a conference with the title 'Homage to Emmanuel Levinas', he found this a peculiarly difficult task. The oration, published as 'Adieu' in the volume of the same name, continues the sequence of eulogies for dead friends, each one singular, but each one bearing the traces of personal as well as public loss. It is, of course, wholly affirmative in its dealings with Levinas's thought. Here's a representative sample:

> Each time I read or reread Emmanuel Levinas, I am overwhelmed with gratitude and admiration, overwhelmed by this necessity, which is not a constraint but a very gentle force that obligates, and obligates us not to bend or curve otherwise the space of thought in its respect for the other, but to yield to this other, heteronymous curvature that relates us to the completely other. (9–10)

For the lecture the following year, however, Derrida is speaking from within a different genre: 'A Word of Welcome' is a reading of Levinas that engages with some of the most problematic aspects of his writing. It is still part of an event of homage, however; Derrida is still feeling the obligation not to curve the space of Levinas's thought in its respect for the other. How does he do justice to the complexity of Levinas's work, to his own disagreements with Levinas, to what remains troubling in his legacy, while remaining faithful to the dead man's – the dead friend's – achievement? Although this text has been the subject of some brilliant readings, notably by Geoffrey Bennington, Hent de Vries and Michael Naas,[3] its complexity as a text of mourning demands further analysis.

III

The first thing I want to note is a formula that Derrida employs, with very little variation, several times in 'A Word of Welcome'. Here are the examples that occur in the space of a dozen pages:

> Levinas would probably not say it in this way, but could it not be argued that . . . (23)

> Levinas does not say this, or he does not say it in this way, but I would like to approach him today by way of this non-way. (25)

> Levinas does not say it in exactly this way, but . . . (32)

> Though Levinas never puts it in these terms, . . . (33)

> . . . even if Levinas never puts it this way. (34)

One could add to this list the openings of a couple of sentences in the discussion of Levinas in *On Touching*:

> I am tempted to say, in a language that is no longer Levinas's but does not necessarily betray him either . . . (78)

> Levinas does not say it in this way, to be sure, . . . (79)

What exactly is going on here? If Derrida has a disagreement with Levinas, why does he not come out with it, as he has not hesitated to do before? The offered logic of this recurrent rhetorical move is that Derrida is only making explicit what Levinas would undoubtedly have agreed with even if he never actually said it, and that the difference between them is thus merely a matter of phrasing and not one of substance. We need to look closely at the readings that these phrases introduce if we want to ascertain how far this is actually the case.

Derrida's lecture is, as the title suggests, a discussion of the theme of hospitality in Levinas's work. 'Although the word is neither frequently used nor emphasized within it,' states Derrida, '*Totality and Infinity* bequeaths to us an immense treatise *of hospitality*' (21). Hospitality, of course, is a significant topic in Derrida's own later work, so in saying this he is celebrating the closeness of Levinas's thought to his own. The ethical relation, for Levinas, involves an unconditional welcoming of the other, and Derrida here offers an unconditional welcome to Levinas's thought on this topic. Things get a little more complicated when Derrida responds to Levinas's welcoming of the thought of Descartes – one of the few philosophers in the Western tradition Levinas keeps coming back to as an admired precursor. It's really only one moment in Descartes that Levinas repeatedly fastens on: the claim that the human subject possesses an idea of infinity, which, for Descartes, was evidence for the existence of God as the only possible source of such an idea. Levinas translates this moment in Descartes into his own language: 'But to possess the idea of infinity is to have already welcomed the Other.' It is this, argues Levinas, that saves Descartes from the infinite negation of the sceptic: affirmation comes not from within, but from outside. 'It is not I', notes Levinas, 'it is the other that can say *yes*' (*Totality and Infinity*, 93).

Derrida's manner of reading Levinas is not very different from Levinas's manner of reading Descartes. He quotes this last sentence, commenting that 'One should no doubt extend without limit the consequences of what Levinas asserts' (23) – a statement which implies an ethical duty to extend the Levinasian insights as far as they can be taken (the French is 'On devrait . . .') (52). He then adds in a parenthesis (and this is the first time he uses the phrase I have singled out):

> If one were to pursue these consequences with the necessary temerity and rigor, they would perhaps lead to another way of thinking the responsible decision. Levinas would probably not say it this way, but could it not be argued that, without exonerating myself in the least, decision and responsibility are always *of the other*? (23).

Here Derrida articulates a favourite argument of his own, derived partly from Carl Schmitt: if a decision is truly a decision and not a calculation, it must be a decision of the other, or of myself as other. Levinas's appropriation of Descartes is in turn appropriated by Derrida to claim that their thought runs along the same tracks – although there is nothing in Levinas about decision as decision of the other. Derrida has indeed pursued the consequences of Levinas's thinking with temerity, though one might question the rigour of this gesture.

Levinas's extrapolation from the doubting Descartes, 'It is the other that can say yes', then provides an occasion for Derrida to develop his argument about the priority of the other over the self, presenting the paradox that he has dwelt on before, notably in his reading of the many 'yes's' in Joyce's *Ulysses*.[4] 'There is no *first yes*, the *yes* is already a response': the call 'is first only in order to await the response that makes it come'. 'Despite all the tragic objections that this harsh law might seem to justify', Derrida continues, 'the necessity remains, as imperturbable as death' (24). This is indeed *not* how Levinas would say it, since he represents the demand of the other as coming from wholly outside. (One could relate this difference to the ancient quarrel in Christian theology, notably between Augustine and Pelagius, about the operation of grace.)[5] Derrida is obviously aware that he is overstepping the bounds of faithful interpretation and the paragraph is followed by the second occurrence of the phrase we're tracking: 'Levinas does not say this, or he does not say it in this way, but I would like to approach him today by way of this non-way' (25). Observe the note of caution here: Derrida first admits that Levinas does not say this ('Lévinas ne dit pas cela') and only as a second possibility are we allowed to think that the difference is merely one of wording ('il ne le dit pas ainsi') (54).

Derrida soon moves on to the most important potential area of disagreement: the relation of ethics to politics. Crucial to this question is the notion of 'the third', *le tiers*. The idea of thirdness or the third appears repeatedly in Levinas's work, and a scrupulous analysis of it has to take careful account of the way it is used in different ways at different times. In 'The *I* and Totality', first published in 1954, he uses the terms 'third man' and 'third party' in a discussion of what he calls 'the moral conditions for thought' (*Entre Nous*, 17); but although there are intimations of the arguments to come in his major works, the discourse is not one that maps easily onto the later writing. *Totality and Infinity* (published as *Totalité et Infini* in 1961, and still probably Levinas's most influential book) does not develop the idea of the third at any length, but in a short passage entitled 'The Other and the Others' (212–14) he makes the striking assertion that 'The third party looks at me in the eyes of the Other . . . It is not that there first would be the face, and then the being it manifests or expresses would concern himself with justice; the epiphany of the face qua face opens humanity'. The ethical response – what Levinas calls here 'the prophetic word' – is 'an irreducible movement of a discourse which by essence is aroused by the epiphany of the face inasmuch as it attests the presence of the third party, the whole of humanity, in the eyes that look at me' (213). It's a remarkable way to move from the ethical – in Levinas's sense, as the singular relation of the self and the other – to the political, but it leaves a number of questions unanswered about politics in any practical sense. How, in answering my obligation to the singular other, do I simultaneously act justly with regard to the whole of humanity?

We should also note that the concept of *justice* presented in *Totality and Infinity* is implicit in the relation with the singular other, and does not involve the third:

> Justice consists in recognizing the Other my master. Equality of persons means nothing of itself; it has an economic meaning and presupposes money, and already rests on justice – which, when well-ordered, begins with the Other. Justice is the recognition of his privilege qua Other and is mastery, is access to the Other outside of rhetoric. (72)

If there is an association between the third party and justice it is that both are inseparable from the face-to-face of the ethical relation. In *Otherwise than Being* (first published in French in 1974), however, a major rewriting of the arguments of *Totality and Infinity* (partly in response to Derrida's critique), Levinas reintroduces the idea of the third, but with a significantly different role and importance. Now we hear, not of the third as looking at us through the eyes of the other, as part and parcel of the ethical relation, but rather of the third as a *complication* of the face-to-face rapport. 'The other stands in a relationship with the third party', writes Levinas, 'for whom I cannot entirely answer, even if I alone answer, before any question, for my neighbor' (157). Because the other for whom I am responsible is responsible for other others, the simply intimacy of the ethical relation is breached, and one name Levinas gives to the domain that we enter when we start to take the other others into account is *justice*. In 'A Word of Welcome' Derrida cites a passage from a text from 1984, 'Peace and Proximity', in which Levinas gives a clear account of the relation between the third, in this new sense, and justice. It is worth quoting the citation at length:

> Doubtless, responsibility for the other human being is, in its immediacy, anterior to every question. But how does responsibility obligate if a third party troubles this exteriority of two where my subjection of the subject is subjection to the neighbor? The third party is other than the neighbor but also another neighbor, and also a neighbor of the other, and not simply their fellow. What am I to do? What have they already done to one another? Who passes before the other in my responsibility? What, then, are the other and the third party with respect to one another? Birth of the question.
>
> The first question in the interhuman is the question of justice. Henceforth it is necessary to know, to become consciousness. Comparison is superimposed onto my relation with the *unique* and the incomparable, and, in view of equity and equality, a weighing, a thinking, a calculation, the comparison of incomparables, and, consequently, the neutrality – presence or representation – of being, the thematization and the visibility of the face.[6]

The passage goes on to list various aspects of the interhuman world introduced by the third, ending with 'the political structure of society, subject to laws and thereby to institutions'.

There is thus a distinct shift in Levinas's understanding of justice from *Totality and Infinity* to *Otherwise than Being*. Justice no longer names an aspect of the face-to-face encounter, but is introduced by the super-imposition of the third and everything that follows in its train. While the ethical encounter is 'anterior', it is 'troubled' by the third party. Levinas himself acknowledges the shift in a 1975 interview: when asked about the two different accounts of justice in his work, he says, 'It is not easy to speak of the way in which things were written fifteen years ago . . .' and asserts his revised position: 'The word "justice" applies much more to the relationship with the third party than to the relationship with the other' (*Of God Who Comes to Mind*, 82). In a 1986 interview, he similarly distances himself from his earlier conflation of ethics and justice:

> In *Totality and Infinity* I used the word 'justice' for ethics, for the relationship between two people. I spoke of 'justice', although now 'justice' is for me something which is a calculation, which is knowledge, and which supposes politics; it is inseparable from the political. It is something which I distinguish from ethics, which is primary. ('The Paradox of Morality', 171)

Derrida, however, conflates these different stages of Levinas's thought, and the result is, inevitably, some bafflement. Referring in 'A Word of Welcome' to the same interview, he states:

> The question of the third was not only present, as we see, but developed in *Totality and Infinity*.[7] One is thus a bit surprised by the concession Levinas seems to make to one of his interlocutors during an interview. On the question of the third and justice, he seems to admit that *Totality and Infinity* did not adequately treat these themes. (143, n. 62)

A similar failure to acknowledge the shift in Levinas's thinking occurs in relation to his use of the term 'discourse' in *Totality and Infinity* to refer to the rapport between the I and the Other. Levinas refers to 'Discourse, which in turn has presented itself as justice, in the uprightness of the welcome made to the face' (82). Derrida cites this, as evidence of the link between justice and welcome, then in a note cites another statement from *Totality and Infinity*, set in italics by Levinas: '*We call justice this face to face approach, in discourse*,'[8] adding that Levinas here 'seems to define justice *before* the emergence [*surgissement*] of the third' and asking 'But is there any place here for this *before*?' (136, n. 14). What Derrida is doing is superimposing the language of *Otherwise than Being* onto statements in the earlier book; as we have seen, at that stage of

Levinas's thinking the third does not arrive to trouble the face-to-face and introduce justice: both are implicit in the face-to-face. But neither the third nor justice can be identified with the same terms in the later book. Derrida's somewhat puzzled question – another marker of the distance he feels from Levinas even as he tries to make the other's thought his own – is surely out of place itself, since the *before* is his, not Levinas's.

What doesn't change in Levinas's thinking is the primacy of the encounter with the other; the whole force of his account of ethics as 'first philosophy' rests on the priority of the face-to-face over any consideration of the wider concerns of politics or justice. The language in which he describes the relation between the two and the third repeatedly implies a primary-secondary relationship, and the language is often that of temporal succession, as we have already seen in the passage from 'Peace and Proximity' quoted by Derrida. In a typical statement in *Otherwise than Being*, Levinas comments: 'The responsibility for the other is an immediacy antecedent to questions, it is proximity. It is troubled and becomes a problem when a third party enters' (157). Here are some further examples from the interviews collected by Jill Robbins in *Is It Righteous to Be?*, arranged by date (my emphases):

1983: 'But it is always *starting from* the face, from the responsibility for the other, that justice appears, calling *in turn* for judgment and comparison . . . *At a certain moment*, there is a necessity for a "weighing", a comparison, a thinking' (166).

1986: '. . . the *initial* for-the-other which is contested by the *appearing* of a third, fourth, fifth human being' (51); 'In the face of the other, I hear my responsibility for him . . . But *along comes* a third party: *new* responsibility' (51–2); 'When the third *appears*, the other's singularity is placed in question' (133); '*I pass* from the relation in which I am obligated and responsible to a relation where I ask myself who is the first. I pose the question of justice . . . My search for justice supposes precisely this *new* relation in which every excess of generosity that I should have in regard to the other is submitted to justice' (214).

1990: 'One *steps out* of the register of charity between individuals to *enter* the political' (194).

These examples could be multiplied from many of Levinas's works. However, in spite of the language he uses, it would be a mistake to think that Levinas has in mind an empirical sequence, whereby I first of all acknowledge my responsibility for the singular other and then have to face the existence of other others. As he says in *Otherwise than Being*: 'It is not that the entry of a third party would be an empirical fact, and that my responsibility for the other finds itself constrained to a calculus by the "force of things"' (158). It is not even a logical sequence, as logic belongs to the order of the third. The primacy of the relation to the other lies in the fact that the ethical subject owes its existence to the relation to the other, and the relation to the third is of necessity, therefore, secondary. John Llewelyn gives a good account:

> The ethical as Levinas would have us understand it is de-ontological, dis-ontological, *ent-ontologisch*. It is prior to all structures of being-with. It is prior to all structures, whether these be the categories of Greek philosophy, of Kant, of Hegel, or Husserl, or the structures of structuralism and of linguistic or economic exchange – prior to all system, to symmetry, to correlation, to the will, to freedom and to the opposition of activity and passivity. It is the superlation of passivity. Because it is prior to the third person. (137)

Levinas at times counters the impression given by his rhetoric of an empirical, temporal sequence by emphasising that the third's claims are already pressing when the primary ethical relation is established. Thus in *Otherwise than Being* we find after the sentence just quoted:

> In the proximity of the other, all the others than the other obsess me . . .The other is from the first the brother of all the other men. The neighbor that obsesses me is already a face, both comparable and incomparable, a unique face and in relationship with faces, which are visible in the concern for justice. (158)

And, somewhat misleadingly given his change of vocabulary, he adds a footnote referring back to the section in *Totality and Infinity* on 'The Other and the Others'. In a 1983 interview he states: 'Justice itself is born of charity. They can seem alien when they are presented as successive stages; in reality, they are inseparable and simultaneous, unless one is on a desert island, without humanity, without a third' (*Is It Righteous to Be?*, 168–9). The terms he uses in the 1975 interview are even closer to those of *Totality and Infinity*: 'In the relationship with another I am always in relation with the third party . . . In the very appearance of the other the third already regards me' (82) – though he twice in this paragraph uses the phrase 'from this moment on' in referring to the force of the third. The difficulty Levinas faces, and that is evident in these apparent contradictions, is that he wishes to avoid compromising the primacy of the ethical relation with the singular other, but at the same time to avoid relegating the third and justice to a merely secondary and subsidiary role.[9]

One of the terms Levinas invents in his attempt to describe the relation of the I to the other – and to distinguish his own thought from the closely related thought of Martin Buber – is *illeity*.[10] The relation to the other is not an I–you relationship but an I–it (or I–he relationship, if we are to sustain Levinas's masculinist discourse), even though it has some of the attributes of an I–you relation. In 'The Trace of the Other' from 1963, in a passage repeated in *Humanism of the Other*, Levinas explains the difficult notion of the face as a signifying trace by introducing the term 'illeity' as an indicator of its third-person status. '*Beyond being is a third person* who is not defined by the Oneself, by ipseity . . . The *beyond* whence comes the face is in the third person' (40–1). He returns to the term in *Otherwise than Being*:

> Illeity lies outside the 'thou' and the thematization of objects. A neologism formed with *il* (he) or *ille*, it designates a way of concerning me without entering into conjunction with me. To be sure, we have to indicate the element in which this *concerning* occurs. If the relationship with illeity were a relationship of consciousness, 'he' would indicate a theme, as the 'thou' in Buber's I–thou relation does, probably. (12–13)[11]

Illeity is also associated in a number of places with God, the ultimate other.

Levinas never identifies illeity and the grammatical third person it implies with the third who interrupts the face-to-face relation and introduces the questions of justice and politics; indeed, they are clearly opposed, the second challenging and complicating the direct ethical command of the first. Yet commentators are often tempted to make this identification; Howard Caygill, for instance, in his penetrating study *Levinas and the Political*, says of the 'third person' referred to in 'The Trace of the Other' that it is 'precisely the "third" that earlier in *Totality and Infinity*, and also later in *Otherwise than Being*, represented the order of justice and the state, namely the reduction of alterity . . . Levinas here proposes a thought of the "third" that is beyond, not below, the opposition of ipseity and alterity, and gives it the name "*illeity*"' (146).

Derrida, too, seems to collapse the terms. 'The illeity of the third is thus nothing less, for Levinas, than the beginning of justice' (29), which may be true of the justice of *Totality and Infinity* – justice as implicit in the face of the other – but it's clearly not that earlier concept of justice that Derrida is working with here, since he associates it with the law. Surprisingly he goes on in the same paragraph to cite a sentence of Levinas's that makes it abundantly clear that the similarity between the third person of illeity and the third that introduces justice, law and politics is only a verbal one: '*Otherwise than Being or Beyond Essence*', writes Derrida, 'speaks of this [he now quotes Levinas] "*illeity*, in the third person, but according to a 'thirdness' that is different from that of the third man, from that of the third interrupting the face to face of the welcome of the other man – interrupting the proximity or approach of the neighbour – from that of the third man with whom justice begins"' (29).[12] In spite of this clarification, Derrida continues as if Levinas's two kinds of thirdness – that which characterises the other to whom I am obligated and that which interrupts the one-to-one relation with the other – were the same.

What Derrida wants from Levinas is a combination of his later account of justice – as law, calculation, politics, rights and so on (very different, incidentally, from his own account of justice in a text like 'Force of Law') – with his earlier account of the third – as immediately implicit in the face to face. 'Illeity' offers the latter, and so is conflated with the third of the later Levinas.[13] Thus Derrida can say, 'The third does not wait; its illeity calls from as early as the epiphany of the face in the face to face' (32). His awareness that he is departing from Levinas is perhaps the reason for his insistence on this point; much later in the work, he returns to it:

> It is right endlessly to insist on this: even if the experience of the third, the origin of justice and of the question as a putting into question, is defined as the interruption of the face to face [which is how Levinas defines it in his later work], it is not an intrusion that comes second. The experience of the third is *ineluctable* from the very first moment, and ineluctable in the face. (110)

And, of course, to justify *this* interpretation he cites *Totality and Infinity*. A similar insistence occurs in 'Hostipitality', where Derrida refers to

> the first intrusion of the third in the face-to-face, this intrusion on which we have underscored that it was at once ineluctable and a priori, archi- or preoriginary, an intrusion not occurring to the dual but *connaissant* with it, knowing it and being-born-together with it, insinuating itself in it from the first instant – and immediately poses, without waiting, the question of justice linked to the third. (388)

The seminar of which this is a transcript took place a little over a year after Levinas's death. At one point he does reflect the difference between *Totality and Infinity*'s conception of the third and that of *Otherwise than Being*, but sees them as coexisting alternatives: 'Once again, "illeity", the emergence of the question, of the third, and of justice [again the misconstrual of "illeity"], designates *sometimes* the interruption of the face to face [Levinas's later view], *sometimes* the very transcendence of the face in the face to face [his earlier view]' (60).

Derrida's next move, as he explains why the arrival of the third *has* to be immediate, is extremely interesting, but is even more creative as an interpretation of a text he is committed to honouring: 'For the absence of the third would threaten with violence the purity of ethics in the absolute immediacy of the face to face with the unique' (32). Let us pause to unpack this: for Derrida, Levinas's face-to-face, the foundation of his ethical thought, would be a violent relation if it occurred *without* the intervention of the third, its purity threatened by the very absence of that which must compromise it. What does Levinas himself say? In a passage Derrida has quoted, he says 'In its non-violent transitivity the very epiphany of the face is produced.' And this is a recurrent theme. In *Totality and Infinity* Levinas tells us:

> The face in which the other – the absolutely other – presents himself does not negate the same, does not do violence to it . . . This presentation is preeminently nonviolence, for instead of offending my freedom it calls it to responsibility and founds it . . . It is peace. (203)

It is certainly the case that in developing the notion of 'substitution' in his later work Levinas draws on language with implications of violence: the self in substituting for the other is taken hostage, experiences trauma, persecution, obsession. But if this is violence, it is the violence that constitutes the ethical self; 'The word *I*', as he puts it in *Otherwise than Being*, 'means *Here I am*, answering for everything and for everyone' (114).

If there is a violence that poses a threat to ethics in Levinas's view, it is the violence brought onto the scene by the arrival of the third, the imperative of justice. Derrida himself detects the accents of Job in what he calls Levinas's 'appeal not *to* justice but *against* it' (30). Levinas elsewhere calls the necessity of taking the third into consideration 'first violence, violence of judgment, transformation of faces into objective and plastic forms', and observes that 'there is a certain measure of violence necessary starting from justice' (*Is It Righteous to Be?*, 115–16, 167). Justice, which 'brings this being delivered over unto the neighbor under a measure', 'is already the first violence' (*Is It Righteous to Be?*, 136).

No wonder Derrida, in claiming that the face-to-face itself is a violent encounter, adds yet another version of our phrase: 'Levinas does not say it in exactly this way' (32). A number of questions follow in which Derrida asks us to consider why Levinas feels the need to say that justice, the emergence of the third, is *necessary* (by using the form of the question he finds another way of introducing a measure of tentativeness into the argumentation): 'Is he not trying to take into account this hypothesis of a violence in the pure and immediate ethics of the face to face? A violence potentially unleashed in the experience of the neighbour and of absolute unicity?' And he concludes: 'The third would thus protect against the vertigo of ethical violence itself' (33).

Derrida thus doubles the violence in the Levinasian ethical encounter, and he is well aware of what he is doing: 'It is true that the protecting or mediating third, in its juridico-political role, violates in its turn, at least potentially, the purity of the ethical desire devoted to the unique. Whence the terrible ineluctability of a double constraint' (33). For Derrida, the advent of the other in its absolute singularity would be a violent assault, but this is prevented by the simultaneous and necessary emergence of the third – this, too, being a violent entry. For Derrida, it is always a question of the lesser violence.[14]

Having sketched this rather forbidding picture, Derrida retreats once more behind one of his wary qualifications: 'Though Levinas never puts it in these terms, I will risk pointing out the necessity of this *double bind* in what follows from the axioms established or recalled by Levinas' (33). The risk is, no doubt, the risk of being accused of misrepresenting the dead other, of posthumous infidelity. A French word for betrayal is *parjure*, which carries a more generalised meaning than its English equivalent, and this is what Derrida detects in the necessary arrival of the third: justice betrays ethics, betrays what Levinas calls the 'uprightness of the face to face'.[15] 'An intolerable scandal', Derrida calls it, but once more qualifies the assurance of his own reading: 'Even if Levinas never puts it this way, justice commits perjury as easily as it breathes' (34).

This is the last time we find the verbal formula I've been highlighting, but the inventive interpretation continues. I'll just mention one moment that is particularly revealing. In 'At This Very Moment in This Work Here I Am' Derrida had taken Levinas to task for his handling of gender difference. Now he cites one of the Levinas's most notorious passages, in which 'the welcoming one par excellence' is named as 'the feminine being'. But before this, we read:

> More than one reading could be given of the few lines I am about to cite. It would be necessary to linger awhile in their vicinity. One approach would be to acknowledge, so as then to question, as I once did in a text to which I do not wish to return here [this, of course, is 'At This Very Moment in This Work Here I Am'], the traditional and androcentric attribution of certain characteristics to woman (private interiority, political domesticity, intimacy of a sociality that Levinas refers to as a 'society without language', etc.). But another reading of these lines might be attempted, one that would not oppose in a polemical or dialectical fashion either this first reading or this interpretation of Levinas. (43)

He then proceeds to develop this 'other approach', which, he claims, not only 'would no longer raise concerns about a classical androcentrism', 'it might even, on the contrary, make of this text of sort of feminist manifesto' (44). (We see here an instance of the increasingly welcoming approach to Levinas that I mentioned earlier, a process that was understandably accelerated with Levinas's death.) I will not attempt to judge here whether Derrida succeeds in rescuing Levinas, or whether he simply lands himself in the same predicament. (He asserts, in his own voice, that the 'welcoming par excellence is feminine'.) What interests me is the rhetoric of this semi-recantation: Derrida claims to keep open the two possible interpretations, while leaving us in no doubt that he now prefers the more generous one.

IV

Unquestionably, then, Derrida, in his homage to Levinas, is being unfaithful to him, an infidelity clearly signalled, at the same time as it is disguised, in his rhetoric.[16] He has, if you like, allowed the third, the necessary betrayal, to intervene in the pure one-to-one relation between himself and the thought of his dead friend – or rather, to adopt Derrida's own view of the matter, the third that is always already implicit in the one-to-one is necessarily complicating the directness of the relation. How might we describe this third? One way of putting it would be to say that it is just Derrida's awareness of the necessity of the third, of the fact that there is no simple, pure reading that would do absolute and final justice to Levinas's thought, however much we might want to honour his memory, since that thought itself is always mediated by a third, by language, by systems of signification, by difference and deferral.[17] (This is one reason why, for Derrida, mourning is never complete.) Levinas's words can only be read in context, and that context, as Derrida has often shown, is unsaturable, infinitely open. In being faithful to Levinas, in doing justice to his words, Derrida is necessarily being unfaithful, doing an injustice.[18]

But we could also say that it is Derrida's awareness of the third in Levinas's more specific sense that produces the pressure on his homage to his friend – his recognition that questions of justice and politics, of the other of the other, can't be kept out of the ethical relation. He therefore carries forward Levinas's insight in *Totality and Infinity* – 'The third party looks at me in the eyes of the Other' – to combine it with the argument in *Otherwise than Being* that the introduction of the third institutes questions of justice and politics. This is why in 'A Word of Welcome' he stresses, more than once, that 'the third arrives without waiting' (29, 32, 33). He is still stressing it in the late interview I mentioned earlier: after noting the risks Levinas took in his thought, he comments:

> The greatest risk presents itself with the question of the third, in particular, of the other of the other, which precedes as much as it interrupts [here's the Derridean spin] the face-to-face of the visages and which, in the 'wholly other', reintroduces, *must* reintroduce (it's also a duty) the same, comparison, reason, universal intelligibility, the institution of law (what Levinas often calls 'justice'), Greek philosophical discourse, etc. ('Derrida avec Levinas', 33)

For Derrida, we are never simply in a one-to-one relation with the other: we are constantly subject to multiple ethical demands, and in answering to one of these we necessarily fail to answer to all the others – an argument he presents with almost comic force in *The Gift of Death*.[19] In the interview he summarises his dependence on and departure from Levinas in this work, referring to an expression I have already cited more than once:

> '*Tout autre est tout autre*', I once responded to Levinas, in a formula that is scarcely translatable, perhaps perverse and the stakes of which can't be mastered. It brings together both the fidelity and the resistance possible in responding to the Levinasian discourse. ('Derrida avec Levinas', 33)

Moreover, in the most striking departure from Levinas's thinking, if the other could present itself to the I *without* any mediation, this would mean, for Derrida, an experience of pure violence: the third protects us 'against the vertigo of ethical violence itself' (*Adieu*, 33).

Had Levinas still been alive when Derrida embarked on this response to his thought, he might have presented his reinterpretation as a critique, as he did in his earlier pieces. Levinas would have been free to rebut the criticisms or to adjust his thinking – both of which he did in response to Derrida's earlier critiques. In his funeral oration Derrida reminds his auditors of a text by Levinas entitled 'Death and Time', in which Levinas often defines death as '*non-response*' (5). He continues: 'Death: not, first of all, annihilation, non-being or nothingness, but a certain experience for the survivor of the "without response"' (6). 'A Word of Welcome', it seems to me, is written in the shadow of that 'without response': Levinas will not answer, will not correct, will not show that his words mean something more than or different from what they have been taken to mean. So, in a sense, Derrida takes up that responsibility, showing that a certain reading of Levinas can move his thought in a direction which he may not have foreseen but which enriches and deepens it.[20] It's perhaps not too strained to cite Derrida's own comments on the inheritance of a tradition as exemplified by Nelson Mandela:

> You can recognize an authentic inheritor in the one who conserves and reproduces, but also in the one who respects the *logic* of the legacy enough

to turn it upon occasion against those who claim to be its guardians, enough to reveal, despite and against the usurpers, what has never yet been seen in the inheritance: enough to give birth, by the unheard-of *act* of a reflection, to what had never seen the light of day. (17)

This is what it means to be hospitable to the other's thought, to welcome it in the fullest sense: both to allow one's own thinking to be transformed by it, as Derrida's certainly was by Levinas's, and also to treat it as still growing, still in the process of fulfilling its potential. The risk, of course, is that this kind of reading may turn out to be an appropriation in the worst sense, a misreading that twists the original to suit the predilections of the reader; but this is a risk that has to be run.[21]

Were Derrida still alive, I might have presented my reading of his reading of Levinas in a more critical spirit; I'm not sure. But Derrida cannot respond, cannot elaborate or revise, and it seems to me that to do justice to his text one has to follow his example and read it for more than just the literal and logical arguments it presents. One has a responsibility to be hospitable to it in the complex fashion I've just described. There's no doubt that my own understanding of writing, of meaning, of ethics has been transformed by Derrida's work, as has that of many others; but it's important that we do not treat that work as an inert body never growing or changing. If mourning is interminable, I would like to think that it's not because it stays frozen in melancholia, but because the memory of the other, and that includes the surviving words of the other, continues to develop and adapt to new contexts. Derrida's conviction that the third arrives without waiting and thus forestalls the violence of the other signals both his fidelity to his dead friend's thought and, as itself a mark of the third complicating that relation, his willingness to let it be remade by his own inventiveness – though Derrida, of course, does not put it in this way.

Notes

1. For a lucid account of the role of the 'constitutive outside' in Derrida's thinking, see Staten, *Wittgenstein and Derrida*, 15–19 and *passim*.
2. An excellent discussion of Derrida's accounts of the infidelity of mourning is given by Pascale-Anne Brault and Michael Naas in their Introduction to *The Work of Mourning*. It is from this Introduction that I have taken the phrase by Proust that forms the title of this chapter.
3. See Bennington, 'Deconstruction and Ethics'; de Vries, *Religion and Violence*, chapter 4, 'Hospitable Thought'; and Naas, *Taking on the Tradition*, 102–14.
4. See 'Ulysses Gramophone', 296–305 and *passim*.

5. An author for whom grace is an important, if elusive, concept is J. M. Coetzee; see my discussion in *J. M. Coetzee*, 177–83.

6. *Basic Philosophical Writings*, 168; quoted in 'A Word of Welcome', 32. Part of this passage is repeated from *Otherwise than Being* (157).

7. This is hardly true: the section of the book dealing with the third extends to two-and-a-half pages only.

8. The translation of *Totality and Infinity* has 'conversation', but the original is 'discours' and the translators of 'A Word of Welcome' give this as 'discourse'.

9. Robert Bernasconi, in 'Justice without Ethics?', an essay comparing Levinas's and Derrida's conceptions of justice, acknowledges the difficulty of squaring Levinas's different statements about the third. Levinas's account of justice in *Totality and Infinity* is called 'anomalous' within the context of his work (61), and the irreconcilability of the demands of ethics and justice termed an 'aporia amounting to a contradiction . . . at the heart of Levinas's thought' (65). De Vries also calls this 'an ambiguity or, rather, aporia' (*Religion and Violence*, 313). Simon Critchley, by contrast, attempts to articulate a consistent position, though his own account betrays a similar tension: the third 'has always already entered into the ethical relation, troubling and doubling it into a political discourse', yet the third party '*introduces* a limit to responsibility' and 'In justice, I am *no longer* myself in relation to an other for whom I am infinitely responsible, but I can feel myself to be an other like the others' (*The Ethics of Deconstruction*, 231, my italics).

10. See, for example, *The Humanism of the Other*, 40–1; *Basic Philosophical Writings*, 119 (where the distancing from Buber is manifest); *Otherwise than Being*, 12–13, 147–50.

11. In *Totalité et Infinité* Levinas uses personal pronouns differently, suggesting that the other is not intimate but at a respectful distance: 'L'interlocuteur n'est pas un Toi, il est un Vous' (104). The English translation cannot capture this distinction: 'The interlocutor is not a Thou, he is a You' (101).

12. Alphonso Lingis, the translator of *Otherwise than Being*, is another who collapses the terms in his mistranslation of this sentence: he has Levinas saying 'This "thirdness" is different from that of the third man, it is the third party that interrupts the face to face of a welcome of the other man . . . it is the third man with which justice begins' (150). Pascale-Anne Brault and Michael Naas, translating *Adieu*, render the passage accurately.

13. This conflation is also evident in Derrida's note 15: '*Totality and Infinity* already welcomes, with such words, the "ineluctable" occurrence of the third as "language" and as "justice"' (136).

14. See Beardsworth, *Derrida and the Political*, *passim*, on the importance of this comparative judgement.

15. *Totality and Infinity*, 202, cited by Derrida in 'A Word of Welcome', 34.

16. In 'Deconstruction and Ethics', Bennington gives an excellent account of Derrida's deconstructive ethics as a radicalisation of Levinas's thought, using a variety of phrases to describe Derrida's proceeding: 'Reading beyond the obvious intention of Levinas's text' (40), 'pushes the text read beyond its own explicit claims' (40), 'through and beyond Levinas' (41), 'explicitly extending (and thereby also, respectfully, contesting) Levinas'

(44). Similarly, de Vries begins a sentence on Derrida's account of the immediacy of the third with 'Pushing his interpretation far beyond commentary . . .' and adds, 'This would be the logic, the argument . . . at work in Levinas's text; without ever being acknowledged, thematized or formalized as such' (*Religion and Violence*, 323).

17. In conversation with Maurizio Ferraris, Derrida adumbrates two conceptions of the third in its most general operation:

> The third term can be taken as the mediator that permits synthesis, reconciliation, participation; in which case that which is neither this nor that permits the synthesis of this and that. But this function is not limited to the form it has taken in Hegelian dialectic, and the third of neither-this-nor-that and this-and-that can indeed also be interpreted as that whose absolute heterogeneity resists all integration, participation and system, thus designating the place where the system does not close. It is, at the same time, the place where the system constitutes itself. (Derrida and Ferraris, *A Taste for the Secret*, 5)

18. In 'Hostipitality' Derrida speaks of the 'infidelity at the heart of fidelity' brought about by the co-presence of the third in the face-to-face of the ethical relation (388).

19. I discuss the apparently extreme examples of ethical choice given in *The Gift of Death* in Chapter 4 above.

20. De Vries describes the relation between the thought of Levinas and that of Derrida as follows:

> These thinkers' writings can be translated *almost* completely into one another, to the point of becoming *almost* interchangeable. While this resemblance is remarkable, on second reading they take different directions as well . . . Their congruity is not that of an overlapping minimal consensus but an intersection that is a chiasmic crossing, and instantaneous substitution of one for the other at an indeterminate point of indifference, albeit one from which all that matters will take its departure. (*Religion and Violence*, 310)

21. Jane Gallop, in an essay on *Adieu*, comments aptly on Derrida's play with underlining and emphasis in his quotations from Levinas. She writes:

> When we quote a text, we are engaged in an act of hospitality, of taking in/lodging (*héberger*) someone else's words. When we underline a text, we are taking possession of it, writing on it. Derrida's hesitation about underlining, his self-consciousness about it, both recognizes that taking possession and resists it with a sense of the words as not his to do with as he likes. The play of underlining, the tense play of rendering it suspect while still doing it, allows us to see Derrida reading, and to see reading as a tension between the will to comprehend/use/possess and the recognition that the text does not belong to us. His self-consciousness makes us aware that reading involves a self and an other – that reading must recognize, negotiate, and respect the space between them. ('Reading', 23–4)

Chapter 8

Roland Barthes's Obtuse, Sharp Meaning and the Responsibilities of Commentary

I

Searching for a name to give to the excessive, exorbitant connotation – what he calls 'the third meaning' – that he senses in certain Eisenstein stills, Roland Barthes comes upon the Latin word *obtusus*, or perhaps more accurately, it comes to him. He explains why it seems just right:

> *Obtusus* means *blunted, rounded* . . . An obtuse angle is greater than a right angle: *an obtuse angle of 100°*, says the dictionary; the third meaning, too, seems to me greater than the pure perpendicular, the trenchant, legal upright of the narrative . . . I even accept, for this obtuse meaning, the word's pejorative connotation: the obtuse meaning seems to extend beyond culture, knowledge, information . . . It belongs to the family of puns, jokes, useless exertions; indifferent to moral or aesthetic categories (the trivial, the futile, the artificial, the parodic), it sides with the carnival aspect of things. *Obtuse* therefore suits my purposes well. ('The Third Meaning', 44)

This comes from an essay first published in 1970, in which Barthes posits two 'obvious' meanings, the informational or communicational meaning and the symbolic meaning, and this third meaning which is not really a meaning at all.

A decade later, seeking a name for an element in the photographic image that escapes all the codes of reading that governs what he now calls the *studium* of the photograph, he is again struck by a Latin word that seems to have exactly the right connotations:

> This element . . . rises from the scene, shoots out of it like an arrow, and pierces me. A Latin word exists to designate this wound, this prick, this mark made by a pointed instrument: the word suits me all the better in that it also refers to the notion of punctuation, and because the photographs I am speaking of are in effect punctuated, sometimes even speckled with these sensitive points; precisely, these marks, these wounds are so many *points*. This second

element which will disturb the *studium* I shall therefore call *punctum*; for *punctum* is also: sting, speck, cut, little hole – and also a cast of the dice. A photograph's *punctum* is that accident which pricks me (but also bruises me, is poignant to me). (*Camera Lucida*, 26–7)[1]

Blunt versus sharp, carnivalesque versus poignant: the metaphorics of these two essays in naming could hardly be more different, even though it is possible to sense strongly in each the satisfaction with which Barthes greets the term when it comes to him. ('The word [obtuse] readily comes to my mind, and miraculously, upon exploring its etymology, I find it already yields a theory of the supplementary meaning' (*TM*, 44); 'the word [*punctum*] suits me all the better in that . . .' (*CL*, 26).) As he elaborates on the notion of the *punctum* in *Camera Lucida*, Barthes makes no reference back to the 'obtuse meaning' of his earlier essay. Furthermore, one essay concentrates on images of actors and emphasises the question of disguise, the other on portraits and historical referentiality. One examines stills and pursues a definition of the 'filmic' (*TM*, 58); the other examines photographs and seeks to establish the 'essence of the Photograph' (*CL*, 73). In 'The Third Meaning' Barthes resists the idea that the excessive effect he is discussing arises from the photograph's recording of the real: it cannot be 'reduced to the persistence which any human body exerts by merely being present' (43); it has 'a distancing effect with regard to the referent' (55). In *Camera Lucida*, the recorded presence of the referent becomes crucial to the entire argument.

Yet in spite of these marked differences, many readers have made a connection between the obtuse meaning and the *punctum*, situating both names in a series of terms employed by Barthes in an attempt to capture a moment of breakdown in the codes of signification to whose elucidation he devoted so much effort: the list includes *jouissance* (notably in *The Pleasure of the Text*), haiku and *satori* (discussed in *The Empire of Signs*), and *signifiance* (in a number of texts).[2] Unlike 'obtuse meaning' and *punctum*, however, the other terms in the series are borrowings, and inevitably come into Barthes's work with a certain amount of foreign theoretical matter clinging to them. I want to focus on the two coinages, since I believe that – precisely as coinages – they play a special role in Barthes's writings on the image.

II

Once we examine Barthes's attempts to explain and exemplify the phenomena to which he is responding in these two pieces of writing, we find that the metaphorical opposition between them begins to collapse.[3]

Obtuse meaning, he tells us, is not so much 'read' as 'received' (*TM*, 42), making us think of the arrow of the *punctum*. It 'can be seen as an *accent*, the very form of an emergence, of a fold (even a crease) marking the heavy layer of information and signification' (*TM*, 56); this sounds very much like the way in which the *studium* is 'traversed, lashed, striped' (*CL*, 40) by the *punctum*. The obtuse meaning is even said at one point to be a 'penetrating feature' (*TM*, 48); conversely, it is the *punctum* that 'bruises' (*CL*, 27). And the following comments on an instance of the *punctum* seem to invoke something like obtuseness as well as acuity: 'The effect is certain but unlocatable, it does not find its sign, its name; it is sharp and yet lands in a vague zone of myself; it is acute yet muffled, it cries out in silence' (*CL*, 52–3).

There are many other similarities between the two accounts. Both phenomena are said to be outside the intention of the artist, and both are described as 'supplements' to the primary cultural meaning. Both have a distinctive emotional force, are associated with love and eroticism, and inhere primarily in details. (Barthes identifies a second *punctum* in *Camera Lucida* which does not inhere in details; I shall return to this somewhat different employment of the term later.) Although Barthes doesn't say so, his choice of examples suggests that both are especially likely to be produced by images of the human body's border zone: its material excrescences or its accoutrements. No fewer than three of the examples, one of obtuse meaning and two of the *punctum*, consist of images of human nails; others include hair, teeth, a ring, a bandage on a finger, facial makeup, shoes and a necklace. Moreover, although most of the account of the obtuse meaning is based on stills involving actors, Barthes adds, as a supplementary example that threatens to cast the entire argument in a new light, a documentary image of Hermann Goering handling a bow and arrow at some Nazi publicity event.

What, then, are we to make of the fact that the *names* Barthes fixes on – with the entire lexicons of more than one language to choose from – are so contradictory? This fact is surely connected to another striking fact about the two pieces: that it is normal for readers to finish them without having gained any specific, clear understanding of what the obtuse meaning and the *punctum are*. I am not denying that we gain a theoretical understanding of the place of obtuse meaning and *punctum* in the account of signification that Barthes provides, but the very nature of these phenomena makes such an understanding limited in its usefulness. To understand them in their specificity could only be to *experience* them *in the examples Barthes gives*, since it is a constitutive feature of both of them that they cannot be conveyed in words. ('We cannot describe the obtuse meaning' (*TM*, 55); 'What I can name cannot really prick me'

(*CL*, 51).) Now, when I look at the image of the two courtiers pouring gold over the young tsar's head with which 'The Third Meaning' begins, I see what Barthes has pointed out – the contrast between the two faces, one refined, the other coarse, and so on – but it produces no special affect in me. When I take in the photograph by James Van der Zee entitled 'Family Portrait' that Barthes reproduces in *Camera Lucida*, I sense a certain pathos in the figure of the sister or daughter deriving from her rather little-girlish outfit, but I don't find the low belt and the strapped pumps piercing me with inexplicable force. I must immediately add that when I look at these images fresh from Barthes's vivid commentary on them I am likely to experience a kind of after-effect, temporarily convincing myself that I am indeed feeling what he felt – but even if I do, this experience is exactly what the obtuse meaning and *punctum* are not: the product of words. How many readers who claim to experience these effects would have done so without reading Barthes's commentary first?

What becomes clear is that the terms 'obtuse meaning' and *punctum themselves* have the status of something like obtuse meanings or *puncta* within Barthes's writing. Their emergence in his discourse is not the product of calculation, but of something more like a happy accident (one that appears 'miraculous' to him), and although he devotes much space to accounts of the terms and gives several examples of their operation, their meaning remains obscure and recalcitrant, having to be revised with each new example and not lending themselves to use in new contexts by the reader. They stand out from or cut into the flow of the discourse, which would be only mildly interesting without them. (After all, the discussions of 'obvious meaning' and the *studium* are not what we most remember in these texts.) They thus only masquerade as technical terms, their specificity and Latinity a ruse functioning to prevent generalisation rather than to facilitate it. They are not the names of concepts but function more like proper names. As with the instances of obtuse meaning and *punctum* in the images, we can understand how the two terms function for Barthes but we can't share with him their specific force. (Again, I must qualify this statement: the reader who has been through several pages of Barthes's explanations and paraphrases of these terms may believe that he or she is deriving from them the same mental and affective content that Barthes did, but I doubt whether, in most cases, this is a very durable impression.)

So we have an explanation for the contradiction between obtuse and sharp; or, rather, we find that it does not require explanation. The rightness of the two names is not, finally, to be explained in terms of etymology and dictionary definitions, but in terms of their special meaningfulness for Roland Barthes at different times of his life and in front of different objects. The contradictions – between the two accounts and within each one – are an indication that we are not dealing with 'obvious meanings', with informational or symbolic codes, with the *studium* of theoretical semiotics, but with a singular response that resists or exceeds what can be discursively conveyed. The quality or qualities to which the two terms refer – a certain kind of thickness that is also a kind of sharpness? Or sometimes one and sometimes the other? – cannot be extracted from the discussion in which Barthes elaborates on their meanings. Like that which they name, the terms themselves have a bluntness, resisting hermeneutic procedures with their obstinate quiddity, and an acuity, piercing the flat surface of the prose with their striking foreignness.[4] An obtuse meaning or *punctum* can be named *only* by a *punctum* or an obtuse name.

The semiotic project of these two texts is therefore an impossible one. The images which Barthes reproduces are provided in order that the reader may have direct access to the experience of the obtuse meaning and the *punctum*, among whose characteristics, we should remember, is the fact that they impose themselves upon the reader. However, the nature of the obtuse meaning and the *punctum* is such that Barthes's readers do not experience them by simply looking at the pictures – if they did, the meaning in question would be an instance of the informational or symbolic levels, part of the shared codes that constitute the *studium*. Barthes is obliged to add a commentary, therefore, but here is the paradox: the more successful he is in conveying to the reader in language the special quality of the features that have moved him, the more he shifts them from the realm of the obtuse meaning and *punctum* to the realm of the coded and cultural. (To anticipate my argument a little: isn't this the difficulty faced by any commentary on a work of art – in any medium?)

Thus the words that Barthes skilfully accumulates in 'The Third Meaning' to convey to us a sense of his response to the two courtiers build up, of their own accord, a meaning that is not evanescent or resistant:

> There is a certain density of the courtiers' makeup, in one case thick and emphatic, in the other smooth and 'distinguished'; there is the 'stupid' nose on one and the delicate line of the eyelids on the other, his dull blond hair, his wan complexion, the affected smoothness of his hairstyle which suggests a wig, the connection with chalky skin tints, with rice powder. (*TM*, 42–3)

These meanings do not, it is true, contribute to the narrative of *Ivan the Terrible*, but they do contribute to the texture of the representation, and Barthes begins to sketch an interpretation of the features he has just pointed out: one courtier 'remote and bored', the other 'diligent', the pair signifying that '"*They are simply doing their job as courtiers*"'. To save the obtuse meaning, he has to assert rather lamely that this herme-neutic exercise 'does not altogether satisfy me' and that 'something in these two faces transcends psychology, anecdote, function, and, in short, meaning' (43). The other examples in the essay are caught in the same double bind.

Barthes is somewhat cannier in *Camera Lucida*, but is still unable to escape the structural predicament his project has placed him in. To take one example, in 'Family Portrait' he first identifies the younger woman's belt and strapped pumps as the location of the *punctum*, but later, to illustrate that the *punctum* can unfold after the photograph is no longer in front of him, revises this to the gold necklace she is wearing. Once more, we are guided toward an understanding of this effect by a commentary:

> It was this same necklace (a slender ribbon of braided gold) which I had seen worn by someone in my own family, and which, once she died, remained shut up in a family box of old jewelry (this sister of my father never married, lived with her mother as an old maid, and I had always been saddened whenever I thought of her dreary life). (*CL*, 53)

This time Barthes makes no attempt to provide an interpretation that the reader can share; the associations of the gold necklace are resolutely private. Nevertheless, he has given us here a domestic narrative which, to the extent to which it *explains* the force of the *punctum* upon Barthes, denies its existence as *punctum*. It becomes part of a recognisable set of codes, including those of psychological associations and gender stereo-types. It is Barthes, in fact, who identifies the necklace as being a 'slender ribbon of braided gold': one can't see this in the reproduction, where it looks white and rather thick – and identical to the other necklace in the picture, from which no *punctum* shoots its piercing arrow. This discrepancy is of no account, however; even if we did see what Barthes describes, we would remain impervious to the *punctum*'s laceration.

Barthes is, of course, aware of the impossibility of his task, even if this awareness is not theoretically articulated. His presentation of examples is studded with remarks that allude to the private nature of his responses, including the frequently repeated phrase 'for me'. The fact that his readings are presented as *narratives* of his readings (embracing, in both texts, narratives of past readings) testifies to their personally and historically determined nature. Not, in other words, 'This detail means x . . .' but 'This detail has, or had, x effect on me . . .' Of the first example of the obtuse meaning – the courtiers pouring gold – he says: 'I am not certain whether my reading of this third meaning is justified – if it can be generalized' (*TM*, 43). Later in the essay he draws a touching analogy between his fascination with incommunicable properties of images and Saussure's compulsive search for anagrams:

> The obtuse meaning is not structurally situated, a semantologist would not acknowledge its objective existence (but what is an objective reading?), and if it is evident to me, this is *still* perhaps (for the moment) because of the same 'aberration' which compelled the unfortunate Saussure alone to hear an enigmatic, obsessive, and unoriginated voice, that of the anagram in ancient poetry. (*TM*, 54–5)[5]

In *Camera Lucida* Barthes stresses the private nature of the *punctum*: 'I dismiss all knowledge, all culture, I refuse to inherit anything from another eye than my own' (*CL*, 51) – a gesture which may sound like a classical phenomenological *epoch* but in fact has nothing to do with the postulation of a universal subject. And of course, most tellingly of all, he does not reproduce the Winter Garden photograph out of which the whole of Part Two arises:

> It exists only for me. For you, it would be nothing but an indifferent picture, one of the thousand manifestations of the 'ordinary'; it cannot in any way constitute the visible object of a science; it cannot establish an objectivity, in the positive sense of the term. (*CL*, 73)

The withholding of the picture of his mother is entirely consistent with the logic of the *punctum*; for us, it provides no evidence for the effect, and the affect, he is trying to describe. But the same logic would demand the removal of all the images in which a *punctum* is said to operate; the only point in providing them would be to discuss the *studium*, which we can be expected to share with the author, and in which, at this stage of his career, Barthes is not really interested.

III

If Barthes is aware of the necessary incommunicability of the effect he is discussing, why does he reproduce images and write commentaries that strive to make us see the obtuse meaning or the *punctum*? Partly, perhaps, because he never gives up the hope that somehow it will be possible to communicate exactly what one of these details makes him feel – for without such communication (even to himself), the experience lacks substance. This hope that somehow, against the logic of absolute singularity which governs the phenomenon he is discussing, a sharing of the experience will be possible emerges overtly at one point in 'The Third Meaning':

> If you look at these images I am talking about, you will see the meaning: we can understand each other about it 'over the shoulder' or 'on the back' of articulated language: thanks to the image . . ., indeed thanks to what in the image is purely image (and which, to tell the truth, is very little indeed), we do without speech yet continue to understand each other. (*TM*, 55)

This dream of understanding without the mediation of a code is a familiar utopian (or Edenic) fantasy, which does not mean that it can simply be ignored. In *Camera Lucida,* the most potently affecting photograph for Barthes – the one we do not see – generates in him just this utopic experience, which he calls 'the impossible knowledge of the unique being' (*CL*, 71).

But it is not just stubborn hope that drives Barthes here. One aspect of the experience Barthes is attempting, impossibly, to describe and exemplify is a *demand* for translation: the details that bruise or pierce him call out to be made known, to be transferred from the singular to the general, from the idiosyncratic to the communal.[6] Indeed, it might be said that they are only fully constituted in their incomprehensibility in the necessary attempt to render them comprehensible, that their specificity actually depends on the words (or other codings) by which the viewer acknowledges and attempts to articulate them – in the first place, to himself or herself. They thus appear only in the moment of disappearance. (Think again of the terms *obtusus* and *punctum*: how much of Barthes's elaborate description of the photographic elements they claim to name in fact *derives from* his lexicographic and etymological research?)

So we should not simply think of Barthes's examples and commentaries as so many manifestations of the failure of his endeavour. His narratives do achieve the *signalling* of certain effects that are crucial to the affective power of images, and they succeed in doing this precisely through their inability to specify those effects in such a way as to enable others to experience them. Barthes here joins a long tradition of commentary on the arts, or 'aesthetic experience' more generally, in which the impossibility of exhausting the power of an image, a text or an object receives testimony in the failure of commentary to do justice to it. Indeed, the very institution of Western art, as it has existed for centuries, demands that there be some region inaccessible to the calculations of codes and semes. The work cannot sustain its moving power if that power is charted and explained; we are not in general sympathetic to the notion that a sufficiently complex program would allow a computer to produce new artworks as forceful or as touching as those we already value. Almost all of a work's effectiveness may be accounted for by means of cultural codes, as long as there remains a tiny enclave that refuses all accounting. However tiny this reservation, it functions as a supplement in the full Derridean sense: apparently a little extra ingredient beyond the mass of culturally coded material, it is the one single thing that the work could not do without.[7] (Recall that both the obtuse meaning and the *punctum* are called 'supplements' by Barthes.)

One response to this long history of the supplementary *je ne sais quoi* or 'nameless grace' that becomes the work's animating principle is to undertake a complete demystification, to show that this property of the work always functions culturally, or ideologically, or psychologically, or somatically, or some combination of these, and that its apparent mysteriousness is due only to our ignorance or self-delusion. Hence the projects of structuralism, the sociology of art, much Marxist criticism, some of what is labelled 'cultural studies' – and much of Barthes's early work. But the importance of Barthes's oeuvre taken as a whole is that it demonstrates, in its dogged pursuit of such explanations, both their value and their necessary failure (and the value of that failure). The pursuit is an essential part of the process, since that which remains inexplicable can be most fully apprehended *through* the activity of analysing that which can be explained. Barthes observes in 'The Third Meaning':

> We can perceive the filmic [which Barthes has identified with the obtuse meaning] only after having traversed – analytically – the 'essential', the 'depth', and the 'complexity' of the cinematic work – all riches belonging only to articulated language, out of which we constitute that work and believe we exhaust it. (*TM*, 59)

I may seem to have generalised too hastily from Barthes's specific focus on the photographic image to the arts and even more widely to something as vague as 'aesthetic experience'; he himself insists at several points on the uniqueness of the photograph in relation to other fields of artistic production. So I must emphasise once more that the supplementary force I am talking about here, though its effects are everywhere to be felt, is *not* a generalisable phenomenon; it inheres in the particular and the contingent, it cannot be programmed or predicted, it arises out of an encounter between a work and a consciousness in a given time and place. Barthes, in these two texts, has described some aspects of the particular form it takes in photography; the sheer materiality of bodily excrescences, for instance, is more likely to play a part in our response to photographs than to other kinds of art or image.

The *punctum* of the photograph is by no means always an apprehension of bodily matter, however; Barthes's examples include a number of other aspects of the image. (The comic potential of a Highlander holding Queen Victoria's horse, for instance, or the dirt road of a Central European scene.) The fact that there is in *Camera Lucida* 'another *punctum*' (*CL*, 96), somewhat different from the first, begins to suggest the plurality of the effects that he is discussing. As I've already noted, the two terms I'm focusing on exist in a chain of terms that take us well outside the photograph. None of them is interchangeable with any other, necessitating a careful regard for the individuality of each, but all of them are related to one another.

Let us look for a moment at the second *punctum*, which seems to lead to a more theoretical understanding of the nature of photography. It rests on what Barthes argues (as he had done in earlier essays) is the photograph's unique relation to the referent. The 'photographic referent' is 'the *necessarily* real thing which has been placed before the lens, without which there would be no photograph' (*CL*, 76). The photograph says, 'Ça a été', 'This has been'. It is from this sheer contingency, this unmediated reference, as Barthes portrays it, that there arises the 'new *punctum*' (*CL* 96): the intense apprehension of Time and what it implies – the actuality of a life that existed and, twisted inseparably with it, the inevitability of the death that lay in wait for it.

The story of Barthes's progression to this moment of recognition is moving and compelling, and once again it is important to stress that it could be told only as a personal history since it is not essentially a *theoretical* argument. To respond fully to Barthes's text, however, is to attempt to extend its range and prolong its life by trying to carry over his terms and his thought. We have already seen that neither the instances of obtuse meaning and *punctum* that Barthes puts before us, nor the very terms 'obtuse meaning' and '*punctum*', carry over without loss, and that this is part of what defines them. Is the same true of the 'new *punctum*', of the photographic *ça a été*? The theoretical content is certainly much greater; the argument, not original with Barthes, that the distinctiveness of photography lies in the mechanical and chemical processes that register the real existence of an object, making it, in Peirce's terms, an index rather than an icon or symbol, is sound as far as it goes, and helps to account for the different reactions we have to paintings and to photographs. However, in a gesture rather similar to those which Derrida has traced in a number of writers, Barthes quickly dismisses the apparently marginal cases in which the photograph we see is *not* the unmediated result of light striking a chemically sensitised surface: 'The Photograph is indifferent to all intermediaries: it does not invent; it is authentication itself; the (rare) artifices it permits are not probative; they are, on the contrary, trick pictures: the photograph is laborious only when it fakes' (*CL*, 87). By contrast, Barthes's early essay 'The Photographic Message' had devoted a section to 'Trick effects'.

What, then, if the girl in the Winter Garden photograph was *not* Barthes's mother, but, say, a unknown cousin who looked very like her? Would this mean that Barthes's intense apprehension of a truth about his mother (and himself, and photography) was invalid or deceptive? What if that expression of kindness on her face was in fact the result of a speck of dust in the darkroom? Perhaps if Barthes had lived on into the age of digital photographic images, no longer analogically bound to the referent and therefore open to infinite manipulation, he would not have been so ready to assert that photographs are self-authenticating, that 'every photograph is a certificate of presence' (*CL*, 87). (It is surprising that Barthes appears to take no account of the fact that many of his examples depend for their effect on information – which could always be false – external to them, such as the information that a certain portrait is of Lewis Payne before his execution and that another one is of William Casby, born a slave.) The photograph, as Derrida might say, can always *not* be the direct effect of the referent on sensitised paper, and this fact has to be taken into account in any attempt to say what photography is.

Yet perhaps Barthes has acknowledged this fact in the medium by means of which he has presented his 'discovery' of the essence of photography, through his choice of the autobiographical narrative, which, partaking as it does of the literary, can itself always not be true. (Recall the handwritten epigraph to *Roland Barthes by Roland Barthes*: 'It must all be considered as if spoken by a character in a novel'; and see Chapter 6 above.) What if there is, and was, no Winter Garden photograph? Barthes's moving and memorable exploration of the distinctive qualities of photography would not thereby be revealed as vacuous, though we might revise our estimate of the author's practices.[8] Similarly, if it turned out that Barthes was mistaken about the picture he took to be the unmediated image of his mother, this would not disqualify the insights we might have gained from it – unless our reading of *Camera Lucida* took it to be a scientific treatise or a work of philosophy. Barthes's practice thus shows that the referent is not the source of photography's special power – though the *referential* may indeed be crucial. Derrida effects this subtle but transformative shift in Barthes's argument in a parenthesis in 'The Deaths of Roland Barthes':

He first highlighted the absolute irreducibility of the *punctum*, what we might call the unicity of the *referential* (I appeal to this word so as not to have to choose between reference and referent: what adheres in the photograph is perhaps less the referent itself, in the present effectivity of its reality, than the implication in the reference of its having-been-unique). (288)

Derrida produces a more consistent (and more Derridean) Barthes, but one that lacks the force of a *desire* for unmediated access to the real which animates and complicates Barthes's writing and is part of the lasting power of *Camera Lucida*.

IV

I noted earlier that the obtuse meaning and the *punctum* depend on the very codes they resist. The result is a short-circuiting of cause and effect, a thwarting of chronological progression. Although these aspects of the image convey a feeling of priority, this feeling is itself a product of the operation of the primary codes: a place where these codes slip, contradict one another, fissure, fall into an infinite regression. (Barthes himself wrote in many places about these moments in texts.) If human nails, for instance, have a special potency in certain images, it may be not because of the substance of which they are made, recorded on sensitised paper, but because of their liminal status between our categories of live and dead matter. Obtuse meaning and *punctum* thus stage a certain undecidability between activity and passivity, an undecidability which extends to the other terms in the chain, such as *scriptibilité, jouissance* and textuality.[9]

The contingency and referentiality which Barthes talks about in photographs is thus an *effect* – not a controlled and calculated 'reality-effect' of the type Barthes himself analysed so brilliantly,[10] nor a completely random byproduct, but the product of something which he calls 'luck', though it has other names too. Hence *punctum* and *studium* are interrelated and interdependent; contingency and singularity are not separable from codedness and generality; the experience of the wholly private significance would not be possible without the functioning of public meaning. If Barthes does succeed in conveying to his readership one of the *punctum* effects he is discussing, and thereby abolishes it, a transformation in the shared *studium* is produced, opening up possibilities for new *puncta*. The passage of time – and the work of artists, critics and readers – is thus continually altering the relations of coded meanings and uncoded effects.

Doing justice to a work of art, a family photograph, the performance of a song, an autobiographical essay, a memoir, a theoretical text involves a response to what is singular and untranslatable in it – the obtuse meaning, the *punctum*, the grain of the voice, the moment of *jouissance*, the supplementary force, the secret without depth. Such a response necessarily attempts the impossible: respecting that singularity while generalising it, turning the other into the same without losing its otherness, making the obtuse obvious while retaining its obtuseness, converting the *punctum* into *studium* without putting an end to its role as *punctum*. Impossible not because the singularity in question is a hard, resistant, unchanging nugget but, on the contrary, because it is completely open, always answering to the structuring properties of culture and ideology in a particular time and place, always borne on, and born from, the contingency of a particular encounter between an object and a viewer, listener or reader, and always ready to yield to a codifying procedure that effaces precisely what made it singular. Barthes attempted this impossible task many times and in many different ways, and it seems fitting that his last book is, for many readers, the one that comes closest to fulfilling it while simultaneously – and I have tried to show that this amounts to the same thing – demonstrating its impossibility.

Notes

1. I shall refer to these two works as *TM* and *CL* in the rest of this chapter. The translations have occasionally been modified.
2. Among the commentators who have linked a number of these terms are Moriarty, *Roland Barthes,* 203–4; Clark, 'Roland Barthes', 104–5; Brown, *Roland Barthes*, 278–80; and Haverkamp, 'The Memory of Pictures', 265, n. 9.
3. The original subtitles also signal by the use of the word 'note' that they are not offered as finished theoretical statements: 'Notes de recherche sur quelques photogrammes de S. M. Eisenstein'; *Note sur la photographie.* (Only the first of these survives in the translation.) The use of 'note' is less an apology on Barthes's part than an indication of the nature of the project itself.
4. In German they would be called *Fremdwörter;* see Chapter 5 above.
5. In 'The Grain of the Voice', Barthes also experiences the solitariness of the interpreter of uncodifiable meaning – in this case, the 'phonetics' of Panzéra's singing – and adduces 'Saussure's work on anagrams' (272).
6. Derrida has discussed this demand for translation in 'Des Tours de Babel'.
7. See Attridge, *Peculiar Language,* for a discussion of this supplementary logic at work in accounts of literature from the Renaissance onward.
8. Diana Knight (in 'Roland Barthes') has suggested that the photograph of Barthes's mother to which he responded so strongly is actually the one reproduced in *Camera Lucida* with the title, 'The Stock', and that the conservatory setting described by Barthes is a fiction.
9. There is also a sexual dimension to this undecidability, which functions as part of a long sequence of partly concealed, partly overt references in

Barthes's work to his homosexuality. (See Miller, *Bringing Out Roland Barthes*.) We may also note that Barthes describes the obtuse meaning in sexual terms that appear to distinguish it sharply from *jouissance*: 'It maintains itself in a state of perpetual erethism; in it desire does not attain that spasm of the signified which usually causes the subject to sink voluptuously into the peace of nomination' (*TM*, 56).

10. See 'The Reality Effect'.

Chapter 9

Nothing to Declare: J. Hillis Miller and Zero's Paradox

I

'The critic keeps wanting to add just one more word, in the futile hope of making it all clear'. Thus Hillis Miller, in an essay entitled 'Zero' (388). Miller is talking about the effect, and the effectiveness, of Henry James's story 'The Altar of the Dead', but might he not, also, be talking about the impulse that has kept him producing literary criticism over so many decades, discussing author after author, text after text, passage after passage? For even though he has often engaged with the most recalcitrant and elusive of writers and writings – Kleist, James, Nietzsche, Derrida, de Man and many more – and even though his topic is very often the inexpressible or the inherently ambiguous, there is always that perceptible drive, one might even call it a compulsion, to explain, to make clear, to render as perspicuous as the intractability of the material will allow. Knowing that a hope is futile does not diminish its force and productivity, of course, and, like James's story, Miller's extraordinary career provides ample evidence of this truth.

It's not surprising, therefore, that the statement in 'Zero' that I began with is followed by an assurance which is offered as a reassurance to the reader: 'This impossibility of clear understanding or expression is, on the terms of the story, a lucky thing, since to understand fully, to fill the gap, would be to be dead' (388). Miller's drive for clarity is founded on a paradoxical acknowledgement of the impossibility of clarity, or at least of the kind of clarity which would mean that that text or that topic need not be revisited, that the work of understanding and responding is over. All his careful analyses pronounce, at some level, their own failure; yet it is failure that guarantees success, since it enacts, performatively, the central point – that the literary cannot be exhausted by analysis.[1]

Why not simply announce this fact and spare readers the details of the many analyses? Because, I am guessing Miller would tell us, it is not quite a fact, or is more than a fact. Without the specific engagements with texts, the assertion that 'the literary cannot be exhausted by analysis' amounts to something like a tautology, a purely analytic statement that tells us nothing we did not know already. For the point is not so much that the literary *resists* analysis, but rather that it *invites* it, endlessly and inexhaustibly (and rewardingly). And only by pursuing the analysis, with as much rigour and precision as possible, in a wide range of examples, only by developing a vocabulary that will resituate the problematic of literature's inexhaustibility in a shared present, can the assertion be given content and purchase.

Inexhaustibility is not a synonym for richness or complexity, however. *Finnegans Wake* is inexhaustible, certainly, but so is a six-line poem by Celan. And although the *Wake* may have enough accumulated meanings and allusions to keep the professors busy for several hundred years, its inexhaustibility as literature lies not in this sheer mass of interpretable signification but in the undecidabilities produced by its remarkable dealings with language. When Hillis Miller sets out to clarify a literary work, or to demonstrate the constitutive impossibility of clarity by being as clear as he can, it is the moments of undecidability he focuses on, the moments where one thing is said but another is done, where language refers to itself as well as to the world and thus complicates the very process of referentiality, where meaning appears and disappears in the same gesture. Mere difficulty or density in a work requires only the following through of the work's own logic and the conventions of reading to reach understanding. The target of clarification, as Miller practises it, is the unclarifiable.

Hence his fascination with zero, a fascination which goes a long way back. In 1987, in a discussion of *Adam Bede*, he stated:

> Realism inserts an infinite zero as multiplier or divisor into the circuit of the equation moving away from reality and back to it. The zero is something without ground or substance that nevertheless has the power to make something happen. Its efficacy makes it dangerous, a force perhaps for good, perhaps for ill. (*The Ethics of Reading*, 77)

The existence of zero shows that it is possible for an entity to be and not be at the same time, or to be two different things, each of which makes the other impossible. If zero is a number, it can't be the absence of number, and vice versa. I'm reminded of one of Miller's early essays in a deconstructive vein, 'Ariachne's Broken Woof' (published in 1977), in which he showed that the hero's difficulty in Shakespeare's *Troilus and Cressida* is that the fundamental condition of self-identity upon which Western metaphysics rests has, for him at least, collapsed. As Troilus puts it in the play, with perfect Millerian clarity, 'This is, and is not Cressid' (V.ii.145; Miller cites the Variorum text (45)). And we can't even say whether the anti-conceptual concept of zero was something that always existed and only had to be discovered, or is the product of human invention.

The master of this kind of thinking was, of course, Paul de Man, and I'm sure Miller would be the first to agree that de Man's distinctive operation of the logical double-bind, the machine that never lets you off the hook no matter which way you twist, is something whose influence he has never shaken off and probably has no desire to shake off. When Miller tells us that there is an implacable law of this or that aspect of language or literature – and he often does – we hear de Man turning the handle of this contraption in the background. There are laws, it seems, and there are implacable laws. One might even say that Miller is fascinated by the stony gaze of implacability, but it is no Medusa for him, since it has given rise to some of his most creative work.[2]

II

To see this creative fascination in operation, I want to turn to what I think is one of Hillis Miller's most important books, although one of his shortest: *The Ethics of Reading*, from which I've already quoted and whose contents were first given as the Wellek Library Lectures in 1985. We have all become so used to the debate about ethics that it's hard to recall the time when it was a word little used and treated with much suspicion in literary studies, especially on the left (including the deconstructive left). But de Man had used it in *Allegories of Reading* in 1979 – no doubt at the time sending his political stocks even lower than they had been – and this interest in ethics and ethicity was one of Miller's starting points for the Wellek Lectures a few years later. Miller's argument in the book is that 'there is a necessary ethical moment in [the] act of reading as such, a moment neither cognitive, nor political, nor social, nor interpersonal, but properly and independently ethical' (*Ethics of Reading*, 1). By the 'ethics of reading', Miller tells us,

> I mean that aspect of the act of reading in which there is a response to the text that is both necessitated, in the sense that it is a response to an irresistible demand, and free, in the sense that I must take responsibility for my response and for the further effects, 'interpersonal', institutional, social, political, or historical, of my act of reading. (43)

Later in the book he asserts:

> Each reading is, strictly speaking, ethical, in the sense that it *has* to take place, by an implacable necessity [you can hear the screw turning], as the response to a categorical demand, and in the sense that the reader *must* take responsibility for it and for its consequences in the personal, social, and political worlds. (59).

Let me take the second of Miller's two senses of 'the ethics of reading' first: the fact that I *must* take responsibility for my reading and for its consequences. At first sight, this obligation seems no different from my obligation to take responsibility for all my actions and their consequences, unless I can claim to have been under duress or walking in my sleep or otherwise incapable of exercising my will. I don't even have to *take* responsibility: I *am* responsible – that is, I can be called to account, made to answer for, what I have done, as long as it is the case that I *chose* to do it. Responsibility thus entails freedom of choice. Accepting responsibility means accepting that one was a free agent in doing what one did.

But Miller's account of the 'implacable necessity' that governs the response to the text, his first sense of 'the ethics of reading', denies the possibility of responsible action in this sense. Reading, in his description, sounds much more like a matter of acting under duress than of freely choosing – and if that is the case, how can I, as reader, be held responsible for what I do? In order to make sense of this, we have to have recourse to a different understanding of responsibility, and therefore a different sense of ethics, one not tied to freedom of choice. One such understanding would be Levinas's sense of the ethical demand of the other, a demand which we cannot escape by saying 'I didn't *choose* to come face to face with this person or this situation'. For Levinas, ethics lies not in the responsibility implicit in my freely chosen acts but in the responsibility I find myself gripped by, 'taken hostage' by, as he puts it in language close to de Man's.[3]

Yet Miller says that the act of taking responsibility for my reading and for its effects is 'free' (in contrast to the determined character of the reading process itself). To ask a favourite question of Miller's, what can this mean? If it can't mean that I accept the responsibility implicit in my free act of responding to the text, it must mean a more difficult action: I have to accept that, although I had no choice in the way I responded, I am responsible for my response. (For Levinas, if I am free, it is a freedom only to acknowledge or deny the ethical force that already binds me.)

And one can go further: I am responsible for the *ir*responsibility of my response, for in doing justice to the singularity of the text I have to do justice to my own situation as I engage with it in a particular time and place (this is perhaps one aspect of the implacable law to which I am subject as reader), and to do this I have to make the text anew, as it has never been before (and never will be again). As Miller puts it towards the end of *The Ethics of Reading*, the reader is forced 'to betray the text or deviate from it in the act of reading it, in the name of a higher demand that can yet be reached only by way of the text' (120). Here Miller articulates the necessity of infidelity in a faithful reading, a paradox I have already touched on at several points in earlier chapters.

I, as responsible reader, am not, in other words, seeking to reveal an unchanging core of meaning, the text's 'secret' in the conventional sense of an unrecoverable interior, but rather attempting to perform, here and now, an affirmation of its singularity and alterity – a different kind of secret that cannot simply be revealed.[4] If this performative response is to do justice to the singularity of the text, to countersign its signature, it must itself be singular and inventive – not merely an act of obedience to a law. It must, that is, be irresponsible as well as responsible, or, more accurately, must deconstruct the opposition between these concepts.[5]

It may sound now as if I am disagreeing with Miller on the question of the text's implacable demand: I am suggesting that irresponsibility is as important as responsibility in the face of that demand, which implies that there is a certain freedom involved, that my response is not entirely determined by the text. To clarify this apparent disagreement, let us remind ourselves of the reason why reading is not, for Miller, a question of choosing whether to obey or disobey the demand being made by the text. It is that it is not possible to know this demand *in itself*: we cannot state it as a law, and it does not present itself to us as an injunction we might decide to disregard. All we can do is tell stories about our experience of it, stories which inevitably translate into an ontological register the linguistic necessity that reading, and the text being read, have to obey. All our critical commentaries, that is to say, are *stories*, no matter how logical and precise and clear we try to be. (Barthes's descriptions of instances of the third meaning and the *punctum* would be examples of such stories.) Indeed, as I've suggested, the more logical and precise and clear we succeed in being – and Miller's tales aim always at logic and precision and clarity – the more evident it will be that we have not escaped story-telling.

So in exercising our freedom to tell stories about the text – to performatively countersign its singular signature in our best attempt to do justice to it for our place and time – we are obeying the text's injunction: be responsible in your irresponsibility, tell my secrets with as much care and respect as you can even though you know they will remain secret, let my inventiveness be validated in your inventiveness. This, at least, is what good reading would be, if there is such a thing – and Hillis Miller's readings come closer than most to this ideal.

III

In his essay on zero, Miller refers to Borges, Svevo, Shakespeare, Kleist and Joyce, and gives a typically brilliant Millerian reading of 'The Altar of the Dead'. One writer he does not mention, but who might well have been included among those who exemplify the paradoxes of zero, is Samuel Beckett. We may turn to an author strongly influenced by Beckett for an articulation of this conjunction:

> The art of Samuel Beckett has become an art of zero, as we all know. We also know that an art of zero is impossible. A thousand words under a title and a publisher's imprint, the very act of moving pen over paper, are affirmations of a kind. By what self-contradictory act can such affirmations be deprived of content? By what act can the sentences be, so to speak, erased as they flow from the pen?

So writes J. M. Coetzee in an early essay on Beckett's style ('Samuel Beckett', 43). The first example Coetzee gives is the following sentence from Beckett's 'Imagination Dead Imagine' (whose title alone suggests a process of writing at or from zero): 'Islands, waters, azure, verdure, one glimpse and vanished, endlessly, omit'. Coetzee notes that 'the sentence thus embodies neatly two opposing impulses that permit a fiction of net zero: the impulse toward conjuration, the impulse toward silence' (43). However, as Miller has helped us appreciate, zero is not merely the result of a process of positing and cancellation: it is itself two contradictory things, a number and the absence of number, just as Beckett's sentence is both an affirmation and a denial.

When, at the beginning of *Endgame*, Hamm asks Clov what he has just seen out of the window, he replies 'Zero' (94). Hamm, however, takes this as an affirmation of some kind, since his response is 'It'd need to rain', as if nothing could burgeon into something with a little appropriate sustenance. In Beckett's fiction, as in mathematics, zero is never just nothing. But in this respect at least, Beckett's writing is no different from any other literary attempt to represent zero. To adapt the line by Wallace Stevens that could provide Miller with his epigraph (and did in an earlier version of the essay), zero is never merely 'not there'; it is always 'the nothing that is'. Few writers, however, have managed to give the failed endeavour to attain zero as much substance as Beckett, or the reader as much pleasure in that failure.

Critics, however, are put on their mettle by the Beckettian zero; in the stories they tell, few avoid the trap of reinstating the meaningfulness that Beckett has so assiduously evacuated.[6] Derrida, in explaining why he has avoided publishing texts on Beckett, hints at the way he might go about writing a commentary:

> The composition, the rhetoric, the construction and rhythm of his works, even the ones that seem the most 'decomposed', that's what 'remains' finally the most 'interesting', that's the work, that's the signature, this remainder which remains when the thematics is exhausted. ('"This Strange Institution"', 61)

The exhaustion of thematics, of semantic import, does not leave mere emptiness: as Miller so elegantly demonstrates, zero is a number after all, albeit one which challenges the foundations of number.

Notes

1. When Miller says that Derrida's 'intuition (though that is not quite the right word) of a certain unsayable or something unavailable to cognition is . . . the motivation of all his work' ('Derrida and Literature', 76), he could be speaking of his own work. The passage continues, quoting an unidentified text of Derrida's: '"The inaccessible incites from its place of hiding". It incites speech or writing in an interminable, never successful, never satisfactory, never complete, attempt to "get it right", or "do it right"'. Barthes's adumbration of a 'third meaning' or *'punctum'*, discussed in the previous chapter, is another version of this insistence on a productive but ungraspable element in the work of art.
2. Although de Man is the writer in whose work a sense of implacable laws is strongest, Derrida has commented, in the course of an interview, on the importance of the term in his own thinking: 'All of a sudden, the word *implacable* comes to me. That cannot be appeased, assuaged, quenched [*désaltérer*] (and with good reason), but, for the same reason (following the drift of the derivation) that one can in no sense abandon or give up [*plaquer*]. The trace of the implacable: that is what I am following and what leads me by the nose to write' (Derrida, '*Ja*, or the *faux-bond* II', 47–8).
3. See, for example, Levinas, *Otherwise than Being*, 99–129.
4. On the secret of literature, see Chapter 2 above.
5. I develop this account of the responsible response to literary works in *The Singularity of Literature*.
6. For an instructive discussion of the problems posed by Beckett for the critic and the philosopher, see Critchley, *Very Little . . . Almost Nothing*, 141–80.

Chapter 10

Radical Atheism and Unconditional Responsibility

I

At a Strathclyde University conference in 1986, Derrida brought a questioner up short with the comment, 'I've never said nor thought that the metaphysics of presence was an "evil" . . . I'm inclined to think exactly the contrary, that it's good. There is no "good" outside the metaphysics of presence' ('Some Questions', 257). Jonathan Culler, sensing the consternation among many members of the audience who had heard that deconstruction was an attack on 'the metaphysics of presence', asked Derrida to expand on his remark, and to explain what drives the impetus to deconstruct, which he did, in part, as follows:

> I have to deal with Necessity itself. It is something or someone, some x, which compels me to admit that my desire, for good, for presence, my own metaphysics of presence, not only cannot be accomplished, meets its limit, but *should* not be accomplished because the accomplishment or the fulfilment of this desire for presence would be death itself; the good, the absolute good, would be identical with death . . . Necessity is the drive, or the counterdrive; it's a drive which bars the fundamental drive towards presence, pleasure, fullness, plenitude, etc. The dream beyond Necessity . . . is the plenitude which wouldn't be death. This combination of dream and necessity explains the indefatigable drive for deconstruction. (260–1)

This response probably didn't reduce the perplexity of many in the audience, but it did set out very clearly a nexus that remained central to Derrida's thinking throughout his career. In an important and hard-hitting book, *Radical Atheism*, Martin Hägglund lucidly delineates the argument by means of which Derrida problematises the desire for plenitude in its various guises, and on the strength of this clarity of insight offers trenchant critiques of a number of interpretations of Derridean thought that simplify or distort it. He does ample justice to what Derrida in the comment above calls 'Necessity', though I shall argue that he does not fully account for what Derrida calls 'the dream beyond Necessity'.

Hägglund sets out with admirable clarity the reasoning that leads Derrida from his account of time to the 'law of autoimmunity', which ties possibility to impossibility, success to failure. Briefly, if there can be no such thing as an indivisible 'now' (since the progression to the following 'now' must already be implicit in what is thus a necessarily divided present), time can be seen to possess a trace-structure – the temporal continuity between past, present and future is achieved through a remaining that cannot be purely in the dimension of time but must involve space (since only something spatial can last), while space is temporalised, as a trace of the past left for the future. This becoming-space of time and becoming-time of space (captured by Derrida in the neologism *différance* and the notion of arche-writing, for example) means that exposure to the future, and therefore to potential erasure as much as to potential fulfilment, is constitutive of time. None of this is new, though its implications are often overlooked, and Hägglund goes on to show in a sharper light even than Derrida elected to do how it provides the basis for the latter's treatment of the most far-reaching topics, starting with life itself (hence the subtitle of the book, *Derrida and the Time of Life*).

We may think we desire immortality, Hägglund argues, but what we really yearn for is *survival*: we want our mortal lives to continue. Autoimmunity is the law that governs our existence: that which safeguards is also that which destroys, and an entity has no way of protecting itself against possible attack by its own immune system. Immortality would, therefore, like presence or the absolute good in the comments quoted above, be 'identical with death'. Hägglund works through some of the grounds and implications of this argument in chapters on Derrida's engagement with Kant and with Husserl, and in the three chapters that follow he mounts his critique of three fields in which a failure to grasp the essentials of the trace-structure and autoimmunity have led to misunderstandings of Derrida's use of such terms as 'God', 'hospitality' and 'justice': the fields of theology, ethics and political theory. *Radical Atheism* has provoked a great deal of discussion from specialists in these fields and others,[1] but Hägglund's account of what so often goes wrong in adopting or adapting Derrida has a great deal of force. The argument that the possibility of evil is inherent in the constitution of the good, that, for example, a promise would not be a promise if it could not become a threat, nor democracy democracy if it did not contain the potential to become totalitarian, offends both cherished ideals and the logic of identity. It is all too easy to pull out one strand of the double or triple knot to make Derrida a negative theologian by overlooking the centrality of finitude in his philosophy, or a normative Levinasian by ignoring the importance of arche-violence in his account of relations with the other, or a latter-day Schmittian by misunderstanding his theory of the autoimmunity implicit in sovereignty. Nevertheless, it needs to be said that many of these remade versions of Derrida do reflect important if incompletely understood aspects of his thinking, and constitute significant contributions to their own fields – that Hägglund does not deal with Agamben, for example, may be because the latter's misapprehensions are not particularly fruitful.

II

There may be a problem of one-sidedness in Hägglund's own thinking, however. To get at this, let us look at one key term in his, and Derrida's, discussions of the relation to the other: *hospitality*. Like autoimmunity in its various manifestations, a concern with the other (which is, in fact, at the heart of autoimmunity) permeates Derrida's work from first to last: the deconstruction of presence, supplementarity, originary pervertibility, destinerrence, spectrality – all involve the insinuation of the other into the terrain of the same, without which the same would not be what it is (which means it is not quite what it is usually taken to be). In order for the same to be constituted as what it is, therefore, it has to be open to the other: an other which, by definition, cannot be judged in advance to be constructive or destructive. (As we have seen, Hägglund traces this argument to the fundamental constitution of time, and therefore of life, itself.)

Hägglund rightly insists throughout his book that this openness to the other is a necessary fact; without it, nothing at all would happen. An event – as an unpredictable occurrence – can come about only through exposure to an unknown, unknowable other. So there is a sense in which hospitality to the other (and this, of course, is the only kind of hospitality there can be if the word is to have any force) is just what occurs; it is necessity. When, at the Strathclyde conference, Derrida referred to Necessity as something 'which compels me to admit that my desire . . . for presence, not only cannot be accomplished . . . but *should* not be accomplished' he was referring to this unavoidable intrusion of otherness, barring fulfilment and plenitude – but also to the positive importance of this intrusion, without which my desire would not even be partially satisfied. As Hägglund points out, the 'should' in formulations like this one does not convey moral obligation, but desirability:

fulfilment, were it possible, would not in fact be something we would find to our liking. Hospitality to the other is an inescapable, and indispensable, feature of life.

But we might ask: isn't 'hospitality' a slightly odd word to use in a context of mechanical necessity? It's not unusual, of course, to be invited by Derrida to reinvest familiar words with new senses or values; in fact it's an important part of Hägglund's argument to alert us to the danger of responding only to the negative connotations of words like 'contamination' or 'perversion'. 'Hospitality', however, is one of a chain of words with strong normative associations to which Derrida gave increasing attention; others include 'the gift', 'forgiveness', 'democracy', 'responsibility', 'invention' and 'justice'. In every case, Derrida argued that these terms, understood in their most complete sense, name an act or a state or a response that is impossible, not just for empirical reasons but essentially so, while at the same time having an indissociable relation to the more common-or-garden acts or states or responses to which we give these names in our daily lives. At first sight, these concepts (a term I use *faute de mieux* and with some circumspection in this context) may seem to operate in Derrida's writing in the same manner as one of the most fundamental terms appearing in deconstruction's sights: 'presence'. Presence, too, as we experience or perceive it in our lives or as it has been used in the Western philosophical tradition, names an impossibility, thanks to the working of *différance*; but at the same time it is only thanks to the working of *différance* that anything like presence is possible.

Now it is true that 'hospitality', 'justice' and the other words in this series are internally divided in the same way as 'presence' is. If hospitality, in the fullest sense of the word, were possible, it would not look anything like what we call hospitality in a friend or an institution, since it would be without any invitation, any restriction, any nomination; a gift 'worthy of the name' (as Derrida liked to say) would not be apprehensible, as any consciousness of giving by either party would render it imperfect. But our desire for presence is in fact the opposite of the desire for hospitality, for openness to the other, and its realisation would not just result in something very different from the presence we dream of but would mark the end of life, time and space. Immortality, another mode of resistance to alterity, would produce the same result. We are saved from their terminal destructiveness only by the necessary interposition of the other.

Derrida's normative terms work differently. It is not the case that a desire for hospitality (whether as giver or receiver) does not *really* mean a desire for a limited hospitality – what Derrida calls a 'conditional hospitality' (Derrida and Dufourmantelle, *Of Hospitality*, 25) – in the same way that a desire for immortality could be said really to mean a desire for survival. A desire for justice is not *really* a desire for law. Derrida's handling of these and similar concepts suggest a rather different relation between the impossible, unconditional, unconditioned sense and the limited, law-governed, sense. For a full understanding of his treatment of normative terms it may be as necessary to discriminate among them as it is to bring out their shared structural logics – as it is necessary to discriminate among arche-writing, *différance*, the trace, supplementarity, the *pharmakon*, autoimmunity and so on, even though they bear strong structural similarities to one another.

One version of the relation between unconditional and conditional senses is ruled out repeatedly and forcefully by Derrida: the former does not operate as a Kantian regulative idea; it does not stand as a remote ideal that, as finite beings, we can never hope to reach but that we can imagine. Hägglund is very firm on this point, as is Derrida himself – here the latter is discussing what he calls 'the im-possible':

> It is not the inaccessible, and it is not what I can indefinitely defer: it announces itself; it precedes me, swoops down upon and seizes me *here and now* in a nonvirtualizable way, in actuality and not potentiality. It comes upon me from on high, in the form of an injunction that does not simply wait on the horizon, that I do not see coming, that never leaves me in peace and never lets me put it off until later. Such an urgency cannot be *idealized* any more than the other as other can. This im-possible is thus not a (regulative) *idea or ideal.* (*Rogues*, 84)

In his repeated attempts to articulate the notion of our relation to unconditional hospitality (repeated attempts because, like justice or forgiveness, it is strictly unthinkable and unarticulable), Derrida pushes at the limits of conceptual language and of conventional morality:

> Absolute hospitality requires that I open up my home and that I give not only to the foreigner . . . but to the absolute, unknown, anonymous other, and that I *give place* to them, that I let them come, that I let them arrive, and take place in the place I offer them, without asking of them either reciprocity (entering into a pact) or even their names. (Derrida and Dufourmantelle, *Of Hospitality*, 25)

> To be hospitable is to let oneself be overtaken [*surprendre*], *to be ready to be not ready*, if such is possible, to let oneself be overtaken, to not even *let* oneself be overtaken, to be surprised, in a fashion almost violent, violated and raped [*violée*], stolen [*volée*], . . . precisely where one is not ready to receive – and not only *not yet ready* but *not ready, unprepared* in a mode that is not even that of the 'not yet'. ('Hostipitality', 361)

But he also asserts repeatedly the inseparability of this absolute hospitality from conditional hospitality, and the insufficiency of the latter without its relation to the former. It will be worth quoting several examples of his attempts to specify the connection between the two:

> Just hospitality [i.e. unconditional hospitality] breaks with hospitality by right [i.e. conditional hospitality]; not that it condemns or is opposed to it, and it can on the contrary set and maintain it in a perpetual progressive movement; but it is as strangely heterogeneous to it as justice is heterogeneous to the law to which it is yet so close, from which in truth it is indissociable. (Derrida and Dufourmantelle, *Of Hospitality*, 25–7)

> Conditional laws would cease to be laws of hospitality if they were not guided, given inspiration, given aspiration, required, even, by the law of unconditional hospitality. (Derrida and Dufourmantelle, *Of Hospitality*, 79)

> Only an unconditional hospitality can give meaning and practical rationality to a concept of hospitality. Unconditional hospitality exceeds juridical, political, or economic calculation. But no thing and no one happens or arrives without it. (*Rogues*, 149)

> It is as if there were a competition or a contradiction between two neighboring but incompatible values: *visitation* [i.e. unconditional hospitality] *and invitation* [i.e. conditional hospitality] . . . These two hôtes that the visitor and the invited are, these two faces of hospitality, visitation and invitation, are not moments of hospitality, dialectical phases of the same process, the same phenomenon. Visitor and invited, visitation and invitation, are simultaneously in competition and incompatible; they figure the non-dialectizable [*non-dialectisable*] tension, even the always imminent implosion, in fact, the continuously occurring implosion in its imminence, unceasing, at once active and deferred, of the concept of hospitality. ('Hostipitality', 362)

> It is a question of knowing how to transform and improve the law, and of knowing if this improvement is possible within an historical space which takes place *between* the Law of an unconditional hospitality, offered *a priori* to every other, to all newcomers, *whoever they may be*, and *the* conditional laws of a right to hospitality, without which *The* unconditional Law of hospitality would be in danger of remaining a pious and irresponsible desire, without form and without potency, and of even being perverted at any moment. ('On Cosmopolitanism', 22–3)

Introducing this last comment, on the question of immigration, Derrida states that 'all these questions remain obscure and difficult and we must neither conceal them from ourselves nor, for a moment, imagine ourselves to have mastered them' (22). It is a comment which could no doubt be applied to all these formulations.

We have, therefore, two kinds of hospitality, heterogeneous yet indissociable, incompatible yet coupled; and the inevitably limited hospitality that we exercise or receive in our lives is in some way informed by (set and maintained by, guided and given inspiration by, given meaning and practical rationality by, to repeat some of the expressions Derrida uses) the impossible, unthinkable, unconditional twin. The struggle to articulate the relationship between the two faces of hospitality indicates its resistance to thought, and it is not surprising that in extrapolations of Derrida's argument the relationship often slips into the more easily apprehensible structures of regulative idea or dialectical interchange – indeed, Derrida's own language often comes very close to these alternatives.

'Deconstruction', writes Derrida, 'is hospitality to the other' ('Hostipitality', 364), just as he writes 'Deconstruction is justice' ('Force of Law,' 15) (whereas he would not have written 'Deconstruction is presence'). Which version of hospitality is this? Clearly, it must be unconditional hospitality; there would be no deconstruction if it set limits to its openness in advance, if it knew who or what would arrive, if the event it brought about were in any way predictable. Of course, its absoluteness is immediately compromised: impossible 'pure' deconstruction, in its very openness to the other, is impure from the start. Similarly, justice, always a matter of singular judgements made in the context of general rules, is at once absolute and compromised by laws and rights, memory and consciousness.[2] And, as Hägglund rightly insists, such openness can always lead to the worst as well as the best.

Now let us examine Hägglund's account of hospitality. For him, a hospitality worthy of the name is not Derrida's unconditional hospitality but a distinctly conditional hospitality:

> If I did not discriminate between what I welcome and do not welcome, what I find acceptable and unacceptable, it would mean that I had renounced all claims to be responsible, make judgments, or pursue any critical reflections at all . . . An ethics of unconditional hospitality would short-circuit all forms of decisions and be the same as a complete indifference before what happens. (*Radical Atheism*, 103).

Accordingly, for Hägglund, unconditional hospitality exerts no ethical claims – indeed, he asserts that Derrida deconstructs the ethics of unconditional hospitality (103–4), on the model, presumably, of the deconstruction of presence.

We recognise here the logic of the absolute as death exemplified in Derrida's Strathclyde comments. We may desire to exercise unconditional hospitality, but if we could, it would be disastrous; fortunately, Necessity – the necessity of limits, rights and so on – prevents us from achieving this ultimate perfection. Hägglund's formulations make good sense, but they don't sound quite like Derrida's; they don't give the impression of grappling with an unthinkable relation, they don't struggle to articulate the necessary link between the unconditional and the conditional. Going back to those Strathclyde comments, we recall that Derrida's answer to Culler's question about the drive to deconstruct was an appeal to a combination of necessity and dream, the necessity of limits and laws and the dream of a 'plenitude that wouldn't be death'. Even after the deadliness of plenitude has been exposed there remains a dream that it might be otherwise; and even after the emptiness of immortality or the riskiness of hospitality have been made evident the desire they provoke remains strong.

Hägglund is insistent that Derrida's representations of justice, hospitality, the gift have no ethical content; unconditional hospitality may have terrible consequences as well as wonderful ones. But Hägglund's careful arguments do have ethical implications. For instance, he explains the problematic indissociability of conditional and unconditional hospitality on the grounds that 'it is the exposure to the visitation of others that makes it necessary to establish conditions of hospitality, to regulate who is allowed to enter' (*Radical Atheism*, 104). The moral appears to be: be circumspect when you welcome a stranger, because the unruly force of unconditionality can always disrupt your careful plans. Similarly, because 'a gift *must* be contaminated in order to be a gift' (37), any act of giving had better not strive for purity. The judge in her exercise of justice needs to be aware that 'the risk of injustice is inscribed in the very possibility of justice' (43); fortunately, the law is there to function as 'an immune protection for justice' (42).

To be sure, to put it like this is to push Hägglund's argument further than he intends it to go, but I do it in order to underline the difference between what I can only call the ethical tone of Derrida's writing and his own. We readers of Derrida ought to be grateful to Hägglund for being so severe with us when we move too quickly to derive moral or religious prescriptions from the former's work, and that is not what I am doing here. I am concerned, however, to understand the difference between Derrida's wrestle with the notion of hospitality to the other and Hägglund's resolute anti-ethicism. In order to do so it will be helpful to turn to Levinas.

It's perhaps not much of an argument to say that if Hägglund is correct about the difference between Levinas's and Derrida's arguments, the latter's huge admiration for the former is rather hard to explain. One can assume a certain degree of exaggeration in comments of Derrida's such as 'Before a thought like Levinas's, I never have an objection. I am ready to subscribe to everything he says' (Derrida and Labarrière, *Altérités*, 74); one can allow for the particular circumstances of a funeral eulogy or commemorative conference in assessing the praise expressed in *Adieu: to Emmanuel Levinas*. But there must be some basis for the clear indebtedness Derrida felt to Levinas, and for the frequent references to him when discussing concepts like hospitality and justice. This basis, I would argue, can be found in the power of Levinas's depiction of the ethics of alterity.

III

There is no doubt about the considerable divergences between Levinas's and Derrida's understandings of what 'hospitality to the other' implies; Derrida initially made these differences clear in 'Violence and Metaphysics', first published in French in 1964, and although, as I noted in Chapter 7, the tone in 'A Word of Welcome' (*Adieu*, 15–152), delivered in 1996, has altered significantly, they are still evident. Nevertheless, Levinas's emphasis on an openness to the other that is absolute, a responsibility that is irrecusable, an ethics that is not about prescriptions and moral codes, profoundly influenced Derrida's thought. For Levinas, my encounter with the other is not an encounter with an empirical individual whom I can identify and size up: it is prior to any of the processes of judgement or classification. The other is neither good nor bad, neither deserving nor undeserving; it (rather than he or she – or you; Levinas, as we have seen, uses the term 'illeity' to bring out its 'itness') is an embodied, singular source of a demand which is also an appeal. And I am not invited to take responsibility for it; I *find* myself responsible, my subjectivity in fact constituted by that responsibility. Hägglund's assertion that Levinas 'refuses to realize that alterity cannot be ethical as such' and that 'his philosophy requires that alterity ultimately answers to the Good' (*Radical Atheism*, 90) is misleading, since it is in *responding* to the other that the ethical arises, and part of Levinas's challenge to conventional ethics is his insistence that infinite responsibility is owed to the other *without* consideration of its goodness or badness, without forethought about likely consequences. This 'ethical' response is far from prescriptive, however, since one is infinitely responsible whether one is aware of it or not, whether one accepts it or not. Levinas does argue that everyday morality and politics gains by being informed by the ethics of the face-to-face encounter, but does not succeed in explaining how this works – much as Derrida has difficulty in explaining how his absolutes inspire their limited partners.

Derrida's 'non-ethical opening of ethics', then, is not far removed from what Levinas calls 'ethics'; for both, the encounter with the singular other is pre-prescriptive, and any prescriptions operative in the world are made possible by it. Levinas and Derrida both stress the *passivity* involved in absolute hospitality, and the latter, in a parenthesis distancing his argument from Kant's appeal to duty, associates it with *grace*: 'If I practice hospitality "*out of* duty" . . , this hospitality of paying up is no longer an absolute hospitality, it is no longer graciously offered beyond debt and economy' (Derrida and Dufourmantelle, *Of Hospitality*, 83). But this does not mean that there is no value attached to absolute hospitality, as Hägglund seems to suggest. A purely calculated hospitality (Hägglund's discrimination 'between what I welcome and what I do not welcome') would not be hospitality at all; the decision to be hospitable must, like any decision, pass through the undecidable and hence take place beyond calculation: 'It is the other who decides', as Derrida liked to say. So normativity is indeed at work in Derrida's thinking; his choice of the word 'hospitality', like his choice of the words 'justice', 'forgiveness' and so on, is not made in simple defiance of their normative force. To exercise justice is to carry out the necessary calculation, to weigh and balance and draw on legal and historical knowledge, but it is also to move beyond calculation in inventing the law afresh for a singular case, as Derrida argues powerfully in the first part of 'Force of Law'. We find similar language in Derrida's discussion of unconditional hospitality: 'a hospitality invented for the singularity of the new arrival' (Derrida and Dufourmantelle, *Of Hospitality*, 83).

When Hägglund states that 'Nothing can establish a priori that it is better to be more hospitable than to be less hospitable (or vice versa)' (*Radical Atheism*, 105; and see the very similar statement on 187), he is referring to the calculation of outcomes. But ethics, for Derrida (as for Levinas), is not a matter of calculation, and there can surely be no doubt that hospitality, justice, forgiveness, inventiveness, giving are goods – in an individual, in an institution,[3] in a society – precisely because they involve risk, because their relation to absolutes (difficult though that is to understand or articulate) makes possible actions that are not pre-programmed or secured in the self-same. Hence the importance of deconstruction as *affirmation*; for instance, in an interview with Richard Kearney in 1981, Derrida used strikingly Levinasian language:

> Deconstruction always presupposes affirmation . . . I mean that deconstruction is, in itself, a positive response to an alterity which necessarily calls, summons, or motivates it. Deconstruction is therefore vocation – a response to a call . . . The other precedes philosophy and necessarily invokes and provokes the subject before any genuine questioning can begin. It is in this

rapport with the other that affirmation expresses itself. ('Deconstruction and the Other', 167–8)

Deconstruction's rapport with the other is described in somewhat different terms in 'Psyche', where Derrida describes the 'invention of the other that would come . . . to offer a place for the other, to let the other come':

> I am careful to say 'let it come' because if the other is precisely what is not invented, the initiative or deconstructive inventiveness can consist only in opening, uncloseting, destabilizing foreclusionary structures so as to allow for the passage toward the other. ('Psyche', 341)

Deconstruction as an activity cannot make the other come, but can unsettle existing structures that inhibit its coming. In its openness to the other, it can always lead to evil consequences, as Hägglund would remind us at this point; but Derrida's tone here and in a hundred other places indicates that this risk-taking, affirmative attitude is preferable to its opposite.

Pure justice, absolute forgiveness, unconditional hospitality: all these are impossible and unthinkable, constitutively open to contamination from the first, and without guarantee as to outcome; but without them there would be no justice, forgiveness or hospitality of any kind, there would only be law, calculation, self-interest. Hägglund has shown superbly how Derrida's account of time underlies his explorations of these ethical topics, and how unlike traditional ethical postures the results are; but what is missing from his account is Derrida's reinvention of ethics, a philosophical adventure that was not divorced, as many who knew him can testify, from his own practice of living.

Notes

1. See, for instance, Laclau, 'Is Radical Atheism a Good Name?', and *Living On*, a special issue of the *New Centennial Review* devoted to Hägglund's book.
2. In responding to Levinas's account of the relation between ethics and justice or politics, Derrida repeatedly insists that the latter – 'the third' in Levinas's account – 'does not wait', but is already implicated in the face-to-face ethical relationship. He thus departs significantly from Levinas while claiming to be faithful (see Chapter 7 above).
3. For a clearly normative use of the notion of the unconditional, see Derrida's 'The University without Condition', where he asserts that 'the modern university *should* be *without condition*' (202). (That this is an impossibility doesn't render it a merely imaginary ideal.)

Chapter 11

The Place of Deconstruction: A Conversation with Jean-Michel Rabaté

DA:

In thinking about the place of deconstruction, about deconstruction and place, I'm reminded of some comments made by Jacques Derrida at a conference I attended at the University of Irvine in 1987 entitled 'The States of "Theory"'. Derrida had not noticed at first that 'states' in the title of the conference was in the plural, he told us, and he continued:

> And I thought that the answer to this question – What is the state of theory today? – was then self-evident, it was obvious, *hic et nunc*. The state of theory, now and from now on, isn't it California? And even Southern California? ('Some Statements and Truisms', 63)

Derrida insisted that this was not just a joke (though it certainly had the audience laughing), and that the double meaning of 'state' would have to be taken on board in any analysis of the conference in which we were all participating, an analysis that would necessarily include a consideration of what he called 'the geography and politics of theory'. Such an analysis would show that it was not just by chance that a conference on theory – including 'deconstructive theory' – was happening in Southern California.

Deconstruction, as Derrida uses the word, is not something anyone chooses to undertake but rather something that happens, and there is presumably no place that has any special privilege over others when it comes to the event of deconstruction in this sense. Nevertheless, it is the case that different places have, at different times, been more hospitable to the event of bringing-to-consciousness and setting-to-work (or play) of deconstruction. Conferences, in Southern California or in Paris, are one sign of this hospitality. If we had a globe into which we stuck a flag for every conference on deconstruction the result would be a highly uneven distribution of flags – and Paris, which is in some sense (that we might want to explore further) the 'home' of deconstruction, would not have the thickest clustering.

The question I'm raising, then, is this: when a deconstructive event is staged or brought to light – the holding of a conference, the teaching of a class, the writing of an essay, the publication of a book – in a particular place, what is the role of that place in the event? If deconstruction is a matter of taking the fullest account of idiomaticity and context, of an undermining of philosophy's claims to universality, how can we take account of the particularity of the spatial setting – the country, the city, the building – within which it occurs? Is the deconstruction that is talked about in Irvine identical to the deconstruction that is talked about in New York or Luton? And what about the deconstruction that surfaces on the World Wide Web or, like this conversation, on e-mail that traverses continents? What difference does it make that I am in the UK as I write these words and that you will read them, and respond to them, in the USA?

And – one more issue we might want to consider – how is the reception and institutionalisation of deconstruction in a particular place affected by the presence or absence of Jacques Derrida in person? (One motivation for this question is my sense that the willingness to adopt a positive attitude to deconstruction at my own university, the University of York, increased significantly after a visit from Jacques, during which he turned out to be neither the fierce boa-deconstructor that some had expected, nor the clownish jester that others had him down for, but a polite, thoughtful, animated interlocutor.)

J-MR:

Like you, I have taught in Europe (in England and France) and the Americas (Canada, Mexico and the US), and I have found very different attitudes facing not only deconstruction but the whole issue of what is called 'Theory'. The usual institutional site for which the clash between linguistic skills and an ability to 'philosophise' about texts is played out again and again is comparative literature. (In other departments like English or French, the worries focus more often on the risk, glibly denounced, of students abandoning literature for the sake of an all too abstract theory; for instance, one often hears complaints that students who do too much theory stop reading poems and novels and therefore lose most of their literary competence by the time they finish a PhD.) Indeed, a choice between languages or theory was the first alternative that I found when I became acquainted with comparative literature departments in the US and Canada in the mid-1980s. This choice had something of the options facing Achilles (the choice between a long but obscure life or a short but glorious career as a hero): Theory would provide a rapid fix but was doomed to an early demise, while the patient or laborious acquisition of linguistic skills would prepare students for long-term academic prospects. There was then a divide between departments stressing linguistic skills with all the attendant cultural expertise, and those stressing Theory as offering a unifying discourse.

As I had been teaching in France, my American colleagues believed that I would 'do' theory the way Monsieur Jourdain would speak 'prose'. It took me some time to realise that scholars who referred often to Plato, Hegel, Derrida, Cixous or Kristeva were automatically enrolled in the camp of Theory at a time when antagonisms ran high. While in France, on the other hand, I had the simple illusion that I and my friends were being 'modern' or just 'young' if not 'radical' by contrast with older and more humanistic styles of literary discourse. Besides, as we were rather close to some major actors in what we would call 'philosophy' or 'the human sciences', we had to be more aware of important divergences between camps like those of the Deleuzians, the Derrideans, the feminists or the Lacanians. On the whole, being in France made it more difficult to produce a syncretic or globalised concept of Theory. When I was invited to teach as a visiting professor in the Department of Comparative Literature of the University of Montreal in 1989, I still found traces of this alternative, although the department insisted on both types of competence for its graduate students. Although I need to say that quite a few of my colleagues there would command many languages while being fluent in Theory – which then encompassed a wide spectrum, from semiotics to Heidegger, from Derrida and de Man to Deleuze.

It is clear to me that today neither deconstruction nor Theory as such can play the role of a unifying set of concepts or procedures that would underpin the diverse fields or corpuses corresponding to our forced specialisations. On the other hand, we have come closer to Derrida's idea that what matters is to be able to speak at least two (if not more) languages at once. Are these to be understood as two idioms (like say French and English) or two discourses (like literature and philosophy)? In a revealing passage of 'Deconstructions: The Im-possible', Derrida writes: '. . . if, God forbid, I had to provide a minimal definition of deconstruction, it would be "more than a language"; that is several languages, more than one language' (28–9). I'll just note in passing that in this remarkable essay, Derrida gives a very trenchant critique of deconstruction as practised in American campuses. When summing

up the process leading to the transformation of deconstructive problematics into a methodology that would be repeatable and applicable
everywhere, Derrida seems to provide his own parody of Descartes's
Discourse on Method. He describes the introduction into American
literature departments of paradigms he had launched but that then turn
into 'possibilities', 'powers', 'rules' and 'laws' to be systematically and
immediately implemented:

> Among the examples of these procedural or formalizing formulae that I had
> proposed . . . there was the reversal of a hierarchy. After having reversed a
> binary opposition, whatever it may be – speech/writing, man/woman, spirit/
> matter, signifier/signified, signified/signifier, master/slave, and so on – and
> having liberated the subjugated and submissive term, one then proceeded to
> the generalisation of this latter in new traits, producing a different concept,
> for example another concept of writing such as trace, *différance*, gramme,
> text, and so on. (19)

It is rare to see the originator of a critical method offer such an ironi-
cal assessment of what has been, it is true, too often systematised into
simple conceptual tricks under the guise of deconstruction. Not that
Derrida engages in debunking pastiche or contorted self-parody; the
assessment of what passed as deconstruction nevertheless attests to the
validity of the problematics – what is unbearable is that it turns into an
easy refrain, and can 'function' almost regardless of the text taken as
example or simple pretext.

Thus, to return to the question of place, I would like to point out a
radically historicised origin in order to go beyond this history. Derek,
you asked about the rationale of crucial differences in countries, with the
impact of location on deconstruction, and in that context I would like to
point out that deconstruction, in its very origins and conditions of possibility, appeared at first inseparable, in its very idiom and procedures,
from French phenomenology. The language of deconstruction has been
the language of French phenomenology, that is, a very particular and
exciting moment in the history of thinking that always presupposed two
languages, the French and the German. It would be too long to retrace
them here, but Derrida's roots are intertwined with those shared jointly
by Bataille, Blanchot, Sartre, Levinas, Merleau-Ponty, Beaufret, Michel
Henry and a few others, that is, a typically French way of negotiating
among Hegel, Husserl and Heidegger. All this would not be understandable without the importance of Sartre's *oeuvre*, which functioned much
more as an epistemological obstacle leading to the need felt by younger
philosophers to apologise for what they saw as embarrassing distortions
of Hegel, Husserl and Heidegger.

This story is complicated by the fact that most of the initial impact of deconstruction on English-speaking countries returned to that same spot, but twenty years later, in so far as it had to do with the lack of a philosophical culture shared by undergraduates. Still today, most French students who opt for the humanities can situate, even approximately, Plato, Descartes, Kant and Nietzsche (to quote standard references). Thus, in so far as Anglo-American universities still need to enlarge their libraries so as to include the history of philosophy from, say, Plato to Heidegger, in so far as they are open to translations of the Franco-German dialogue that dominated in the middle of the last century, there is no reason why deconstruction would not continue, if only less visibly so. To sum up, something like British or American monolingualism would be the real enemy, much more than intellectual parochialism or an exclusive reliance on philosophies of language in the Anglo-Saxon mode. And today, another episteme seems to emerge from the same site: the until then massive reference to Heidegger translated into French or English leaves room for another tradition within phenomenology in which one returns to Husserl or rereads Levinas in the light of Rosenzweig, Buber, Benjamin, Scholem, Kierkegaard or Patočka. To sum up, the central question for me becomes this: what room (*place*) is left for thought in the conflict of these languages?

DA:

Your reminder of the place of language, or rather languages, in deconstruction is a valuable one – though I think it's also important to stress that 'plus d'une langue' would also mean 'no more of a language, something that exceeds language'. Deconstruction is that which makes any language at all both polylingual and other to itself, *a* language only in so far as it is at the same time *more than* a language. The idiomaticity of a language, in other words, is premised upon its having porous borders, both to other languages and to what Derrida has called 'the "other" of language' ('Deconstruction and the Other', 173). 'I have only one language', says Derrida at several points in *Monolingualism of the Other*, 'yet it is not mine'.

I wonder if it would be useful to distinguish between two uses of the term 'deconstruction' at this point. There is the philosophical, or quasi-philosophical, movement or mode of reading (one would not want to call it a programme, though it has its programmatic aspect) which one associates with the work of Jacques Derrida, and which has its roots, as you say, in French phenomenology. When it becomes wholly a programme or a method, the appropriate term is 'deconstruction-ism' (a term Derrida discussed, with ironic disapproval, in the same Irvine conference talk that I quoted from earlier). But there is also the deconstruction that happens, the *event* of deconstruction. To quote Derrida's 'Letter to a Japanese Friend' (and we might note that 'place' plays a role here), 'Deconstruction takes place, it is an event that does not await the deliberation, consciousness or organization of a subject, or even of modernity. *It deconstructs itself. It can be deconstructed* [Ça se déconstruit]' (4).

Derrida acknowledged these twin meanings in a conference discussion in 1986:

> Of course deconstruction today designates not only this principle of disinte-gration or dislocation in any question within a system, but a way of thematis-ing this possibility; and to analyse the specific modernity, or post-modernity, of deconstruction as an explicit – or to some extent explicit – endeavour you would have to describe the entire western situation, the European situation [you have begun to do this in your comments, Jean-Michel], the American situation, and so on. But this has to do with the difference between the term 'deconstruction' for the explicit project (if it's a project today) and the inner possibility of deconstruction which is present everywhere. ('Some Questions and Responses', 263)

To discuss the place of deconstruction, or the taking-place of decon-struction, it seems to me, one has to explore precisely that difference, the difference between the ubiquity, in temporal as well as geographical terms, of the deconstructive event, and the very uneven distribution of what Derrida calls the 'thematising' of that event.

So wherever there is language – and it is not merely a matter of verbal language – there is deconstruction, there is 'plus d'une langue'; but are there particular situations in which the 'inner possibility of decon-struction' is more likely to manifest itself. How are these situations determined? Why Southern California, for instance, to go back to the comment I started with? And a related question: how far would we be willing to acknowledge this manifestation of the deconstructive taking-place that is everywhere *under other names*? It is easy to answer 'yes' for names like Nietzsche, Blanchot, Levinas, Bataille; perhaps too for Plato, Kant and Hegel, though one might want to say that this is so in spite of themselves. But I wonder about other kinds of name. For instance, is 'literature' or 'the literary' sometimes a name for the deconstructive event of language? (Even if most literary criticism works hard to conceal the event.)

These questions have a bearing too on the future of 'theory', which you raised. I entirely agree with you that such a future has to be diverse and multilingual, which means that it has to respect the deconstructive potential of all language, the absence of any monolanguage (in spite of many attempts to reduce language to a single nationally-based system). It may not always be the thematisation going by the name 'deconstruction' that offers the best way, in new contexts, of showing that respect. And it may be that in different places, different kinds of thematisation work best. So a final question would be: although there is a huge disparity in the public attention given to deconstruction-as-thematisation in various countries of the world, do other kinds of reading, other kinds of thinking, carry on the same work under different rubrics?

I seem to be doing nothing but multiply questions. I hope you might be able to point us toward some answers . . .

J-MR:

You write – let me know whether I am not simplifying – that 'wherever there is language, and it is not merely a matter of verbal language, there is deconstruction', adding that there would be situations in which the possibility of such a latent but 'always already there' movement of deconstruction' would be more likely to manifest itself.

I personally would resist the generalisation of the principle of a deconstruction taking place everywhere and all the time under other names, precisely because I think that one cannot limit the list to a few obvious 'usual suspects' like Plato, Kant, Hegel, Nietzsche, Blanchot, Levinas and Bataille. I do not see any ground for refusing this status to any writer whose texts articulate important issues about origins, distance, immediacy, reflexivity, comedy, tragedy, the social, religion, ethics and so on. This is a real question: Do you see one? Graham Greene? Blake? Molière? Marguerite Duras? Let us try . . . If one fails and then has to grant that such a list cannot be limited, it follows that this movement always exists, has existed and will exist wherever there is a 'text', i.e. literature as thinking beyond language as rhetoric.

The danger is now a complete de-historicisation. For me, this generalisation (unlike Bataille's famous opposition between a restricted and generalised economy) to 'literature' or 'the literary', as being equivalent to the 'deconstructive event of language', begets the risk of weakening deconstructive approaches by bringing them uneasily close to the position taken by Paul de Man in his earlier essays (such as those in *Blindness and Insight*). Literature has always already thought the deconstructive undoing or opening Derrida started because it contains a hidden, latent, unknown knowledge about itself. No need to 'deconstruct' these texts since they already deconstruct themselves by themselves.

This 'strong' position is too strong, literally unassailable, but thus paints itself in a corner, as it collapses deconstruction with the conditions of possibility of literature as such. This, in my view, reduces the very possibility of an 'event' implied by deconstructive encounters with texts. For me, Derrida's increasing insistence on 'events' and 'eventuality' (after, say, 'Shibboleth') would correspond to a more and more marked distance from the de Manian position (even though he refused to condemn or abandon de Man at the time of the crisis, a position that I find extremely honourable).

The 'event' should surprise anything that looks like the presupposition of an essential reflexivity at work in texts always already thinking/ writing their own contradictions, paradoxes, meta-textual overcomings of metaphysical hierarchies or binaries. Part of the reason why this whole approach quickly looked 'too easy' was contained in the circularity of the argument: if the work of deconstruction has already been 'done' (thought, written, performed) by the text alone, why do it again? Thus the unnerving redundancy of early 'deconstructive readings' of this or that author that became entirely predictable or scripted after page 2 . . .

DA:

We certainly don't want to replay those arguments of the 1970s about literature as self-deconstruction (or, even more reductively, literature as self-deconstruction understood as simple self-reflexivity), and I'm not suggesting that the body of texts that goes under the name 'literature' (though without any historical consistency) should be regarded as occupying a privileged position vis-à-vis deconstruction. Certain literary works may stage deconstructive events in peculiarly compelling ways, and it's easy to start that list – Mallarmé, Joyce, Artaud, Beckett and so on; but as you point out it's not easy to stop it, one reason being that it always remains open to a reader to demonstrate, or to countersign, the deconstructive potential in a text that has hitherto seemed completely resistant to such readings. So it's not a matter of separating the literary from the non-literary or the philosophical – we would find ourselves saying exactly the same about philosophical texts.

In introducing the question of literature, I was suggesting that to the extent that all linguistic events are deconstructive events (and I'll come back to the question of what that statement could mean) they might be called 'literary' events – admittedly stretching the meaning of the word somewhat, but I believe in line with Derrida's thinking in texts such as 'The Double Session' and 'Passions'. The implication is that the cultural domain termed 'literature' by Western culture, and to some extent sealed off by it – the domain governed, as Derrida says, by the principle of *'tout dire'*[1] – in so far as it resists the dominant mode of metaphysical thought (to use a too-simple label) does so by exploiting or highlighting the deconstructive valence of language. But that resistance is also marked in a number of other texts going under a number of other names besides 'literature'.

I agree with you that it's important to insist on the distinction between de Man's particular valorisation of literature and Derrida's much more complex account of the literary and its relation to deconstruction. In *Of Grammatology*, Derrida states that 'literary writing has, almost always and almost everywhere, according to some fashions and across very diverse ages, lent itself to this *transcendent* reading, in that search for the signified which we here put in question' (160). It's hard to imagine de Man saying that.

Now to get back to the question of deconstruction as 'plus d'une langue', as 'an inner possibility which is present everywhere', as 'an event that does not await the deliberation, consciousness or organisation of a subject, nor even of modernity': if I understand you correctly, you're worried that in comments like these Derrida implies a wholly dehistoricised universal principle. But I don't think that is necessarily the case. Even if these are generalisations about any and all language, indeed about all signs, all production and reception of meaning, they don't have the status of trans-historical, context-free generalisations: because the excess, the remainder, the differing and deferring, which are the marks of deconstruction at work, manifest themselves in singular, thoroughly historical ways, and only through specific readings. I find it significant that Derrida stresses, in the interview I held with him and published in *Acts of Literature*, that 'Potentiality [he is talking about deconstructive potentiality] is not hidden in the text like an intrinsic property' and says:

> Even given that some texts appear to have a greater potential for formalization . . . works whose performativity, in some sense, appears the greatest possible in the smallest possible space, this can give rise only to evaluations inscribed in a context, to positioned readings which are themselves formalizing and performative. ('"This Strange Institution"', 46–7)

In other words, only through historically situated readings is the deconstructive potential made manifest, and not as something perpetually latent which is brought out on a particular occasion but as a chance, a possibility, a risky 'perhaps' that different historical contexts will offer in different ways.

This is why those mechanical, so-called 'deconstructive' readings you refer to are so unproductive, isn't it? Far from responding to the deconstruction-at-work in the text, as its condition of possibility and impossibility if you like, which could only happen in a singular counter-signature which respected the singularity of the text as it is encountered in a particular historical (and geographical) context, they operate as a procedure or a method that ignores context. Derrida's own readings always attempt to respect the context within which they are produced, which is part of the singularity of what he reads and what he writes.

What, then, does it mean to say that 'deconstruction takes place', *la déconstruction a lieu*? (The place of deconstruction is, after all, our topic.) This formulation reminds us that, as you say, deconstruction is an event, and an event which ruptures the fabric of those norms and conventions and habits which govern comprehension. But to say it 'takes place' also reminds us of its situatedness, a situatedness which arises from the fact that it is not a general principle of signification but an opportunity, a risky opportunity, to be seized, always in a particular time and place. And this, perhaps, gets us back to the question of the different places (as well as the different times) where the event of deconstruction, by which I mean the singular making-manifest, the performing, of the deconstructive possibility of language, has occurred.

The particular place associated with the deconstructive event in my own experience is Southampton: although I had read some of Derrida's early work in the late 1960s while a student at Cambridge it wasn't until I was a member of the English Department at the University of Southampton that my relation to literature and literary criticism was transformed by a close engagement with his writing. It happened, by one of those chains of chance events that bring a group of people together in one place, that the Southampton English Department became one of the beachheads for deconstruction in the United Kingdom in the late 1970s and early 1980s. (I use a military metaphor advisedly, since we were repeatedly told that deconstruction and other European theoretical practices were aliens whose invasion we should be resisting, not aiding.) Robert Young, Maud Ellmann, Isobel Armstrong, myself and some others (including some of the best students in the department) organised reading groups and conferences that explored deconstruction and other developments in philosophy and literary theory in France, and introduced this thinking into our teaching and writing. *The Oxford Literary Review*, partly edited in the department, was one of the vehicles for publication of translations of important French work and original articles, and the 1987 book, *Post-structuralism and the Question of History*, containing papers from the second of our 'Theory and Text' conferences held in 1983, has remained influential (it is, somewhat to our surprise, still in print). A particularly significant event for me was the International James Joyce Symposium in Dublin in 1982, as I was invited to join a group of British and French academics on a panel that deliberately challenged the reigning methodologies in Joyce criticism. That was how I met you, Jean-Michel, as well as a number of other French scholars, and it was the occasion on which I first presented a reading that was in any way 'deconstructive'.

The strong point of the work that was carried out at Southampton in that period was, I think, its diversity. Whereas in the United States, as you have said, there was a tendency to homogenise a number of very different philosophical strands into a single 'theory' (when I taught in the United States I quickly became tired of dissertation proposals in which the student planned to 'use the theories of Derrida, Kristeva, Lacan and Foucault' to undertake a particular project), our experience was of a number of different discourses that often challenged one another. Robert Young's 1981 anthology, *Untying the Text*, is the best indication of the range of the group's interests; it includes essays by, among others, Barthes, Foucault, de Man, Etienne Balibar and Pierre Macherey, Michael Riffaterre, Barbara Johnson, Jeffrey Mehlman and J. Hillis Miller, but although it relates them to one another as a series of challenges to dominant modes of literary and cultural criticism, it does not attempt to homogenise them.

Ten years later the Southampton group was scattered: Robert Young at Oxford, Maud Ellmann at Cambridge, Isobel Armstrong at Birkbeck College, London, and myself at the University of Strathclyde, Glasgow, and then Rutgers University, New Jersey. Our students were teaching in a number of other universities, and Southampton English became something different again. But I don't think it's an exaggeration to say that literary criticism in the United Kingdom went through a seismic shift in the 1980s that was in part the result of what happened in that particular place.

One more comment before I hand over to you. There is, of course, a historical dimension to our discussion itself. I don't just mean that both you and I, perhaps for largely contingent reasons, found ourselves exposed at an impressionable age to the work of Derrida and others working in close relation to him, and have, for further complicated historical reasons, taught classes on deconstruction on both sides of the Atlantic. I mean the fact that the word 'deconstruction' is dominating our discussion, rather than one of the many other words associated with Derrida's thinking that we might use, is the result of a certain history of publishing, reading, journalism, teaching and so on. And that word, whose supremacy over the other terms is something Derrida has said he finds surprising, seems to many to carry with it connotations of an active process whereby *something is done to a text*. Thus it is not uncommon to hear assertions like 'Derrida deconstructs Plato's *Phaedrus*', 'Barbara Johnson deconstructs *Billy Budd*', 'The students deconstruct whatever text you give them', and it is often not easy to convince those who utter them that they cannot be talking about *Derrida*'s deconstruction.

But what if a different word had caught on? A word like *différance*, or supplementarity, or hymeneality, or contra-band? Wouldn't it be harder to talk in terms of a reader's activity? Wouldn't we be more inclined to talk in terms of the properties of language, the processes of signification and what kinds of reading they make possible? This particular misunderstanding of Derrida's way, or ways, of reading texts would be less likely. The discussion would be skewed in a different direction, however, and we would need to insist once more that these aren't general principles but are manifested only in particular readings or particular stagings of language, always singular readings in particular times and places.

J-MR:

I'll first go back to the expression you have just used, Derek ('The students deconstruct whatever text you give them'), just because it struck me that it is not an expression I would use to describe my pedagogical practice. I am always happy to see my students actively *do* something to a text, but I would be wary of either giving them tools to deconstruct instead of simply 'reading' whatever comes to them, without any preconceived ideas. It would be equivalent, for me, to teaching a class on Freud and then to tell them to go and 'psychoanalyse' some texts. All this may be a mere question of terminology, or my exacerbated sensitivity to the programmatic weight of certain verbs. This is why I would like to be a little playful now: I note that what makes 'deconstruction' such an appealing term (which may be why it has not been supplanted and perhaps never will) is that it balances the negative and the positive meanings in its prefix (de-) and radical (construction). If we agree that the beginning and the end of the word 'decon-' and '-tion' tend to annul one another, then what do we have in the middle? Just *struc*, or *ce truc*, in other words a little 'thingummy' or 'thingumajig', whatever translation you find adequate for the idiomatic French word of 'truc' (suggesting also 'trick' and 'knack'). In French, you might say, with some exasperation: *La déconstruction, mais qu'est-ce que c'est que c' truc?* Here I wish to suggest the most colloquial form of ontological wonder, as it were a low Parisian version of Plato's question, 'What is this, what is being?' (*ti to on, ti to esti?*). It is therefore not a coincidence that deconstruction began not just as a variation on French or Heideggerian phenomenology, as I said earlier, but also more precisely as a phenomenological interrogation addressed to the then dominant discourse of French structuralism; these questions aimed at releasing the playful 'trick' hidden behind an all too serious or pseudo-scientific 'structure'.

Which is not to say that Derrida is a happy trickster, a view that Rorty tried to promote for a while. Rorty was trying to locate the *non-place* of deconstruction as a *bon-lieu* (discharge, excuse). Not having any recognisable place, deconstruction was condemned to be irresponsible. I am indeed attempting to do something different, the opposite perhaps; and this is why, if I wonder what 'place' deconstruction can inhabit, I have first to look at the area of Paris I live in when I am in France: right above 'Place des Abbesses'. I like the name as it is a word that means the same thing and is spelled in the same way in English and French, whereas the English pronunciation makes it sound very much like 'abysses'. Deconstruction is in love with abysses, its foundations are 'abysmal' in Heidegger's sense, that is it inhabits an *Ungrund*. But then thinking of the metro itinerary I took to reach this place, leaving from Place des Abbesses en route to the Charles V section of Paris VII university in the Marais, I had to change at Place de la Concorde. Another great French square, with the phallic obelisk and the traffic jams, the echoes of the national celebrations invented by the French Revolution, this looked like a better, a more positive choice. But no, deconstruction will never extol 'concorde', especially when the word calls up the name of a now scrapped Franco-British supersonic plane bound for New York. In fact, if there was a real place for deconstruction, it would be near Paris, in the village where Maurice Blanchot once lived: Place des Pensées. Jacques whispers to me that this square commemorates Pascal's masterpiece and not the glories of suburban horticulture. After all, it was Pascal who had written: *Se moquer de la philosophie, c'est vraiment philosopher* ('To deride philosophy, that is really to philosophise').

What I am suggesting is that the geographical chance allows us to conclude that the 'place' of deconstruction is to leave a new place for thinking. This thinking owes a lot to Heidegger, who was always ready to shift from *Denken* to *Danken* (to thank) but also to *Dichten* (to write poetry). But we cannot just be thankful for 'being here' (*Da-Sein*)! By taking up the challenge offered by these semantic glides in the high

German of 'thinking', a language that replaces the Greek of olden times according to Heidegger, deconstruction rewrites them in more than one vernacular, and yet no vernacular is assured of leading us to an absolute space for thinking. This is not just being ungrateful to Being. In poetry as in philosophy, in the end, *rien n'aura eu lieu que le lieu*, nothing will have taken place but the place, but having a real place to work from, a new place opening to new vistas: that can change everything.

DA:

I recognise the deconstructive signature in your words, and my wish is to countersign it as a final contribution to this dialogue. To countersign a deconstructive signature (a signature is, of course, an event marking a particular place) is to take full account of the *here*, the *ici*, the *hic*. The *hic* is also a *hiccup* – as we say, 'there was a hiccup in the proceedings as one of the microphones failed to work'. Deconstruction is the *hic* as hiccup. It is also, Derrida has said, a *fête*, a party: I would like to add that in English we talk about a *party-line* and a *party-wall*, where sharing occurs, where one telephone line, one wall, serves two people or two families, where that which connects also divides and vice versa. Deconstruction doesn't simply *take place*; it takes 'place' away from place. Hence the inadequacy of a purely 'objective' sociological analysis of the place, and places, of deconstruction: not that they are invalid, but that they leave many questions still in place . . .

Note

1. See Derrida, '"This Strange Institution"', p. 36.

Bibliography

Adorno, Theodor W. *The Jargon of Authenticity*, trans. Knut Tarnowski and Frederic Will. Evanston, IL: Northwestern University Press, 1973.

———. 'Words from Abroad', in *Notes to Literature*, vol. 1, ed. Rolf Tiedemann, trans. Shierry Weber Nicholsen. New York: Columbia University Press, pp. 185–99.

Agamben, Giorgio. 'Friendship', *Contretemps* 5 (December, 2004): 2–7.

———. *Stanzas: Word and Phantasm in Western Culture*, trans. Ronald L. Martinez. Minneapolis, MN: University of Minnesota Press, 1993.

Anidjar, Gil. 'Hosting', in *Derrida and Religion: Other Testaments*, eds Yvonne Sherwood and Kevin Hart. New York: Routledge, 2005, pp. 63–72.

Attridge, Derek. 'The Art of the Impossible?', in *The Politics of Deconstruction: Jacques Derrida and the Other of Philosophy*, ed. Martin McQuillan. London: Pluto Press, 2007.

———. 'Derrida and the Questioning of Literature', Introduction to Derrida, *Acts of Literature*, pp. 1–29.

———. *J. M. Coetzee and the Ethics of Reading: Literature in the Event*. Chicago: University of Chicago Press, 2004.

———. *Joyce Effects: On Language, Theory, and History*. Cambridge: Cambridge University Press, 2000.

———. 'Modernist Form and the Demands of Politics: Otherness in Coetzee's *Age of Iron*', *Aesthetics and Ideology*, ed. George Levine. New Brunswick, NJ: Rutgers University Press, 1994, pp. 243–63.

———. *Peculiar Language: Literature as Difference from the Renaissance to James Joyce* (1988), 2nd edn. London: Routledge, 2004.

———. Review of Martin Hägglund, *Radical Atheism: Derrida and the Time of Life*. *Derrida Today*, 2 (2009): 271–81.

———. *The Singularity of Literature*. London: Routledge, 2004.

———. 'The Singular Events of Literature', *British Journal of Aesthetics*, 50 (2010): 81–4.

Attridge, Derek, Geoff Bennington and Robert Young (eds). *Post-structuralism and the Question of History*. Cambridge: Cambridge University Press, 1987.

Banfield, Ann. *Unspeakable Sentences: Narration and Representation in the Language of Fiction*. Boston: Routledge & Kegan Paul, 1982.

Barthes, Roland. *Camera Lucida: Reflections on Photography*, trans. Richard Howard. New York: Hill & Wang, 1981.

———. *Criticism and Truth*, trans. and ed. Katrine Pilcher Keuneman. London: Athlone Press, 1987.

———. *The Empire of Signs*, trans. Richard Howard. New York: Hill & Wang, 1982.

———. 'The Grain of the Voice', in *The Responsibility of Forms*, pp. 267–77.

———. 'The Photographic Message', in *The Responsibility of Forms*, pp. 3–20.

———. *The Pleasure of the Text*, trans. Richard Miller. New York: Hill & Wang, 1975.

———. 'The Reality Effect', in *The Rustle of Language*, trans. Richard Howard. Oxford: Blackwell, 1986, pp. 141–8.

———. *The Responsibility of Forms: Critical Essays on Music, Art, and Representation*, trans. Richard Howard. New York: Hill & Wang, 1985.

———. *Roland Barthes by Roland Barthes*, trans. Richard Howard. New York: Hill & Wang, 1977.

———. 'The Third Meaning: Research Notes on Several Eisenstein Stills', in *The Responsibility of Forms*, pp. 41–62.

Beardsworth, Richard. *Derrida and the Political*. London: Routledge, 1996.

Beckett, Samuel. *Endgame. The Complete Dramatic Works*. London: Faber & Faber, 1986, pp. 89–134.

Bennington, Geoffrey. 'Deconstruction and Ethics', in *Interrupting Derrida*. London: Routledge, 2000, pp. 34–46.

Bernasconi, Robert. 'Justice without Ethics?', *PLI: Warwick Journal of Philosophy*, 6 (1997): 58–69.

Bernasconi, Robert and David Wood (eds). *The Provocation of Levinas: Rethinking the Other*. London: Routledge, 1988.

Bhabha, Homi K. *The Location of Culture*. London: Routledge, 1994.

Brown, Andrew. *Roland Barthes: The Figures of Writing*. Oxford: Oxford University Press, 1992.

Caputo, John D. *Against Ethics: Contributions to a Poetics of Obligation with Constant Reference to Deconstruction*. Bloomington, IN: Indiana University Press, 1993.

———. 'Instants, Secrets, and Singularities: Dealing Death in Kierkegaard and Derrida', in *Kierkegaard in Post/Modernity*, eds Martin J. Matustik and Merold Westphal. Bloomington, IN: Indiana University Press, 1995, pp. 216–38.

———. *The Prayers and Tears of Jacques Derrida: Religion without Religion*. Bloomington, IN: Indiana University Press, 1997.

Caputo, John D. and Jacques Derrida. *Deconstruction in a Nutshell*. New York: Fordham University Press, 1997.

Caygill, Howard. *Levinas and the Political*. London: Routledge, 2002.

Cixous, Hélène and Jacques Derrida. 'Bâtons rompus', in *Derrida d'ici, Derrida de là*, eds Thomas Dutoit and Philippe Romanski. Paris: Galilée, 2009, pp. 177–221.

Clark, Timothy. *The Poetics of Singularity: The Counter-Culturalist Turn in Heidegger, Derrida, Blanchot and the Later Gadamer*. Edinburgh: Edinburgh University Press, 2005.

———. 'Roland Barthes, Dead and Alive', *Oxford Literary Review*, 6.1 (1983): 7–107.

Coetzee, J. M. *Age of Iron.* London: Secker & Warburg, 1990.
———. *Boyhood: Scenes from Provincial Life.* London: Secker & Warburg, 1997.
———. 'Confession and Double Thoughts: Tolstoy, Rousseau, Dostoevsky', in *Doubling the Point*, pp. 251–93.
———. *Disgrace.* London: Secker & Warburg, 1999.
———. *Doubling the Point: Essays and Interviews*, ed. David Attwell. Cambridge: Harvard University Press, 1992.
———. *Dusklands* (1974). London: Secker & Warburg, 1982.
———. *Foe.* London: Secker & Warburg, 1986.
———. *The Lives of Animals.* London: Secker & Warburg, 1999.
———. *The Master of Petersburg.* London: Secker & Warburg, 1994.
———. 'Samuel Beckett and the Temptations of Style', in *Doubling the Point*, pp. 43–9.
———. *Summertime: Scenes from Provincial Life.* London: Secker & Warburg, 2009.
———. *Youth.* London: Secker & Warburg, 2002.
Cohen, Tom. *Jacques Derrida and the Humanities: A Critical Reader.* Cambridge: Cambridge University Press, 2001.
Colebrook, Claire. 'Literature', in *Understanding Derrida*, eds Jack Reynolds and Jonathan Roffe. London: Continuum, 2004, pp. 75–83.
Cornell, Drucilla, Michel Rosenfeld and David Gray Carlson. *Deconstruction and the Possibility of Justice.* New York: Routledge, 1992.
Critchley, Simon. *The Ethics of Deconstruction: Derrida and Levinas.* Oxford: Blackwell, 1992.
———. *Ethics – Politics – Subjectivity.* London: Verso, 1999.
———. *Very Little . . . Almost Nothing: Death, Philosophy, Literature.* London: Routledge, 1997.
Culler, Jonathan. 'Derrida and the Singularity of Literature', *Cardozo Law Review*, 27 (2005): 869–75.
———. *Literary Theory: A Very Short Introduction.* Oxford: Oxford University Press, 1997.
———. *On Deconstruction: Theory and Criticism after Structuralism.* Ithaca, NY: Cornell University Press, 1982.
———. *Structuralist Poetics: Structuralism, Linguistics and the Study of Literature.* London: Routledge & Kegan Paul, 1975.
Culler, Jonathan and Kevin Lamb (eds). *Just Being Difficult? Academic Writing in the Public Arena.* Stanford, CA: Stanford University Press, 2003.
Deconstruction and the Possibility of Justice. Special issue of *Cardozo Law Review* 11.5–6 (1990).
de Man, Paul. *Allegories of Reading: Figural Language in Rousseau, Nietzsche, Rilke and Proust.* New Haven, CT: Yale University Press, 1979.
———. 'Autobiography as De-Facement', in *The Rhetoric of Romanticism.* New York: Columbia University Press, pp. 67–81.
———. *Blindness and Insight: Essays in the Rhetoric of Contemporary Criticism*, 2nd edn. Minneapolis, MN: University of Minnesota Press, 1983.
———. 'Heidegger's Exegeses of Hölderlin', in *Blindness and Insight*, pp. 246–66.

de Vries, Hent. *Religion and Violence: Philosophical Perspectives from Kant to Derrida*. Baltimore, MD: Johns Hopkins University Press, 2002.

Derrida, Jacques. *Acts of Literature*, ed. Derek Attridge. New York: Routledge, 1992.

———. *Adieu: à Emmanuel Lévinas*. Paris: Galilée, 1997.

———. *Adieu: to Emmanuel Levinas*, trans. Pascale-Anne Brault and Michael Naas. Stanford, CA: Stanford University Press, 1999.

———. 'Afterword: Toward an Ethic of Discussion', in *Limited Inc*, pp. 111–60.

———. *The Animal That Therefore I Am*, ed. Marie-Louise Mallet, trans. David Wills. New York: Fordham University Press, 2008.

———. 'Aphorism Countertime', in *Acts of Literature*, pp. 414–33.

———. 'At This Very Moment in This Work Here I Am', in *Psyche*, vol. 1, pp. 143–90.

———. 'A Word of Welcome', in *Adieu*, pp. 15–123.

———. *The Beast and the Sovereign*, The Seminars of Jacques Derrida, vol. 1, trans. Geoffrey Bennington. Chicago: University of Chicago Press, 2009.

———. 'Before the Law', in *Acts of Literature*, pp. 181–220.

———. 'Circumfession', in *Jacques Derrida*, by Geoffrey Bennington and Jacques Derrida, trans. Geoffrey Bennington. Chicago: University of Chicago Press, 1993, pp. 3–315.

———. 'The Deaths of Roland Barthes', in *Psyche*, vol. 1, pp. 264–98.

———. 'Deconstruction and the Other', in Kearney, *States of Mind*, pp. 156–76.

———. 'Deconstructions: The Im-possible', in *French Theory in America*, eds Sylvère Lotringer and Sande Cohen. New York: Routledge, 2001, pp. 13–31.

———. 'Derrida avec Levinas: "Entre lui et moi dans l'affection et la confiance partagée"', Interview with Alain David in *Le Magazine Littéraire*, 419 (April 2003): 30–4.

———. *Donner la mort*. Paris: Galilée, 1999.

———. 'The Double Session', in *Dissemination*, trans. Barbara Johnson. Chicago: University of Chicago Press, 1981, pp. 173–285.

———. '"Eating Well", or the Calculation of the Subject: An Interview with Jacques Derrida', with Jean-Luc Nancy, in *Who Comes after the Subject?*, eds Eduardo Cadava, Peter Connor and Jean-Luc Nancy. New York: Routledge, 1991, pp. 96–119.

———. 'Force of Law: The "Mystical Foundation of Authority"', in Cornell, Rosenfeld and Carson (eds), *Deconstruction and the Possibility of Justice*, pp. 3–67.

———. *The Gift of Death (Second Edition) & Literature in Secret*, trans. David Wills. Chicago: University of Chicago Press, 2008.

———. *Given Time: 1. Counterfeit Money*, trans. Peggy Kamuf. Chicago: University of Chicago Press, 1992.

———. *Glas*. Paris: Galilée, 1974.

———. *Glas*, trans. John P. Leavey, Jr and Richard Rand. Lincoln, NE: University of Nebraska Press, 1986.

———. 'Hostipitality', in *Acts of Religion* by Jacques Derrida, ed. Gil Anidjar. New York: Routledge, 2002, pp. 356–420.

———. 'An Idea of Flaubert: "Plato's Letter"', *MLN*, 99 (1984): 748–68.

———. 'I Have a Taste for the Secret', in *A Taste for the Secret* by Jacques Derrida and Maurizio Ferraris, trans. Giacomo Donis. Cambridge: Polity, 2001, pp. 1–92.

———. '*Ja*, or the *faux-bond* II', in *Points* . . ., pp. 30–77.

———. 'The Law of Genre', *Acts of Literature*, pp. 221–52.

———. 'Letter to a Japanese Friend', in *Psyche*, vol. 2, pp. 1–6.

———. *Limited Inc*, ed. Gerald Graff, trans. Samuel Weber and Jeffrey Mehlman. Evanston, IL: Northwestern University Press, 1988.

———. 'Limited Inc a b c . . .', in *Limited Inc*, pp. 29–107.

———. 'Literature in Secret: An Impossible Filiation', *The Gift of Death*, pp. 117–58.

———. 'Mallarmé', in *Acts of Literature*, pp. 110–26.

———. *Memoirs of the Blind: The Self-Portrait and Other Ruins*, trans. Pascale-Anne Brault and Michael Naas. Chicago: University of Chicago Press, 1993.

———. *Monolingualism of the Other; or, The Prosthesis of Origin*, trans. Patrick Mensah. Stanford, CA: Stanford University Press.

———. *Of Grammatology*, trans. Gayatri Chakravorty Spivak. Baltimore, MD: Johns Hopkins University Press, 1976.

———. *Of Spirit: Heidegger and the Question*, trans. Geoffrey Bennington and Rachel Bowlby. Chicago: University of Chicago Press, 1989.

———. *On Cosmopolitanism and Forgiveness*, trans. Mark Dooley and Michael Hughes. London: Routledge, 2001.

———. 'On Cosmopolitanism', in *On Cosmopolitanism and Forgiveness*, pp. 1–24.

———. *On the Name*, ed. Thomas Dutoit, trans. David Wood and John P. Leavey. Stanford, CA: Stanford University Press, 1995.

———. *On Touching – Jean-Luc Nancy*, trans. Christine Irizarry. Stanford, CA: Stanford University Press, 2005.

———. *The Other Heading: Reflections on Today's Europe*, trans. Pascale-Anne Brault and Michael B. Naas. Bloomington, IN: Indiana University Press, 1992.

———. 'Passions: "An Oblique Offering"', in *On the Name*, pp. 3–34.

———. *Points* . . .: *Interviews 1974–94*, ed. Elisabeth Weber, trans. Peggy Kamuf. Stanford, CA: Stanford University Press, 1995.

———. *Politics of Friendship*, trans. George Collins. London: Verso, 1997.

———. *Positions*, trans. Alan Bass. Chicago: University of Chicago Press, 1981.

———. 'Psyche: Invention of the Other', in *Acts of Literature*, pp. 310–43.

———. *Psyche: Inventions of the Other*, 2 vols, eds Peggy Kamuf and Elizabeth Rottenberg. Stanford, CA: Stanford University Press, 2007–8.

———. 'Remarks on Deconstruction and Pragmatism', in *Deconstruction and Pragmatism*, ed. Chantal Mouffe. London: Routledge, pp. 77–88.

———. *Rogues: Two Essays on Reason*. Stanford, CA: Stanford University Press, 2005.

———. 'Sauf le nom (Post-Scriptum)', in *On the Name*, pp. 35–88.

———. 'Shibboleth: For Paul Celan', in *Sovereignties in Question* by Jacques Derrida, eds Thomas Dutoit and Outi Pasanen. New York: Fordham University Press. 2005, pp. 1–64.

————. 'Signature Event Context', in *Margins of Philosophy*. Chicago: University of Chicago Press, pp. 307–30.

————. 'Some Questions and Responses', in *The Linguistics of Writing: Arguments between Language and Literature*, eds Nigel Fabb et al. Manchester: Manchester University Press, 1987, pp. 252–64.

————. 'Some Statements and Truisms about Neologisms, Newisms, Postisms, Parasitisms, and Other Small Seismisms', in *The States of 'Theory': History, Art, and Critical Discourse*, ed. David Carroll. New York: Columbia University Press, 1990, pp. 63–94.

————. *Specters of Marx: The State of the Debt, the Work of Mourning, & the New International*, trans. Peggy Kamuf. New York: Routledge, 1994.

————. *Speech and Phenomena and Other Essays on Husserl's Theory of Signs*, trans. David B. Allison. Evanston, IL: Northwestern University Press, 1973.

————. 'Structure, Sign and Play in the Discourse of the Human Sciences', in Macksey and Donato (eds), *The Structuralist Controversy*, pp. 247–65.

————. '"This Strange Institution Called Literature": An Interview' with Derek Attridge, in *Acts of Literature*, pp. 33–75.

————. 'The Time of a Thesis: Punctuations', in *Philosophy in France Today*, ed. Alan Montefiore. Cambridge: Cambridge University Press, 1983, pp. 34–50.

————. 'Des Tours de Babel', in *Psyche*, vol. 1, pp. 191–225.

————. 'Ulysses Gramophone: Hear Say Yes in Joyce', in *Acts of Literature*, pp. 256–309.

————. 'The University without Condition', in *Without Alibi* by Jacques Derrida, ed. Peggy Kamuf. Stanford, CA: Stanford University Press, 2002, pp. 202–37.

————. 'Violence and Metaphysics: An Essay on the Thought of Emmanuel Levinas', *Writing and Difference*, trans. Alan Bass. Chicago: University of Chicago Press, 1978, pp. 79–153.

————. 'White Mythology', in *Margins – of Philosophy*, trans. Alan Bass. Chicago: University of Chicago Press, 1982.

————. *The Work of Mourning*, trans. Pascal-Anne Brault and Michael Naas. Chicago: University of Chicago Press, 2001.

Derrida, Jacques and Giovanna Borradori. 'Autoimmunity: Real and Symbolic Suicides: A Dialogue with Jacques Derrida', in *Philosophy in a Time of Terror: Dialogues with Jürgen Habermas and Jacques Derrida*. Chicago: University of Chicago Press, 2003, pp. 85–136.

Derrida, Jacques and John D. Caputo. *Deconstruction in a Nutshell*. New York: Fordham University Press, 1997.

Derrida, Jacques and Anne Dufourmantelle. *Of Hospitality*, trans. Rachel Bowlby. Stanford, CA: Stanford University Press, 2000.

Derrida, Jacques and Maurizio Ferraris. *A Taste for the Secret*, eds Giacomo Donis and David Webb, trans. Giacomo Donis. Cambridge: Polity, 2001.

Derrida, Jacques and Pierre-Jean Labarrière. *Altérités*. Paris: Osiris, 1986.

Derrida, Jacques and Mustapha Tlili (eds). *For Nelson Mandela*. New York: Henry Holt, 1987.

Derrida, Jacques and Gianni Vattimo (eds). *Religion*. Cambridge: Polity Press, 1998.

Dickinson, Emily. *Poems*, ed. R. W. Franklin. Cambridge, MA: Harvard University Press, 1999.

Douzinas, Costas (ed.). *Adieu Derrida*. London: Palgrave Macmillan, 2007.

Dutoit, Thomas and Philippe Romanski (eds). *Derrida d'ici, Derrida de là*. Paris: Galilée, 2009.

Eagleton, Terry. *The Ideology of the Aesthetic*. Oxford: Blackwell, 1990.

Edelman, Lee. *Homographesis*. New York: Routledge, 1994.

Esposito, Roberto. *Bíos: Biopolitics and Philosophy*, trans. Timothy Campbell. Minneapolis, MN: University of Minnesota Press, 2008.

Fowler, H. W. *A Dictionary of Modern English Usage*, 2nd edn, rev. Ernest Gowers. London: Oxford University Press, 1965.

Gallop, Jane. 'Reading Derrida's Adieu', *Differences: A Journal of Feminist Cultural Studies*, 16.3 (Fall 2005): 16–26.

Gasché, Rodolphe. 'A Relation Called "Literary"', in *Of Minimal Things: Studies on the Notion of Relation*. Stanford, CA: Stanford University Press, 1999, pp. 285–308.

———. 'On Responding Responsibly', in *Inventions of Difference: On Jacques Derrida*. Cambridge, MA: Harvard University Press, 1994, pp. 227–50.

———. *The Tain of the Mirror: Derrida and the Philosophy of Reflection*. Cambridge, MA: Harvard University Press, 1986.

Genette, Gérard. 'Fictional Narrative, Factual Narrative', *Poetics Today*, 11 (1990): 755–74.

Hägglund, Martin. 'The Arche-Materiality of Time: Deconstruction, Speculative Materialism, and Radical Atheism', *Theory after 'Theory'*, eds Jane Elliott and Derek Attridge. London: Routledge, forthcoming.

———. *Radical Atheism: Derrida and the Time of Life*. Stanford, CA: Stanford University Press, 2008.

Hallward, Peter. *Absolutely Postcolonial: Writing between the Singular and the Specific*. Manchester: Manchester University Press, 2001.

Harrison, Nicholas. *Postcolonial Criticism: History, Theory and the Work of Fiction*. Cambridge: Polity, 2003.

Hartman, Geoffrey. *Saving the Text: Literature/Derrida/Philosophy*. Baltimore, MD: Johns Hopkins University Press, 1981.

Haverkamp, Anselm. 'The Memory of Pictures: Roland Barthes and Augustine on Photography', *Comparative Literature*, 45 (1993): 258–79.

Heidegger, Martin. 'Letter on Humanism', in *Basic Writings*, ed. David Farrell Krell. New York: Harper & Row, 1977, pp. 189–242.

Heath, Stephen, Colin MacCabe and Christopher Prendergast. *Signs of the Times: Introductory Readings in Textual Semiotics*. Cambridge: Granta, 1971.

Hill, Leslie. *Radical Indecision: Barthes, Blanchot, Derrida and the Future of Criticism*. Notre Dame, IN: University of Notre Dame Press, 2009.

Johnson, Barbara. 'Melville's Fist: The Execution of *Billy Budd*', in *The Critical Difference: Essays in the Contemporary Rhetoric of Reading*. Baltimore, MD: Johns Hopkins University Press, 1980, pp. 79–109.

Johnson, David E. 'As If the Time Were Now: Deconstructing Agamben', in *Late Derrida*, Special Issue of *South Atlantic Quarterly*, ed. Ian Balfour, 106 (2007): 265–90.

Kamuf, Peggy. *A Derrida Reader: Between the Blinds*. New York: Columbia University Press, 1991)

———. '"Fiction" and the Experience of the Other', in *Book of Addresses*. Stanford, CA: Stanford University Press, 2005, pp. 135–53.

Kant, Immanuel. *The Conflict of the Faculties*, trans. Mary J. Gregor. New York: Abaris Books, 1979.

———. *Religion within the Limits of Reason Alone*, trans. Theodore M. Greene and Hoyt H. Hudson. New York: Harper & Row, 1960.

Kearney, Richard. *States of Mind: Dialogues with Contemporary Continental Thinkers*. New York: New York University Press, 1995.

Kierkegaard, Søren. *Fear and Trembling; Repetition*, trans. Howard V. Hong and Edna H. Hong. Princeton, NJ: Princeton University Press, 1983.

Knight, Diana. 'Roland Barthes, or The Woman without a Shadow', in *Writing the Image after Roland Barthes*, ed. Jean-Michel Rabaté. Philadelphia: University of Pennsylvania Press, 1997, pp. 132–43.

Kronick, Joseph G. *Derrida and the Future of Literature*. Albany, NY: SUNY Press, 1999.

Laclau, Ernesto. 'Is Radical Atheism a Good Name for Deconstruction?', *Diacritics*, 38.1–2 (2008): 180–9.

Lamarque, Peter. *The Philosophy of Literature*. Malden: Blackwell, 2009.

Leitch, Vincent B. *American Literary Criticism from the 30s to the 80s*. New York: Columbia University Press, 1988.

Levinas, Emmanuel. *Basic Philosophical Writings*, eds Adriaan T. Peperzak, Simon Critchley and Robert Bernasconi. Bloomington, IN: Indiana University Press, 1996.

———. *Entre Nous: Thinking-of-the-Other*, trans. Michael B. Smith and Barbara Harshav. New York: Columbia University Press, 1998.

———. 'Ethics of the Infinite', in Kearney, *States of Mind*, pp. 177–99.

———. *Humanism of the Other*, trans. Nidra Poller. Urbana, IL: University of Illinois Press, 2003.

———. *Is It Righteous to Be? Interviews with Emmanuel Levinas*, ed. Jill Robbins. Stanford, CA: Stanford University Press, 2001.

———. *Of God Who Comes to Mind*, trans. Bettina Bergo. Stanford, CA: Stanford University Press, 1998.

———. *Otherwise than Being, or Beyond Essence* (1981), trans. Alphonso Lingis. Pittsburgh: Duquesne University Press, 1998.

———. 'The Paradox of Morality: An Interview with Emmanuel Levinas' with Tamra Wright, Peter Hughes, Alison Ainley, in Bernasconi and Wood (eds), *The Provocation of Levinas*, pp. 168–80.

———. *Proper Names*, trans. Michael B. Smith. Stanford, CA: Stanford University Press, 1996.

———. *Totalité et infini: Essai sur l'extériorité* (1961). Paris: Livre de Poche, 1996.

———. *Totality and Infinity: An Essay on Exteriority*, trans. Alphonso Lingis. Pittsburgh: Duquesne University Press, 1969.

Living On: Of Martin Hägglund, Special Issue, *CR: The New Centennial Review*, 9.1 (2009).

Llewelyn, John. 'Levinas, Derrida and Others *vis-à-vis*', in Bernasconi and Wood (eds), *The Provocation of Levinas*, pp. 136–55.

Lyotard, Jean-François. *The Differend: Phrases in Dispute*, trans. Georges Van Den Abbeele. Minneapolis, MN: University of Minnesota Press, 1988.

———. *Heidegger and 'the jews'*, trans. Andreas Michel and Mark Roberts. Minneapolis, MN: University of Minnesota Press, 1990.

Macksey, Richard and Eugenio Donato (eds). *The Structuralist Controversy: The Languages of Criticism and the Sciences of Man* (1970). Baltimore, MD: Johns Hopkins University Press, 1972.

Meillassoux, Quentin. *After Finitude: An Essay on the Necessity of Contingency*, trans. Ray Brassier. London: Continuum, 2008.

Michaud, Ginette. 'Literature in Secret: Crossing Derrida and Blanchot', *Angelaki*, 72.2 (2002): 69–90.

Miller, D. A. *Bringing Out Roland Barthes*. Berkeley, CA: University of California Press, 1992.

Miller, J. Hillis. 'Ariachne's Broken Woof', *Georgia Review*, 31 (1977): 44–60.

———. 'The Critic as Host', *Deconstruction and Criticism*, by Harold Bloom et al. New York: Seabury Press, 1979.

———. 'Deconstruction and a Poem', in Royle (ed.), *Deconstructions*, pp. 171–86.

———. 'Derrida and Literature', in Cohen (ed.), *Derrida and the Humanities*, pp. 58–81.

———. *The Ethics of Reading: Kant, De Man, Eliot, Trollope, James, and Benjamin*. New York: Columbia University Press, 1987.

———. 'Literature and Scripture: An Impossible Filiation', in *Exits*, ed. Stefan Helgesson. Amsterdam: Rodopi, forthcoming.

———. 'A Profession of Faith', in *The J. Hillis Miller Reader*, ed. Julian Wolfreys. Edinburgh: Edinburgh University Press, 2005, pp. 282–94.

———. *Speech Acts in Literature*. Stanford, CA: Stanford University Press, 2001.

———. 'Zero', in *Glossalalia: An Alphabet of Critical Keywords*, eds Julian Wolfreys and Harun Karim Thomas. Edinburgh: Edinburgh University Press, 2003, pp. 369–89.

Moriarty, Michael. *Roland Barthes*. Stanford, CA: Stanford University Press, 1991.

Naas, Michael. *Taking on the Tradition: Jacques Derrida and the Legacies of Deconstruction*. Stanford, CA: Stanford University Press, 2003.

Norris, Christopher. 'Deconstruction, Post-Modernism and the Visual Arts', in *What Is Deconstruction?* by Christopher Norris and Andrew Benjamin. London: Academy Editions, 1988.

———. *The Deconstructive Turn: Essays in the Rhetoric of Philosophy*. London: Methuen, 1983.

———. *Derrida*. Cambridge, MA: Harvard University Press, 1987.

Ofrat, Gideon. *The Jewish Derrida*, trans. Peretz Kidron. Syracuse, NY: Syracuse University Press, 2001.

On the Necessity of Violence for Any Possibility of Justice, Special Issue of *Cardozo Law Review*, 13.4 (1991): 1081–349.

Orwell, George. 'Politics and the English Language', in *The Collected Essays, Journalism and Letters of George Orwell*, Vol. 4, *In Front of Your Nose: 1945–1950*, eds Sonia Orwell and Ian Angus. New York: Harcourt Brace Jovanovich, 1968, pp. 127–40.

Owen, Wilfred. *Collected Poems*, ed. C. Day Lewis. London: Chatto & Windus, 1963.

Oxford English Dictionary, 2nd edn, online.

Parry, Benita. *Postcolonial Studies: A Materialist Critique*. London: Routledge, 2004.

———. 'Problems in Current Theories of Colonial Discourse', *Oxford Literary Review*, 9 (1987): 27–58.

Quiller-Couch, Sir Arthur. 'Interlude: On Jargon'', *On the Art of Writing*. Cambridge: Cambridge University Press, 1916, pp. 83–103.

Rabaté, Jean-Michel and Michael Wenzel (eds). *L'Éthique du don: Jacques Derrida et la pensée du don*. Paris: Métailié-Transition, 1992.

Robbins, Jill. 'Visage, Figure: Speech and Murder in Levinas's *Totality and Infinity*', in *Critical Encounters: Reference and Responsibility in Deconstructive Writing*, eds Cathy Caruth and Deborah Esch. New Brunswick, NJ: Rutgers University Press, 1995, pp. 275–98.

Royle, Nicholas. *After Derrida*. Manchester: Manchester University Press, 1995.

———. *In Memory of Jacques Derrida*. Edinburgh: Edinburgh University Press, 2009.

———. *Jacques Derrida*. London: Routledge, 2003.

——— (ed.). *Deconstructions: A User's Guide*. Basingstoke: Palgrave, 2000.

Said, Edward W. *Beginnings: Intention and Method*. New York: Basic Books, 1975.

———. *Orientalism*. New York: Random House, 1978.

Searle, John. 'The Logical Status of Fictional Discourse', in *Expression and Meaning: Studies in the Theory of Speech Acts*. Cambridge: Cambridge University Press, 1979, pp. 58–75.

Sidney, Sir Philip. *An Apology for Poetry*, ed. Geoffrey Shepherd. Manchester: Manchester University Press, 1973.

Singy, Pascal. 'Le vocabulaire médical: jargon ou argot?', *La Linguistique*, 22 (1986): 63–74.

Spivak, Gayatri Chakravorty. *A Critique of Postcolonial Reason: Toward a History of the Vanishing Present*. Cambridge, MA: Harvard University Press, 1999.

———. *In Other Worlds: Essays in Cultural Politics*. New York: Methuen, 1987.

———. *Other Asias*. Malden: Blackwell, 2008.

———. *Outside in the Teaching Machine*. London: Routledge, 1993.

Staten, Henry. *Wittgenstein and Derrida*. Lincoln, NE: University of Nebraska Press, 1984.

Syrotinski, Michael. *Deconstruction and the Postcolonial: At the Limits of Theory*. Liverpool: Liverpool University Press, 2007.

Ulmer, Gregory L. *Applied Grammatology: Post(e)-Pedagogy from Jacques Derrida to Joseph Beuys*. Baltimore, MD: Johns Hopkins University Press, 1985.

Vološinov, V. N. *Marxism and the Philosophy of Language*, trans. Ladislav Matejka and I. R. Titunik. Cambridge, MA: Harvard University Press, 1986.

Williams, Raymond. *Keywords: A Vocabulary of Culture and Society*, rev. edn. London: Fontana, 1983.

Wood, David. 'Much Obliged', *Philosophy Today*, 41.1 (Spring 1997): 135–40.

World Picture, Special Issue: 'Jargon', 1 (Spring 2008). Online at: http://www. worldpicture.com.

Wortham, Simon Morgan. 'Law of Friendship: Agamben and Derrida', *New Formations*, 62 (2007): 89–105.

Young, Robert J. C. *Colonial Desire: Hybridity in Theory, Culture and Race.* London: Routledge, 1995.

———. *Postcolonialism: An Historical Introduction.* Oxford: Blackwell, 2001.

———. *Postcolonialism: A Very Short Introduction.* Oxford: Oxford University Press, 2003.

———. *White Mythologies: Writing History and the West.* London: Routledge, 1990.

——— (ed.). *Untying the Text: A Post-Structuralist Reader.* London: Routledge & Kegan Paul, 1981.

Index

Titles of works originally in languages other than English are given in their English versions

Abraham and Isaac, 46, 47–9, 56–77
Adorno, Theodor W., 80–1, 87n
Agamben, Giorgio, 9, 10–11, 37, 49n, 140
Anidjar, Gil, 48
arche-writing, 82, 139, 142
Aristotle, 16
Armstrong, Isobel, 3, 158–9
Arnold, Matthew, 48
arrivant, 43
Artaud, Antonin, 5, 16, 22
Augustine, St, 103
Austin, J. L., 12
autoimmunity, 139–40, 142

Badiou, Alain, 9, 10, 37, 49n
Bakhtin, Mikhail, 85, 87n
Banfield, Ann, 95n
Barthes, Roland, 2, 10, 13, 23, 33n, 36, 37, 85, 98, 135, 137n
  Camera Lucida, 13, 117–30
  Criticism and Truth, 85, 86–7
  Empire of Signs, The, 118
  'Grain of the Voice, The', 129n
  Pleasure of the Text, The, 118
  'Reality Effect, The', 130
  Roland Barthes by Roland Barthes, 79, 127
  'Third Meaning, The', 117–30
Bataille, Georges, 22, 23, 152, 155
Baudelaire, Charles, 5, 16, 33n, 44–5
Beardsworth, Richard, 115n

Beaufret, Jean, 152
Beckett, Samuel, 23, 136–7, 137n
Bennington, Geoffrey, 38, 101, 115n
Bernasconi, Robert, 115n
Bhabha, Homi, 39–40, 41
Birkbeck College, 159
Bismarck, Otto von, 59
Blanchot, Maurice, 5, 10, 11, 23, 26, 29, 33n, 72, 152
Borges, Jorge Luis, 136
Borradori, Giovanna, 49n
Bourdieu, Pierre, 37
Brassier, Ray, 10
Brault, Pascale-Anne, 114n, 115n
Britten, Benjamin, 74
Buber, Martin 108, 115n
Butler, Judith, 38

Cahiers de l'Herne, 12
Cambridge University, 2, 31n, 158, 159
Cant, Alexander, 84–5
Cant, Andrew, 84–5
Caputo, John D., 74, 75n, 76–7
Cardozo Law School, 53
Casaubon, Isaac, 11
Caygill, Howard, 108
Celan, Paul, 5, 16, 132
Cerisy-la-Salle, 53, 54n, 56
Chaucer, Geoffrey, 82, 89
Chomsky, Noam, 2
Cixous, Hélène, 13, 37
Clark, Timothy, 32n, 50n

Coetzee, J. M., 12, 42–3, 53–4, 96,
115n, 136
Cohen, Tom, 49n
Colebrook, Claire, 32n
Coleridge, Samuel Taylor, 82
counter-signature *see* signature
Critchley, Simon, 62, 76n, 115n,
137n
Culler, Jonathan, 2, 17, 22, 32n, 38,
138, 145

David, Alain, 100
de Man, Paul, 31–2n, 33n, 35, 37, 98,
131, 133, 155–6, 157
de Vries, Hent, 101, 115n, 116n
decision, 60, 65–6, 69, 76n, 102, 147
Defoe, Daniel, 94
Deguy, Michel, 11
Deleuze, Gilles, 37
Derrida, Jacques
Acts of Literature, 6, 12, 32n, 52
Acts of Religion, 42
Adieu, 33n, 38, 42, 75n, 97, 100–16,
146
'Afterword', 32n
Altérités, 68, 75n, 99, 146
Animal that Therefore I Am, The, 38,
42, 49n
'Animal that Therefore I Am, The',
53, 54, 54n
'Aphorism Countertime', 26, 33n,
52–3
'At This Very Moment', 99, 111
'Autoimmunity', 49n
Beast and the Sovereign, The, 14n
'Before the Law', 3, 33n
'"But as for me, who am I
(following)?"', 55n
'Circumfession', 98
'Deaths of Roland Barthes, The',
127–8
'Deconstruction and the Other', 24,
153
'Deconstructions', 152
'Derrida avec Levinas', 100, 113
'Double Session, The', 20, 21–2, 33n,
157
'Eating Well', 53
'Faith and Knowledge', 38

'Force of Law', 33n, 42, 53, 60, 109,
144, 147
Gift of Death, The, 33n, 38, 42, 53,
56–77, 99, 116n
Given Time, 33n, 38, 43, 44–5, 60
Glas, 18, 24, 83
'Hostipitality', 42, 109, 116n, 142–4
'I Have a Taste for the Secret', 46,
50n, 97, 116n
'*Ja*, or the *faux-bond*', 137n
'Law of Genre, The', 54n
'Letter to a Japanese Friend', 154
Limited Inc, 32, 96
'Limited Inc a b c', 14n, 32n
'Literature in Secret', 43, 45, 46, 47,
50n, 54n, 76n
'Mallarmé', 33n
Mémoires, 98
Memoirs of the Blind, 33n
Monolingualism of the Other, 153
Of Grammatology, 21, 22, 24, 30,
38, 40, 157
Of Hospitality, 42, 60, 142–3, 147
Of Spirit, 53
On Cosmopolitanism, 42
'On Cosmopolitanism', 143
On Touching, 99, 101
Other Heading, The, 60, 75n
'Passions', 43, 45, 46–7, 50n, 95n,
157
Points, 44, 47
Politics of Friendship, 11, 38, 60
Positions, 19, 21, 22, 25
'Psyche', 60, 54n, 148
'Remarks', 46
Rogues, 142, 143
'Sauf le nom', 60
'Signature Event Context', 14n, 32n,
95n
Signéponge, 3
'Some Questions', 138, 154
'Some Statements and Truisms', 34,
35, 149
Specters of Marx, 38, 71
Speech and Phenomena, 38, 97
'Structure, Sign and Play', 2
'"This Strange Institution"', 17, 24,
27, 30, 33n, 49n, 96n, 137, 157
'Time of a Thesis, The', 17, 35

'Tours de Babel, Des' 129n
'Ulysses Gramophone', 50, 54n
'University without Condition, The', 148
'Violence and Metaphysics', 12, 14n, 60, 99, 146
'White Mythology', 33n
Work of Mourning, The, 98, 114n
'Word of Welcome, A', 97
Writing and Difference, 14n, 38
Descartes, René, 102, 152
Dickens, Charles, 94
Dickinson, Emily, 56–7
différance, 22, 40, 139, 141, 142, 152, 160
Diogenes Laertius, 11
Donato, Eugenio, 2
Dufourmantelle, Anne, 42; *see also* Derrida, Jacques, *Of Hospitality*

Eagleton, Terry, 31n
Edelman, Lee, 87–8n
Eisenstein, S. M., 117, 121, 129n
Elam, Diane, 38
Eliot, George, 132
Ellmann, Maud, 3, 38, 158–9
Esposito, Roberto, 9, 10
Essex University, 36

Ferraris, Maurizio, 116n
Flaubert, Gustave, 33n
Florian, Jean-Pierre Claris de, 11
Foucault, Michel, 10, 36, 37, 41
Fowler, H. W., 79, 84
Fremdwörter, 80–1, 87n, 129n
Freud, Sigmund, 23, 93

Gallop, Jane, 116n
Gasché, Rodolphe, 18, 22, 30, 32n
Gates, Henry Louis, 38
Genesis *see* Abraham and Isaac
Genet, Jean, 83
Genette, Gérard, 95
Gide, André, 96n
Granta, 2

Habermas, Jürgen, 37
Hägglund, Martin, 13, 138–48
Hallward, Peter, 49n

Hardt, Michael, 10
Harrison, Nicholas, 49n
Hartman, Geoffrey, 32n
Heath, Stephen, 2
Hegel, G. W. F., 12, 16, 152
Heidegger, Martin, 16, 26, 33n, 53, 54n, 75, 80, 99, 152, 153
Henry, Michel, 152
Hill, Leslie, 32n, 33n, 48
Hobson, Marian, 38
Hölderlin, Friedrich, 26, 33n
hospitality, 4, 49n, 60, 101–2, 116n, 140–8
Husserl, Edmund, 10, 16, 152

illeity, 108–9, 146
impossibility, 4, 38, 59–73, 75n, 98–9, 124, 129, 132, 139, 148
Interventions, 39
invention, 2, 7, 8, 51–2, 54, 75n, 135, 147, 148
Irvine, University of California, 3, 149
iterability, 7, 27, 28, 29, 30

Jakobson, Roman, 2
James, Henry, 131, 136
Johns Hopkins University, The, 36
Johnson, Barbara, 38, 43
Johnson, Christopher, 38
Johnson, David E., 14
Johnson, Samuel, 90
jouissance, 45, 118, 128, 129, 130n
Joyce, James, 3, 5, 16, 50n, 87n, 89, 90, 132, 136
justice, 4, 44, 63, 98, 103–12, 115n, 142, 143, 144, 145, 147, 148

Kafka, Franz, 3, 7–8, 16, 29, 93
Kamuf, Peggy, 3, 32n, 38, 94, 95n
Kant, Immanuel, 9–10, 11, 16, 71, 76, 93, 142, 147
Kearney, Richard, 147
Keenan, Thomas, 38
Kierkegaard, Søren, 46, 57–9, 62–3, 65–70, 72, 73, 74, 75n, 80, 99
Kleist, Heinrich, 131, 136
Knight, Diana, 129n
Kristeva, Julia, 36, 37

Lacan, Jacques, 36, 37
Laclau, Ernesto, 148n
Lamarque, Peter, 16, 31n, 95, 95n
Leavis, F. R., 31n
Leavy, John P., 83
Lecercle, Jean-Jacques, 38
Leibniz, Gottfried, 16
Leitch, Vincent, 32n
Levinas, Emmanuel, 12–13, 27, 37,
   53, 54n, 59, 62, 67–8, 72, 75n,
   97–116, 134, 140, 145–7, 152
   Entre Nous, 103
   'Ethics of the Infinite', 77
   Humanism of the Other, 108
   Is It Righteous to Be?, 106, 110
   Of God Who Comes to Mind, 105
   'Other and the Others, The', 107
   Otherwise than Being, 104–15, 137n
   'Paradox of Morality, The', 76n
   'Peace and Proximity', 104
   Proper Names, 75n
   Totality and Infinity, 76n, 102,
   104–15
   'Visage, Figure', 76
Lévi-Strauss, Claude, 12
Lingis, Alphonso, 115n
Llewelyn, John, 107
logocentrism, 16, 20, 21, 24, 25, 32n
Lyotard, Jean-François, 37, 70n, 71, 72

MacCabe, Colin, 2
Macksey, Richard, 2
Major, René, 37
Mallarmé, Stéphane, 5, 16, 21, 22, 23,
   25, 26, 29, 33n
Mallet, Marie-Louise, 49n
Mandela, Nelson Rolihlahla, 113
Marvell, Andrew, 33n
Meillassoux, Quentin, 9–10
Melville, Herman, 43, 72
Merleau-Ponty, Maurice, 152
Miller, J. Hillis, 13, 32n, 37, 48–49,
   86n, 131–7
Milton, John, 33n
Montaigne, Michel de, 11
Montreal, University of, 151

Naas, Michael, 101, 114n, 115n
Nancy, Jean-Luc, 10, 37, 53

Negri, Antonio, 9, 10
New York Times, 42
Nietzsche, Friedrich, 11, 131
Norris, Christopher, 18, 22, 32n, 33n

obtusus, 117, 124
Ofrat, Gideon, 48
Olsen, Regine, 67
Orwell, George, 80–1, 87n
Owen, Wilfred, 74–5
Oxford English Dictionary, 78–9, 82,
   83–5, 87n
Oxford Literary Review, The, 39, 41,
   158
Oxford University, 159

Panzéra, Charles, 129n
Pascal, Blaise, 161
Patočka, Jan, 71
Pelagius, 103
performative, 95n
pharmakon, 142
Plato, 10, 12, 16, 31n, 43, 92
Poe, Edgar Allen, 44
Ponge, Francis, 51
Prendergast, Christopher, 2
punctum, 13, 117–30, 135, 137n

Quiller-Couch, Sir Arthur, 88
Qur'an, The, 75n

Rabaté, Jean-Michel, 13, 56, 149–62
Rancière, Jacques, 9, 10
Rand, Richard A., 3, 83
responsibility, 4–5, 12, 27–8, 42–3,
   57–77, 99, 104, 106–7, 138–48
   of the reader, 4–5, 27, 114, 133–5
   of the writer, 4–5, 12, 46, 54, 85–6
Richards, I. A., 31n
Rilke, Rainer Maria, 26
Robbins, Jill, 106
Rorty, Richard, 161
Rousseau, Jean-Jacques, 12, 32n, 43,
   96n
Royle, Nicholas, 12, 32n, 49n, 52, 53
Rutgers University, 159

Said, Edward, 41
Sartre, Jean-Paul, 152

Saussure, Ferdinand de, 12, 43, 83, 123, 129n
Schmitt, Carl, 140
Searle, John, 14n, 37, 90, 93, 95
Sebeok, Thomas A., 2
secret, the, 43–9, 50n, 65–6, 129, 135
Sedgwick, Eve Kosofsky, 38
Shakespeare, William, 5, 16, 26, 33n, 52, 71, 132–3, 136
Sidney, Sir Philip, 89, 94
signature, 1, 4, 27, 29, 51, 135, 158, 162
Silentio, Johannes de *see* Kierkegaard, Søren
singularity, 7, 28–9, 33n, 50n, 63, 65, 76n, 111, 123–4, 129, 147
   of the literary work, 4, 5, 7, 8, 28–9, 30, 46–7, 134–5, 158
Singy, Pascal, 88n
Sollers, Philippe, 22
Southampton, University of, 3, 36, 158–9
Spivak, Gayatri Chakravorty, 40, 41
Staten, Henry, 114n
Stevens, Wallace, 136
Strathclyde University, 138
studium, 117–21, 123, 128–9
supplement, 40, 119, 125, 129, 140, 142, 160
Sussex University, 36, 39–40

Svevo, Italo, 136
Syrotinski, Michael, 49n

Tate Modern, 5
Thatcher, Margaret, 31n
third meaning, 117–30
Todorov, Tzvetan, 37
tout dire, 30, 46, 96, 157
trace, 21, 82, 108, 139, 142, 152

Ulmer, Gregory L., 32n

Valéry, Paul, 16
Van der Zee, James, 120
Vattimo, Gianni, 38, 97
Vološinov, V. N., 87n

Warwick University, 36
White, Hayden, 37
Williams, Raymond, 87n
Wills, David, 48, 49n, 55
Wittgenstein, Ludwig, 31n
Wood, David, 63–8
Wortham, Simon Morgan, 14n

Yale University, 36
Yeats, W. B., 40
York, University of, 150
Young, Robert J. C., 3, 39, 41–2, 158–9

Žižek, Slavoj, 9, 10, 37, 49n